IMAGES
of America

Around
NEW MARKET

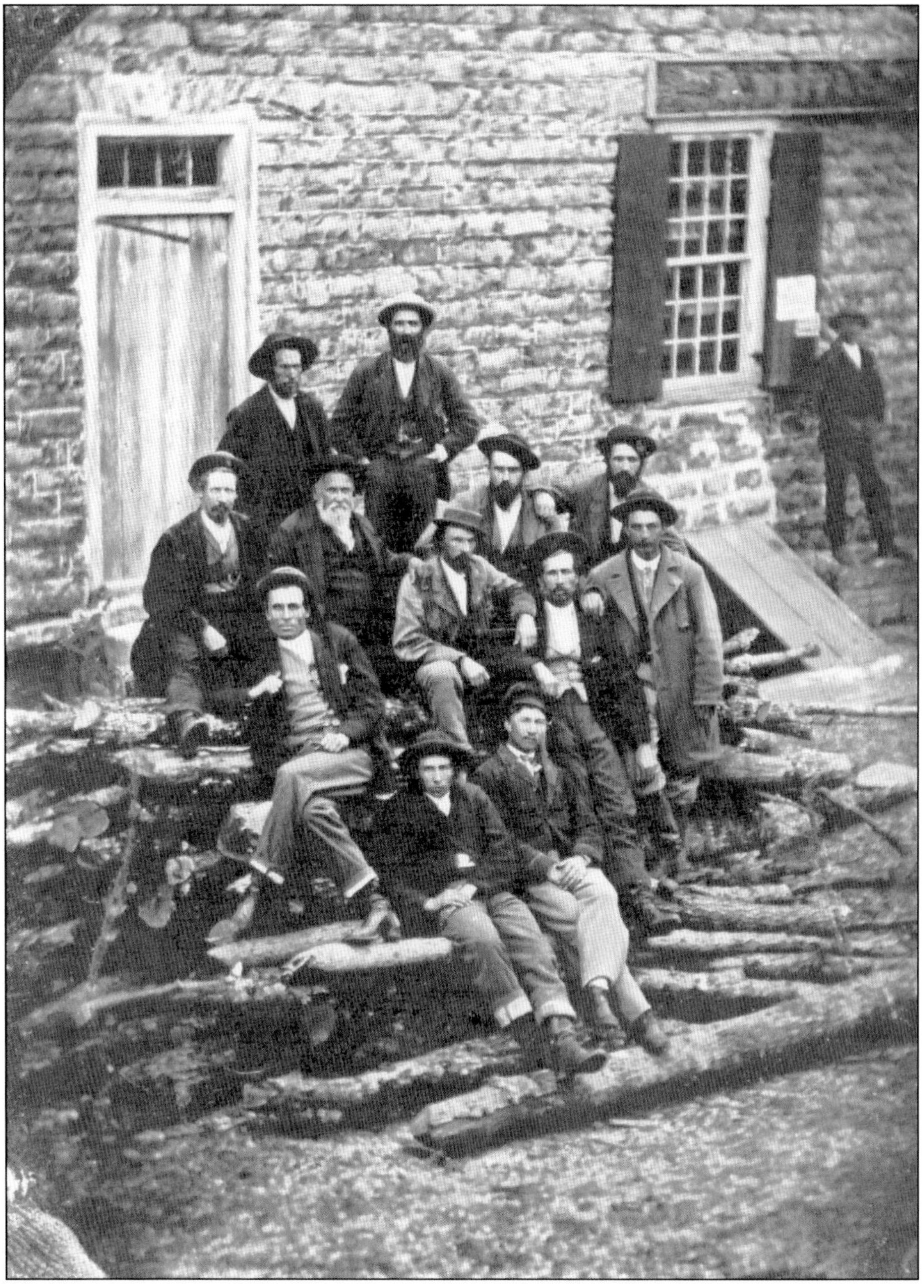

A group of New Market businessmen are seated on logs hauled in behind this prominent stone building anchoring the Crossroads. In the upper right, a sign displaying "A. Neff & Co" can be seen identifying the building as Abraham Neff's mercantile store. A lack of military clothing places the photograph in the late 1850s or early 1860. The men appear to be gathered perhaps for construction of a pole shed for added storage behind Abraham Neff's store. The man second from right in the third row has been tentatively identified as John W. Crim, who was a veteran of McNeill's Rangers during the Civil War, husband of Eliza (Clinedinst) Crim, and great-grandfather of one of the authors. The building survives today as a BB&T branch and still anchors the town's center. (John D. Crim.)

IMAGES
of America

Around
New Market

James R. Graves
and John D. Crim

ARCADIA
PUBLISHING

ISBN 978-0-7385-4280-5

Published by Arcadia Publishing
Charleston, South Carolina

Printed in the United States of America

Library of Congress Catalog Card Number: 2006923107

For all general information contact Arcadia Publishing at:
Telephone 843-853-2070
Fax 843-853-0044
E-mail sales@arcadiapublishing.com
For customer service and orders:
Toll-Free 1-888-313-2665

Visit us on the Internet at www.arcadiapublishing.com

This book is dedicated to the living and loving memory of Nancy Branner Stewart.

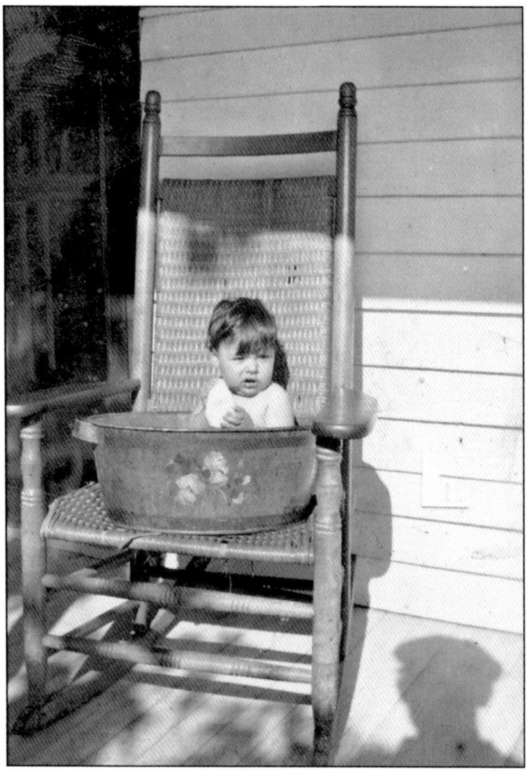

Nancy Branner (Stewart) poses in a hand-decorated, outdoor bathtub in a rocking chair looking onto Congress Street in New Market, Virginia. This little girl would grow to be one of New Market's premier historians, contributing so much to preserving its vivid past. She has written about all of New Market's schools, churches, and historic homes. Many events and places that she discovered would now be lost to history if not for her scholarly research. Thank you for the inspiration, Nancy. (Nancy Branner Stewart.)

Contents

ACKNOWLEDGMENTS

The collection of the images within these pages brought us in contact with some of the finest people in the world, namely our neighbors and our friends. While the written history of the New Market area has been fairly well documented, the pictorial history has been considerably dispersed among the population. Every person approached was willing to share something. Some loaned images; others provided memories and observations as well as stories. Many of our captions indicate the sources of the photographs and information as they were made available. In many cases, the same image was obtained from several different sources; thus final ones chosen were usually the best of several available. Given the circumstances, if we have left a donor's name out of the project, it was unintentional and we sincerely apologize for the oversight. The following people deserve special recognition and we are deeply grateful for their patient assistance: Gary Bauserman, *Shenandoah County Bi-centennial Book*, Edward "Casey" Bilhimer, Barbara Blakey, John Bracken, David Breneman, Grace Brubaker, Henry Buhl, Maxine Burkholder, Anna M. Coffman, George Collins, Dr. Gene Comstock, Luray Caverns Corporation, Phillip Crown, Janet (Theis) Dellinger, William A. "Bill" Good, John H. H, Graves, Betty Booten Grubbs, Elder Richard Harris, Scott Harris, Anna and Cathy Hildreth, Dianne Jacobs, Jean Kite, New Market Area Library, James A. Litten, Harry Long, Nancy R. Long, Cathy (Blackburn) Mauck, John and Helen Neese, Fritzi Orebaugh, Jan Osborne, New Market Battlefield State Historical Park, New Market Rebels Baseball Team, A. B. Rice, John and Nancy (Branner) Stewart, Katie Terry, Virginia Military Institute Archives (Preston Library), Dan Vaughn, and Pat (Funkhouser) Vaughan. We are deeply grateful to our spouses, Isabel Graves and Cindy Crim, for their assistance in preparing our book. We would like to highlight the guidance and encouragement of Luray and Page County friend and Arcadia author Dan Vaughn. For the great photographic repairs, we wish to thank David Breneman. Also many thanks go to the Arcadia staff: Kathryn Korfonta, Courtney Hutton, Lauren Bobier, and Barbie Halaby.

INTRODUCTION

The Shenandoah Valley, the Shenandoah River, and Shenandoah County are words almost instantly recognizable across the North American continent and the world. The name could have come from the Senedo Indian tribe that long ago lived near present-day New Market, or it could have come from a Native American word meaning "Daughter of the Stars." Most likely, both origins are connected, equally correct, and nowhere more evident than at a crisp autumn sunrise or a warm spring sunset when the air is clear and the grass and fields smell sweet. Geographically the Shenandoah lies between the Appalachian Mountains (the Blue Ridge) to the east and the Allegheny Mountains to the west.

In 1716, Virginia's Gov. Alexander Spotswood and his "Knights of the Golden Horseshoe" climbed the Blue Ridge at Swift Run Gap to see this valley for himself and explore a portion of it. He was followed by waves of settlers and immigrants from the east, arriving in the 1720s. They were among the valley's first permanent settlers along with German Lutherans, Mennonites, and other religious followers moving southward along the mountains from Pennsylvania. Additional groups, such as the Moravians, cut their way through the wilderness during the mid-1750s, widening the existing game and Native American trails and bringing through more wagons and settlers. Most early immigrants were drawn not only by the fertile valley, but also by the social and religious freedoms available in the remote frontier, which did not exist in their native countries left so far behind.

The area has served as a natural crossroads for centuries. Wild game created trails moving up and down the valley and crossing it through the mountain gaps. Native American groups followed closely, widening the trails and camping along the Shenandoah and in the flat areas. The area became a cultural crossroads of settlers from Pennsylvania to the north, intersecting with the English, Scotch, and Irish settlers from the Norfolk and Richmond areas to the east. In the 1780s, a small village straddled the crossroads near the valley's midpoint. Nearby, the Shenandoah River flowed northward "down" the valley toward Winchester and the river's blending with the Potomac River at Harpers Ferry in West Virginia. In 1796, the Virginia General Assembly approved incorporating the town of New Market, which, by the mid-1800s, was securely established at the crossing of the Shenandoah Valley Turnpike (now Route 11, still referred to as the Valley Pike) with the New Market–Sperryville Turnpike (now Route 211). The turnpikes sported new macadamized roads (named for inventor John L. McAdam) that provided a harder, more weather-tolerant surface to handle the increasing flow of produce and goods to and from the area. There being no better method of transportation, such as rail service, available until later, the pikes served as well for troop movements during the Civil War.

Travel to and from this new frontier utilized the earliest game trails that, over time, widened into a barely passable road network. The nearby Shenandoah became the principal transportation for lumber, hides, and other produce that were floated north, down the river, on long, narrow flat-bottomed boats called "gundalos" in the local vernacular, which probably came from the word gondola. Gundalos made it possible for very large loads to be carried relatively inexpensively for long distances. Their principal disadvantage lay in that each boat could only be used once, and that was going north or downstream. After each load was sold, the gundalo was broken down and its lumber sold, while back up the river, new ones were being built. Another disadvantage was that there were no major rivers flowing through the valley from east to west. As east-west roads were widened and improved, large wagons were built to carry goods and produce back and forth over the Blue Ridge, opening up new markets for valley residents. No one wagon, however, could match the cargo capacity of one gundalo.

There have been any number of families that have called New Market home either temporarily or permanently over the years, and among them, one family stands out for its spiritual, medical, and educational contributions to the culture of the community. The Rev. Paul Henkel settled his family in the village of New Market about the 1780s. Henkel, a devout Lutheran minister, is remembered (as his father was) as one of the founders of Lutheranism in America. He quickly set up a printing press devoted to Lutheran dialogue, established the Davidsburg Lutheran Church, had traveling gospel lectures, and started a school shortly after his arrival. He was truly a driven man establishing culture in the wilderness of the Virginia backcountry. This remarkable man changed many people's lives for the better.

The Henkel Press (at various times also known as Henkel Printing) was established in 1806 and began printing staggering amounts of Lutheran and non-devotional broadsides, books, and hymnals, including many documents for the Virginia, Tennessee, and North Carolina Synods. Henkel would establish one of the first newspapers west of the Blue Ridge. Early on, he reluctantly began to print in English as well as the more common German he so fervently wanted to preserve. His descendants would become ministers, doctors and pharmacists, printers and educators in the town. The Henkels were the type of individuals who would always make a difference in preserving the community and New Market's integrity in the annals of the Shenandoah Valley's complex history.

Later the entire valley witnessed the ebb and flow of Union and Confederate forces struggle for control of this "bread basket of the Confederacy" for three long years since the Civil War began. On May 15, 1864, the war came home to New Market with a vengeance. Defending the valley, Confederate general John C. Breckinridge faced a Union force that greatly outnumbered his own, forcing him to call out the cadets of the Virginia Military Institute (VMI) to join with his troops near the town. At the height of the battle, Breckinridge gave the order, "Put the boys in, and may God forgive me for the order." The "boys" joined the right flank of the 62nd Virginia Infantry and overran the commanding Union position, winning the battle. For their role in the fighting, VMI had 10 cadets killed out of a total of 258 participating. It remains the only time in American history that a college group fighting as a unit materially affected the outcome of a battle in a time of war.

After the Civil War, the railroad made its final push to complete the North-South link through the New Market area. A number of townspeople, however, wanted no part of its noisy operation, so the railroad and consequently the New Market Depot were located about a mile west of town and across the river. Any major industry wishing to locate to the New Market area would thus have to be well outside the town limits. Long-term, this railroad decision meant that in spite of the turnpikes, the town avoided some of the boom-to-bust cycles of industries closely associated with the railroad. New Market's business climate would principally attract small businesses and stand-alone manufacturers, an atmosphere that continues today.

By the 1920s, the proliferation of automobiles and travelers escaping from the cities were able to enjoy greatly improved road construction and roadways. Local attractions such as Endless Caverns, Shenandoah Caverns, and Luray Caverns geared up for the hundreds of travelers and railroad passengers that passed daily through their gates. New Market as a whole decided to encourage the hospitality and local businesses that served the needs of the traveling public, a practice that continues today and provides a sizable portion of the town's revenues.

While there is significant written history about the town and the Shenandoah Valley, the local pictorial record is considerably dispersed among the population. The collection of images shared within these pages is intended to provide "a short trip on a long road" that is the history of the town of New Market, Virginia.

One

The Crossroads Beginnings

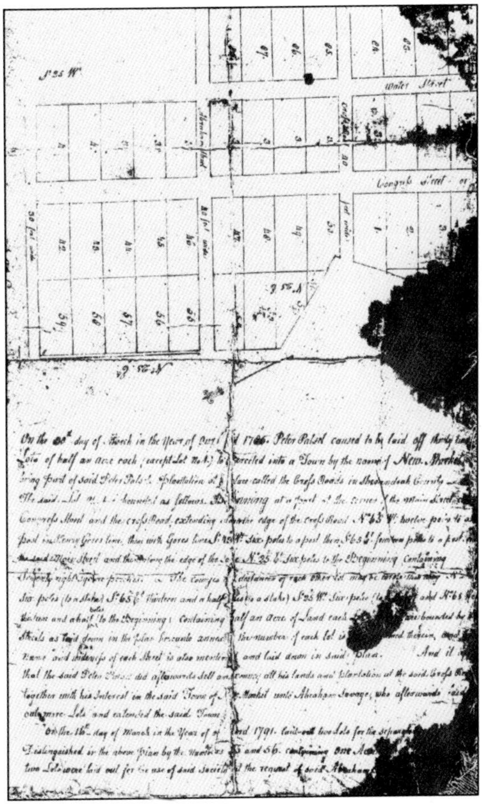

On August 22, 1806, surveyor Jacob Rinker, son of a Swiss immigrant, was employed by the town's trustees to re-survey the town's lots. Green Street (which is Stuart Street today) varied between 34 and 36 feet wide, probably because of building construction. As a result, the town realigned Green Street per Rinker's plat to produce a uniform, 35-foot width that continues today. (John D. Crim.)

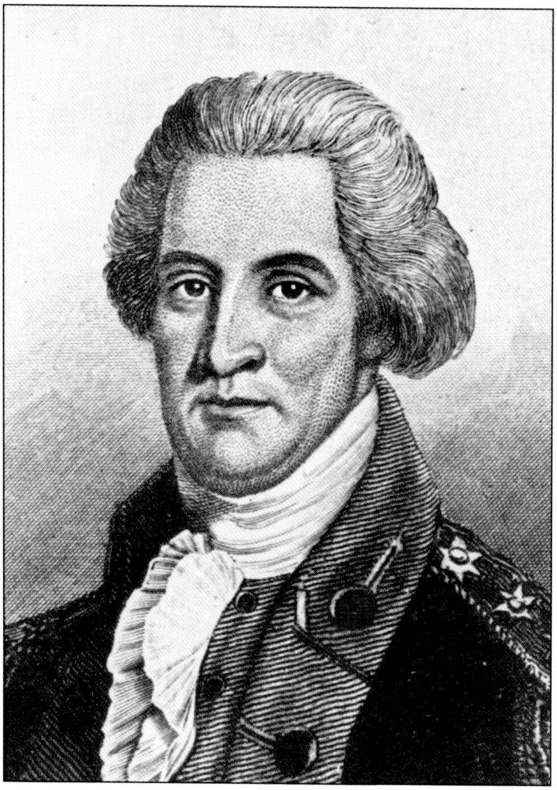

John Sevier was the founder yet short-time resident of New Market, Virginia. Sevier was born in Rockingham County, south of the town, on September 23, 1745. His father, Valentine Sevier, was said to have been from near Mount Jackson, Virginia. John was thought to have a trading post and tavern near the original Crossroads. He would serve under George Washington during the French and Indian War as a revered Native American fighter known by some as "Nolichucky Jack." Just prior to that conflict, he was attracted to the new lands of Tennessee along the Holston River. He would later fight as an American patriot, raising over 1,000 men for the cause for liberty from Virginia and Tennessee. In 1796, Sevier was elected first governor of Tennessee and was reelected again in 1803. He served in the House of Representatives until his death in 1815 while in Alabama on presidential assignment. (Nancy Branner Stewart.)

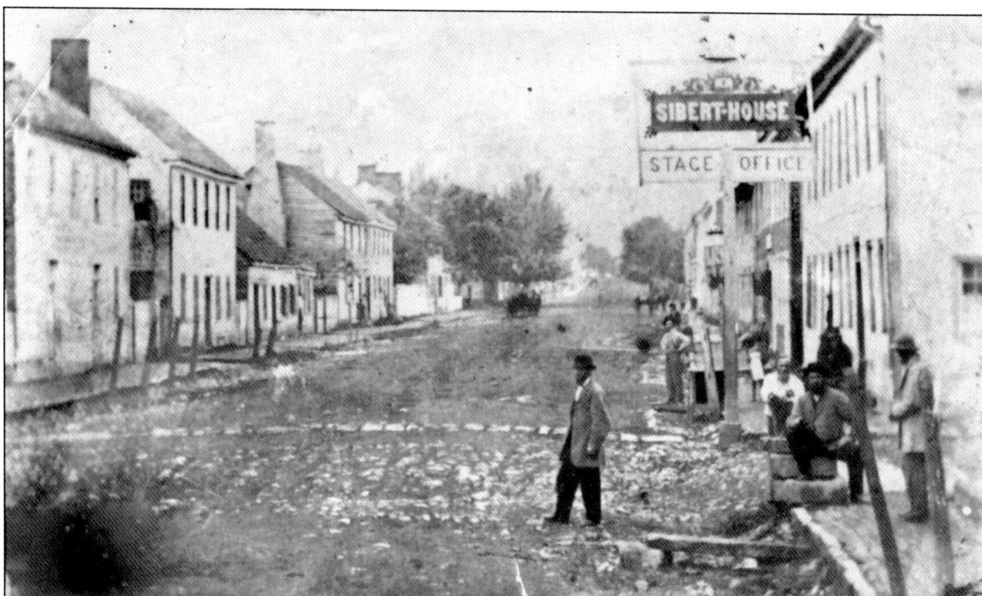

Looking south at the Crossroads, probably just before the Civil War, a man identified only as a Dr. Estridge carefully crosses Congress Street just north of the Stage Office at the Sibert House. The second building from left survives today as Shop Civil War at 9398 Congress Street. The small, one-story building to its right was eventually torn down to make room for the large, brick, two-story that stands today. (New Market Area Library.)

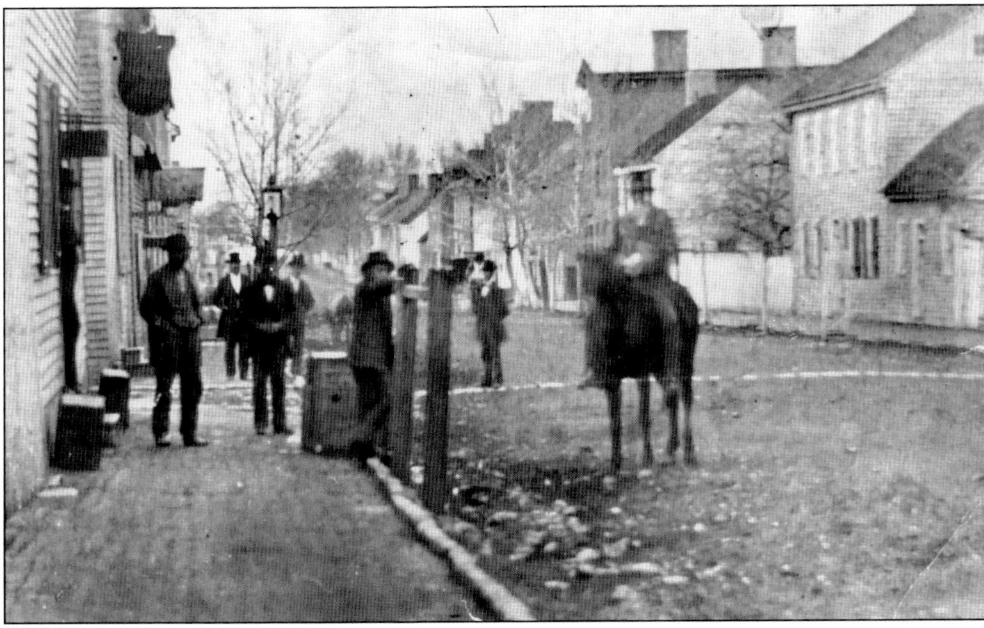

The view looking north on Congress Street includes Dr. Solon Henkel's office and residence in the building at left. Beyond his office stands one of the town's first self-extinguishing street lamps, installed in 1884. Visible at right center behind the rider is the south side of what was then Caspar Henkel's two-story brick residence, which still stands today at 9400 Congress Street. The photograph appears to have been taken during the mid-1880s. (New Market Area Library.)

This American banner is marked "New Market 7th Brigade, 13th Regiment 1799." The flag represents one of the earliest 18th-century American military flags that remain intact today. The construction is silk fabric painted with "Liberty or Death" atop a federal eagle expressing deep pride in the newfound freedom. In 1794, Shenandoah County raised the 13th Regiment in the area. William Bushby was commissioned to paint and sew the standard for the unit as another flag was commissioned to him on November 8, 1787, for the "Shennando" Militia. (Old Salem/Museum of Early Southern Decorative Art Research Center.)

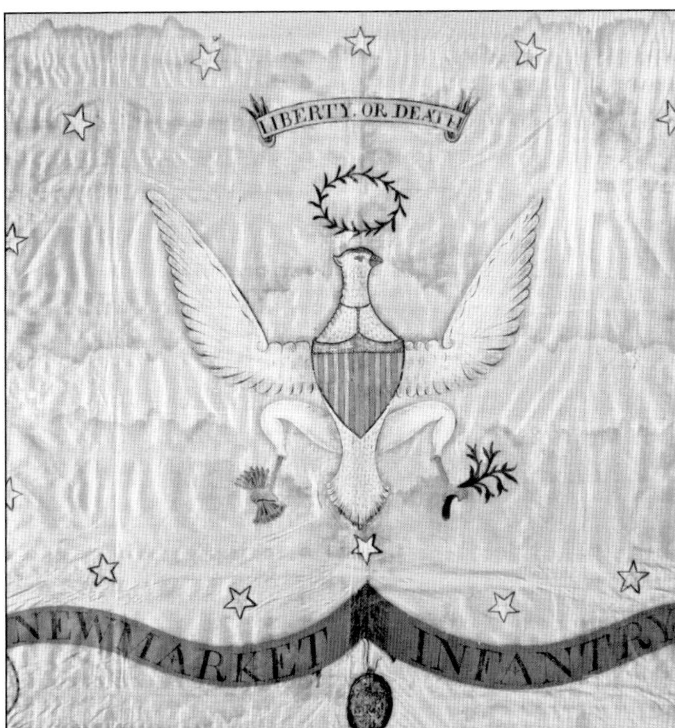

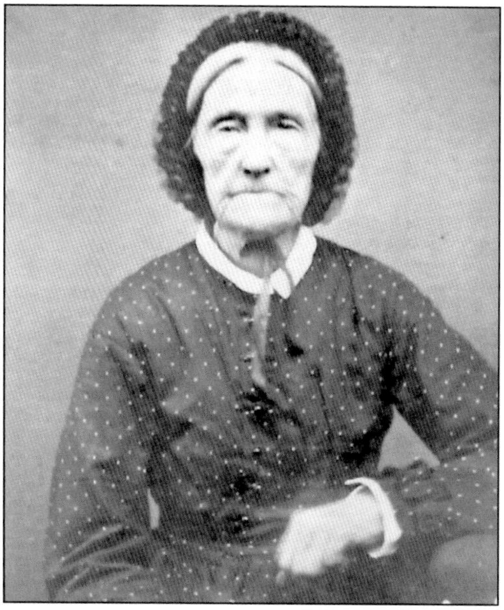

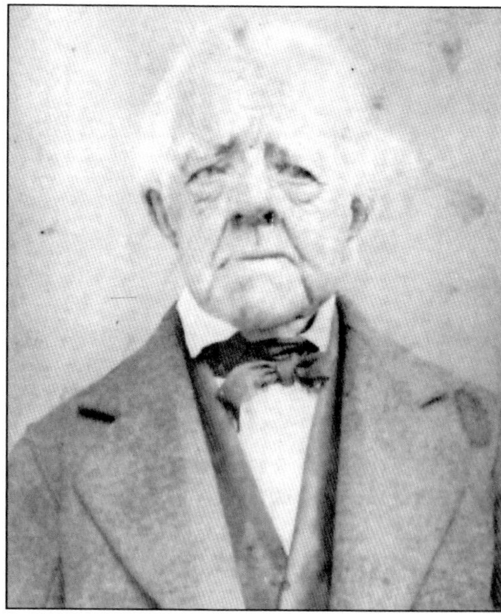

LEFT: Anna Cauldwell (Crim) Pennybacker was a New Market resident in the mid-1800s. She had been widowed around 1827 from Mike Crim, who operated a road wagon, hauling local produce and goods to markets across the mountains. They had two children—David, married to Martha Windle, and Sophia, married to John David Zirkle. Her grandson was John W. Crim. **RIGHT:** George Mayberry Pennybacker married the widow Crim and assisted raising her children. He was extensively engaged in the manufacture of iron in Rockingham, Shenandoah, and Page Counties. Pennybacker built Newman's Liberty Furnace, Pine Forge, River Forge, and the Brock's Gap Forge and assisted in the building of other forges by family members in the Shenandoah Valley. He died in 1880, having lived almost 93 years. (Both images John D. Crim.)

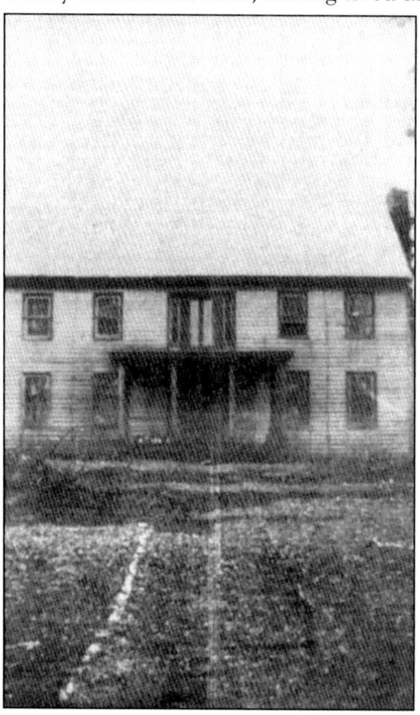

One of the first settlements and established plantations in the New Market area was along Smith's Creek and owned by Andrew Byrd II. Andrew Byrd III was born in 1754, and at that time, his father was establishing a carding and flour mill. Byrd later served as a Virginia Militia captain during the war for American independence. Near this home, currently called Cloverdale Farm, was the 18th-century village of Craney Island, where several of the earliest industries in Shenandoah County were started. Byrd was an ironmaster with one of the first iron forges in the Shenandoah, called Pine Forge. It is believed he had a strong interest as a mold carver for iron furnaces, too. However, his largest efforts were in flour, having started an early mill there. Byrd owned many lands in the area. His father had land transactions with Valentine Sevier, father of New Market founder John Sevier. Byrd would later move south to Rockingham County, Virginia. Records of this early settler were burned by Union troops while on Civil War raids, which destroyed most of the documents and made Byrd historically elusive. (Virginia Historical Society/Phillip Crown.)

The wool industry was a booming business in the Shenandoah, especially in the first half of the 19th century. Most farms had large flocks of sheep. Andrew Byrd of Craney Island incorporated a wool-carding mill along Smith's Creek. It mentions in this 1809 broadside that it would be "an advantage for hatters to have their wool broke by the machine." This helped create material that started a long millinery (or hat) tradition in the New Market area. It mentions that the wool must be greased and cleaned of impurities. Ungreased wool would catch fire from the heavy sparks turning about in the mill, sending the whole operation up in flames. This remarkable printed document produced by the Henkel Press expresses the need at the time for bilingual advertising for the predominantly German element in the county. (Phillip Crown.)

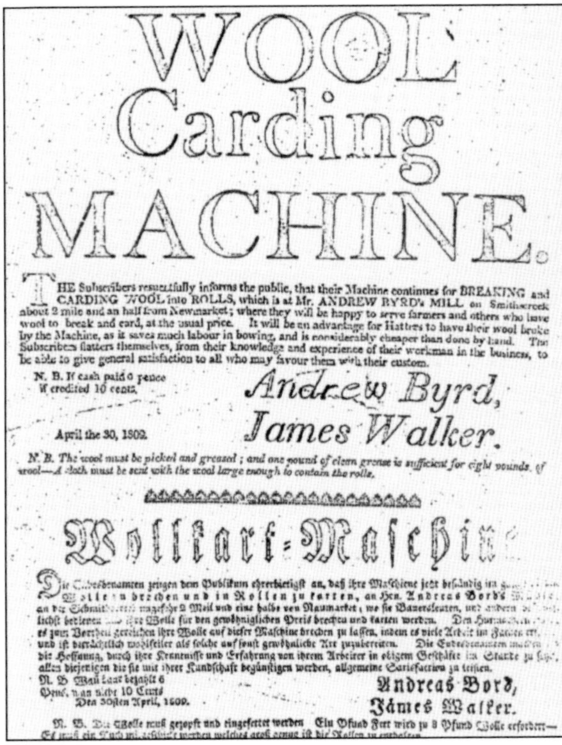

WOOL
Carding
MACHINE.

THE Subscribers respectfully informs the public, that their Machine continues for BREAKING and CARDING WOOL into ROLLS, which is at Mr. ANDREW BYRD's MILL on Smithscreek about 2 mile and an half from Newmarket; where they will be happy to serve farmers and others who have wool to break and card, at the usual price. It will be an advantage for Hatters to have their wool broke by the Machine, as it saves much labour in bowing, and is considerably cheaper than done by hand. The Subscribers flatters themselves, from their knowledge and experience of their workman in the business, to be able to give general satisfaction to all who may favour them with their custom.

N. B. If cash paid 6 pence
if credited 10 cents.

April the 30, 1809.

Andrew Byrd,
James Walker.

N. B. The wool must be picked and greased; and one pound of clean grease is sufficient for eight pounds of wool—A cloth must be sent with the wool large enough to contain the rolls.

Wollkart-Maschin[illegible]

Die [illegible] zeigen dem Publikum ehrerbietigst an, daß ihre Maschiene jetzt beständig im [illegible] Wolle zu brechen und in Rollen zu karten, an Hrn. Andreas Byrd's [illegible] an der Schmit[illegible] ungefähr 2 Meil und eine halbe von Nawmarket, wo sie Bauersleuten, und andern [illegible] lichst bedienen [illegible] ihre Wolle für den gewöhnlichen Preis brechen und karten werden. Den Hut[illegible] es zum Vortheil gereichen ihre Wolle auf dieser Maschine brechen zu lassen, indem es viele Arbeit im [illegible] und ist beträchtlich wohlfeiler als solche auf sonst gewöhnliche Art zuzubereiten. Die Endesbenannten [illegible] die Hoffnung, durch ihre Kenntnisse und Erfahrung von ihrem Arbeiter in obigem Geschäfte im Stande zu [illegible] allen diejenigen die sie mit ihrer Kundschaft begünstigen werden, allgemeine Satisfaction zu leisten.

N. B. Wann baar bezahlt 6
Pens, wann nicht 10 Cents
Den 30sten April, 1809.

Andreas Byrd,
James Walker.

N. B. Die Wolle muß gezopft und eingefettet werden. Ein Pfund Fett wird zu 8 Pfund Wolle erfordert—

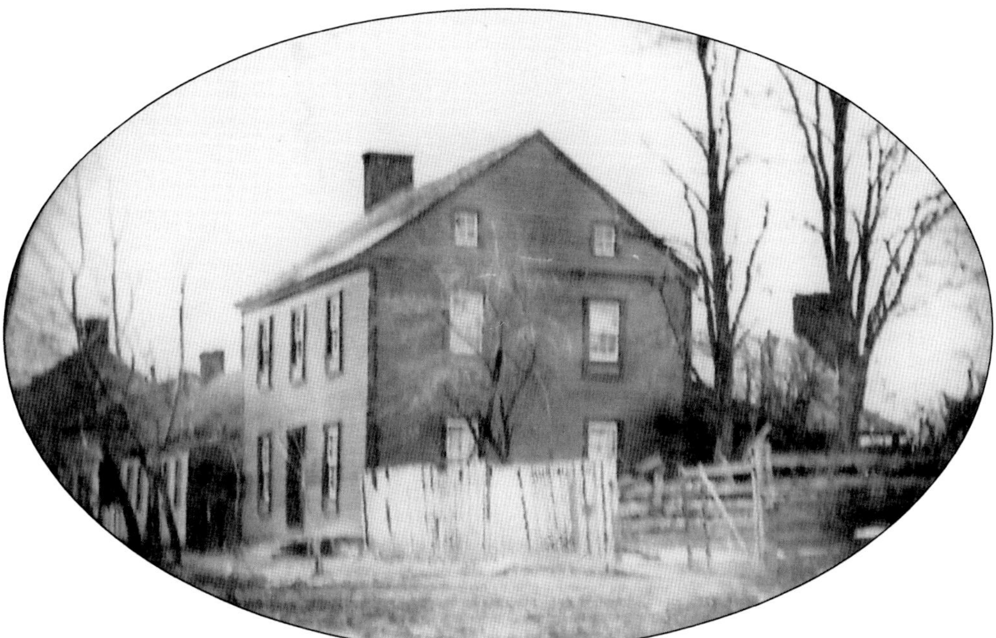

During the late 1800s, this house was purchased by the Rupp family and would be occupied by Charlie and Willie Rupp and George Neese, all bachelors. Neese, a Civil War veteran, authored a book based on his diary titled *Three Years in the Confederate Horse Artillery*. The log home is thought to have been built in the very early 1800s and has been restored today at 9295 Congress Street. (Phillip Crown.)

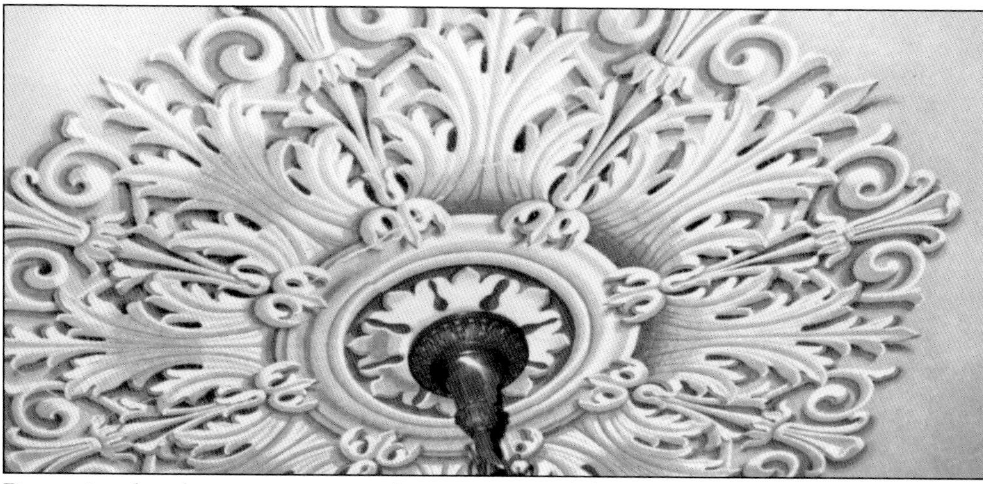

Decorative, faux house painting was becoming quite fashionable in rural Virginia from about 1840 to 1880 as the area became less rustic and more wanting in their sophistications. Around 1857, William Rupp emigrated from Germany and began his fresco work in Shenandoah and neighboring Page County. He was an exceptional painter, decorating many houses and churches in the area. The present-day New Market library has his work preserved in similar trompe l'oeil fashion to this one in frescoed plaster. Creating a fresco was very time-consuming. It took great mechanical and artistic skills to produce the master works Rupp engineered. Many coats of replicated paint were applied to the always-damp plaster to successfully create a sense of the illusionary, three-dimensional space. There are never any margins for error during this process. This particular Rupp work is for a hanging oil lamp in a Page County, Virginia, parlor and is an outstanding example of Southern interiors in America at that time. (Gary Bauserman.)

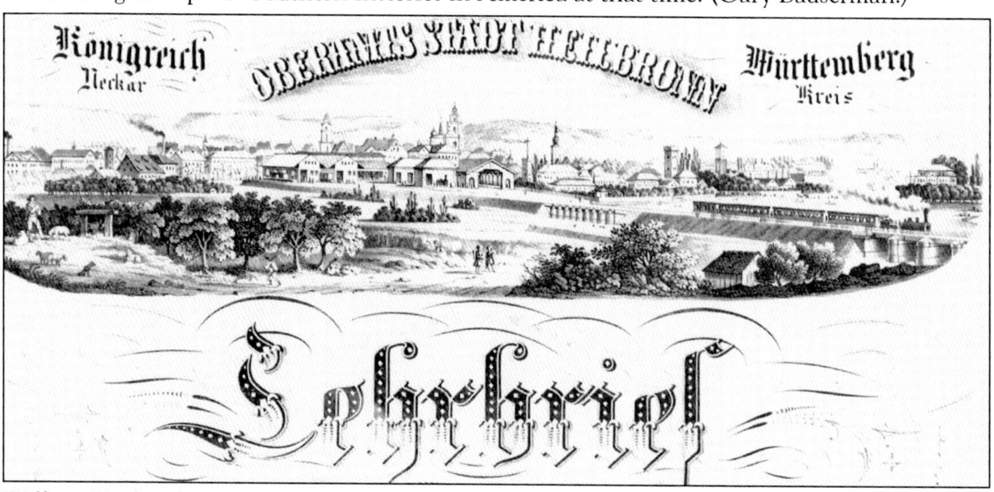

William Frederick Rupp received this diploma or "lehrbrief" from Heilbronn before emigrating from Wurttemberg, Germany, in 1852 for a degree in art. Rupp married into the Spitzer family and lived on Congress Street. He was conscripted into the Confederate States service in the 13th Virginia Infantry when the Civil War began. He was a pacifist and therefore enlisted with the option to serve as a musician in an all-German unit from Fredericksburg on May 12, 1860. After the war, he advertised heavily and continued to practice his fresco work as a professional artist. He was recorded as doing a novel work as the fresco artist for the Virginia Hotel in the post–Civil War years by the *New York Times Vindicator* newspaper. His works are prized still today in many valley homes and churches as fine, local folk art. (Fritzi Orebaugh.)

Lewis Amiss Spitzer, son of Charles Spitzer, the well-known rifle maker of New Market, poses with the famous "Buffalo Bill" Cody (at left) in the late 1800s. The back of this photograph reads, "Col. W. F. Cody (Buffalo Bill) and L. A. Spitzer who was with the firm of Majors, Russell, and Waddell on the Plains in 1857 & 1858." Spitzer would have been with Cody about this time around Leavenworth, Kansas. A gold rush in 1858 stirred up movement to the region. Spitzer's firm was a teamster company that employed over 500 wagons in one of the largest wagon trains in American history. Cody also started the Pony Express. It is not known if Spitzer participated as a mail carrier. Early on, his brother and he sought adventure in the "wild" West and saw many changes along the frontier. Lewis's brother, Moses, tragically died while traveling with the famous Donner Party—freezing to death in the Sierra Nevada. (Laura Collison Ray/Amiss family.)

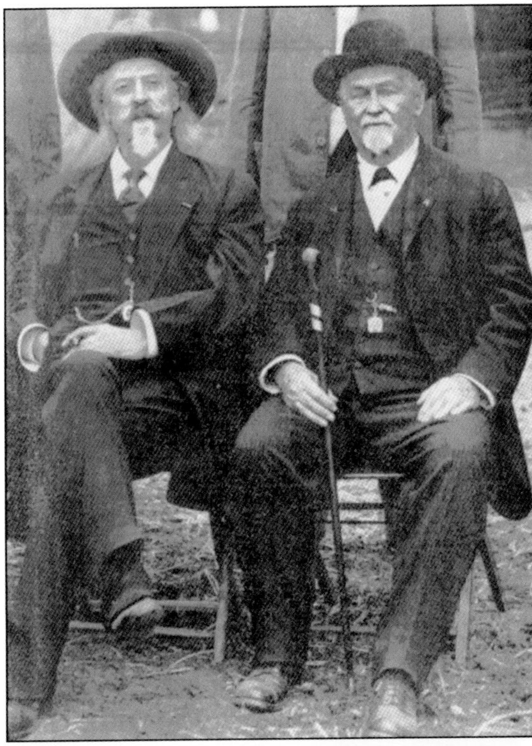

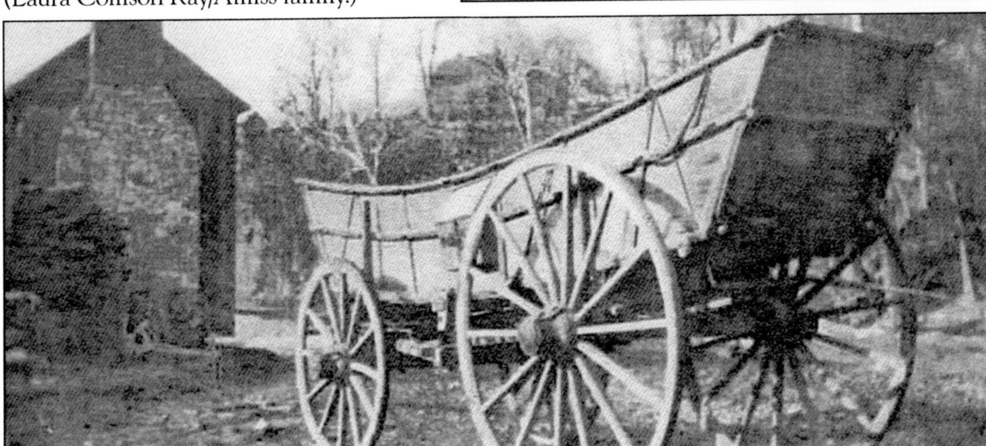

The Zirkle Minnick Waggon is displayed in this *c.* 1910 photograph at New Market's Zirkle-Dale Museum. This was typical of the dory-shaped wagons produced from the Shenandoah region, labeled sometimes as the "Winchester" style, as many were made in that region. They were the masterworks of wheelwrights and blacksmiths. The German influence abounds in the construction of these vehicles, lending an almost Old World appeal. This particular "road waggon" (with two g's to discern it from smaller wagons) is thought to have been manufactured in neighboring Newtown (today's Stephens City), Virginia, about 1796. The teamsters hauled all the vital necessities of life before other forms of transportation abounded, making teamsters wealthy very quickly. Later, after 1833, the railroad was established, and it gradually put waggons out of business after about 1860. This important Colonial/Federal–period Southern waggon still survives and is in the care of the Colonial Williamsburg Foundation, Virginia. (Newtown/Stevens City, Virginia Historical Society, Stone House Museum.)

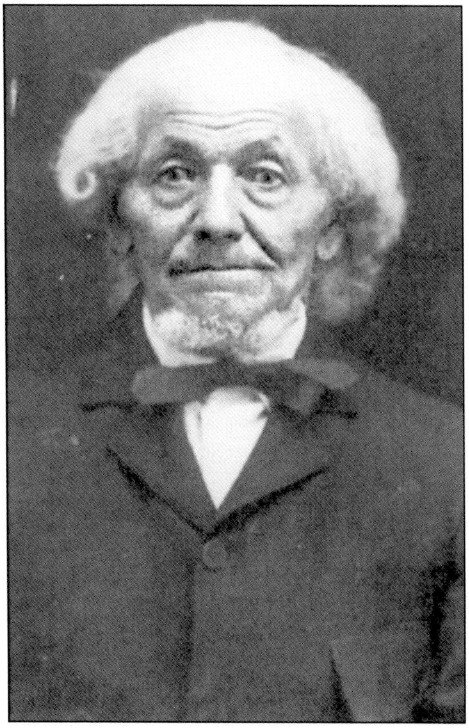

Immigrating from Baden, Germany, John George Schweinfurt landed in Philadelphia in 1855 and moved to New Market about 1857 as a potter. Schweinfurt had worked under several Virginia folk potters, and after about the 1860s, he began his work solo in New Market. His artistic ability as a potter was profound. In form and color, Schweinfurt's pottery was distinctive in the Virginia folk pottery tradition. Most of his work was utilitarian, but he was also known to be bold and unique in many of his recorded works. Compositionally his works stands out from the rest of the Shenandoah Valley potteries during that period. The town had other potteries that preceded his shop, such as Adams and Bodel, all following the famous Rockingham County style in pottery. (Dr. Gene Comstock.)

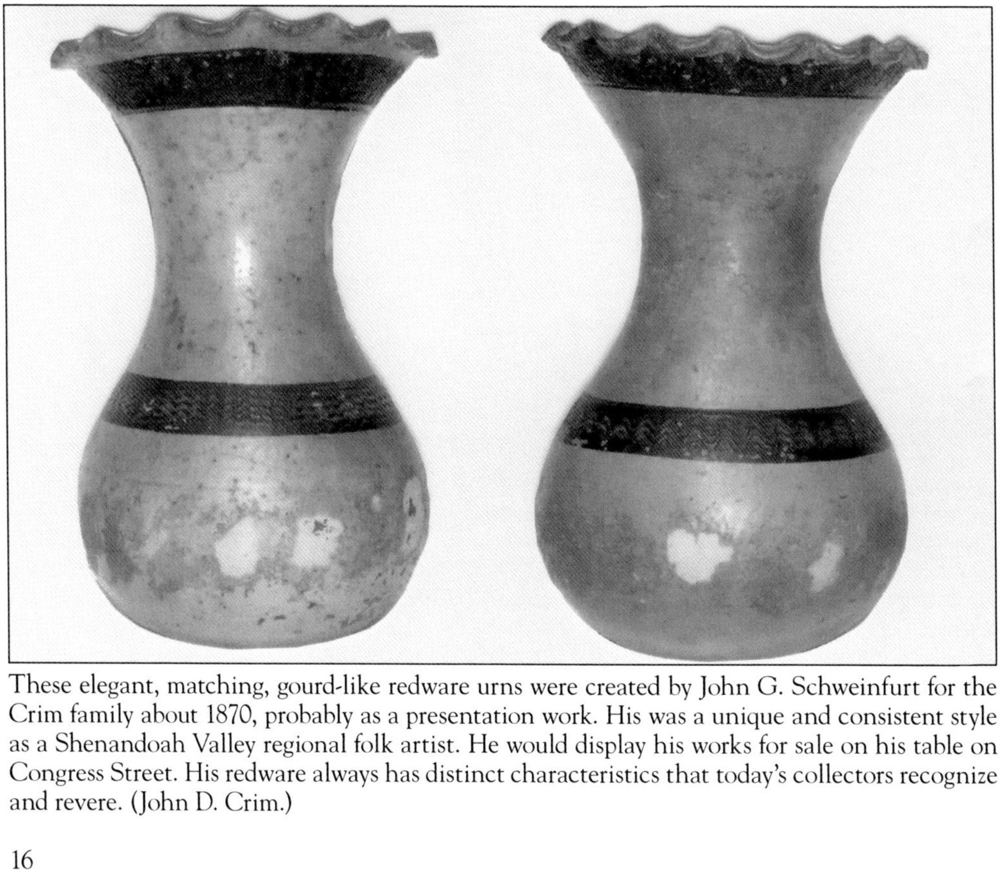

These elegant, matching, gourd-like redware urns were created by John G. Schweinfurt for the Crim family about 1870, probably as a presentation work. His was a unique and consistent style as a Shenandoah Valley regional folk artist. He would display his works for sale on his table on Congress Street. His redware always has distinct characteristics that today's collectors recognize and revere. (John D. Crim.)

Two

The Henkel Legacy

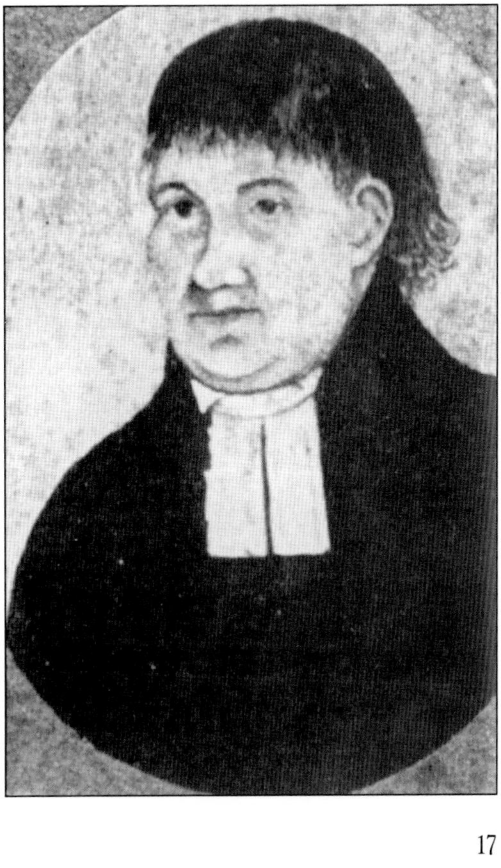

Rev. Paul Henkel hailed from Rowan County, North Carolina. Born in 1754 on Dutchman's Creek near present-day Salisbury, Paulus, as he sometimes wrote his name, became the first North Carolina–born Lutheran minister. He was multi-lingual, and in the year of America's rebellion, 1776, he started his journey as a minister studying Lutheran doctrine and traveling to Fredericktown (now Frederick), Maryland, under the Reverend Andrew Krugh. He graduated and was ordained in Pennsylvania in 1783. He began moving south in mid-1790, arriving in New Market, Virginia, and establishing the German School in late 1805. He wrote and published Christian books and hymnals in town. This began a stellar carrier for Henkel's missionary. He set the stage for the Lutheran Church in Virginia, Tennessee, North Carolina, and Ohio as a traveling minister. His sojourns as a Christian minister established many synods in those states, baptizing hundreds. He had a family of five sons and three daughters who helped establish the positive reputation of Henkel in New Market's history. (Nancy Branner Stewart.)

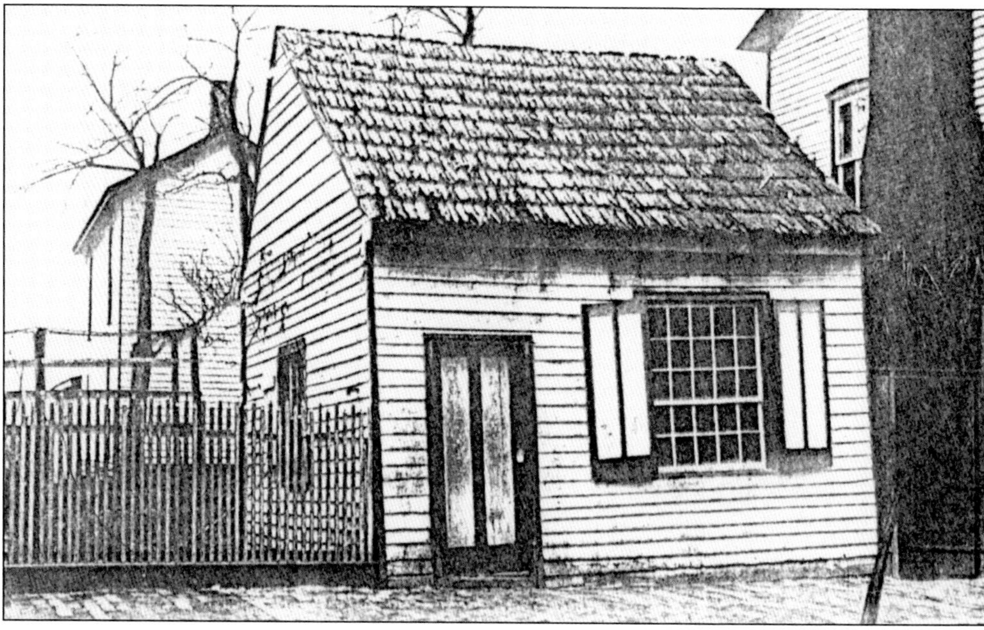

No longer standing, this Federal-style building located by the Henkel house was likely first a bookstore for the Henkel Press books sold in New Market along Congress Street. Some suggest it may have had a brief history as housing the Henkel Press. Other historians suggest that it was one of the locations of an apothecary shop affectionately known to locals as "Solomon's Temple." Perhaps different times justified different business locations for the structure. Within recent memory, it was Russell Clark's shoe repair shop. (A. B. Rice.)

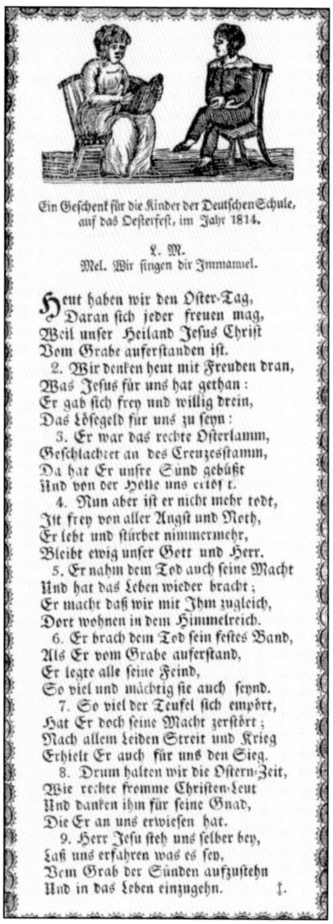

Ein Geschenk für die Kinder der Deutschen Schule,
auf das Oesterfest, im Jahr 1814.

L. M.
Mel. Wir singen dir Immanuel.

Heut haben wir den Oster-Tag,
Daran sich jeder freuen mag,
Weil unser Heiland Jesus Christ
Vom Grabe auferstanden ist.
2. Wir denken heut mit Freuden dran,
Was Jesus für uns hat gethan:
Er gab sich frey und willig drein,
Das Lösegeld für uns zu seyn:
3. Er war das rechte Osterlamm,
Geschlachtet an des Creuzesstamm,
Da hat Er unsre Sünd gebüßt
Und von der Hölle uns erlöst.
4. Nun aber ist er nicht mehr todt,
Ist frey von aller Angst und Noth,
Er lebt und stürbet nimmermehr,
Bleibt ewig unser Gott und Herr.
5. Er nahm dem Tod auch seine Macht
Und hat das Leben wieder bracht;
Er macht daß wir mit Ihm zugleich,
Dort wohnen in dem Himmelreich.
6. Er brach dem Tod sein festes Band,
Als Er vom Grabe auferstand,
Er legte alle seine Feind,
So viel und mächtig sie auch seynd.
7. So viel der Teufel sich empört,
Hat Er doch seine Macht zerstört;
Nach allem Leiden Streit und Krieg
Erhielt Er auch für uns den Sieg.
8. Drum halten wir die Ostern-Zeit,
Wie rechte fromme Christen-Leut
Und danken ihm für seine Gnad,
Die Er an uns erwiesen hat.
9. Herr Jesu steh uns selber bey,
Laß uns erfahren was es sey,
Vom Grab der Sünden aufzustehn
Und in das Leben einzugehn. †.

This broadside was published at the Henkel Press in 1814 by Henkel's son Ambrose for "*Deutfchen Schule*" or "the German School" in New Market founded by the Reverend Paul Henkel in 1805. This might have been the first formal school, and it survived until about the 1820s. Located off Congress Street near present-day Cadet Street, the German School was strictly devoted to old order Lutheranism and Swiss/German culture and spoke only the native German tongue. Before 1840, the German language was the language of choice in the Shenandoah Valley and many parts of the United States because of the social immigration from Europe in the late 18th and early 19th centuries. Tutors in New Market did abound; however, most were inadequate thanks to lack of discipline and the rampant alcoholism of some teachers. Henkel preached heavily against alcohol, dancing, and social change, which were present in town at that time. The German School was one of many successful schools in New Market's vast educational history. (Dr. John Stewart.)

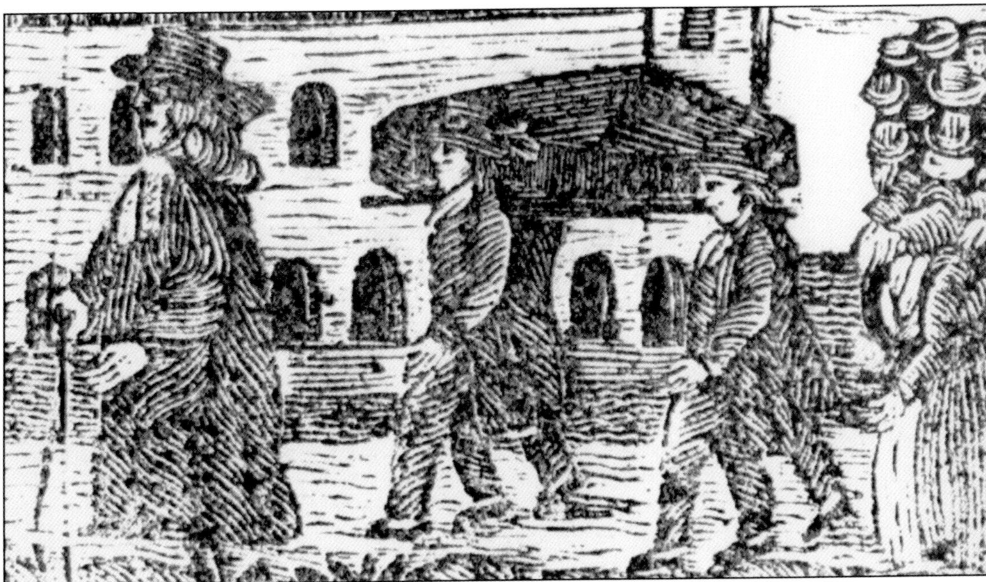

An old Henkel Printing office woodcut portrays an important funeral. Local historian Bill Good believes the woodcut depicts the 1825 funeral procession of Rev. Paul Henkel, New Market's first Lutheran minister, past Davidsburg Church, the first Lutheran church built in New Market. The church split in the 1840s, and Emmanuel Lutheran Church was built in 1848. Reverend Henkel was reburied in Emmanuel Cemetery. (Dr. John Stewart.)

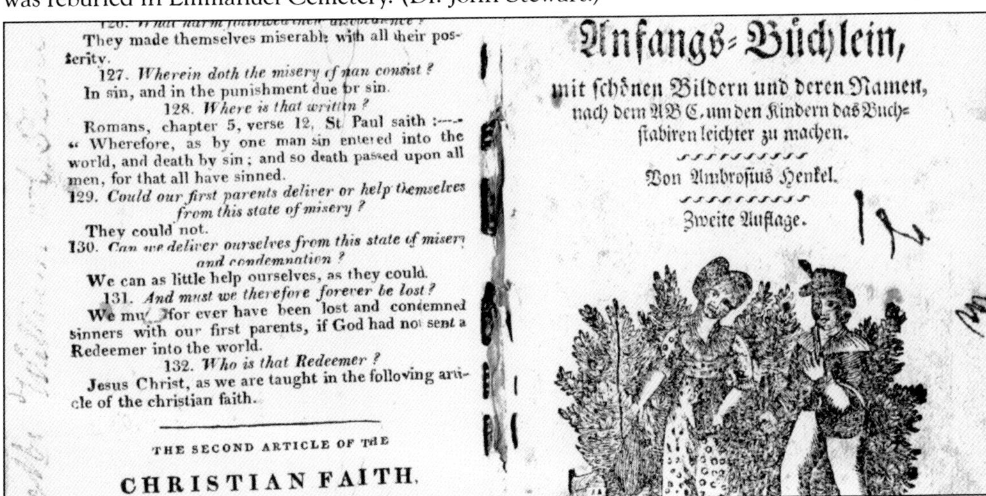

They made themselves miserable with all their posterity.

127. *Wherein doth the misery of man consist?*

In sin, and in the punishment due for sin.

128. *Where is that written?*

Romans, chapter 5, verse 12, St Paul saith :—

"Wherefore, as by one man sin entered into the world, and death by sin; and so death passed upon all men, for that all have sinned.

129. *Could our first parents deliver or help themselves from this state of misery?*

They could not.

130. *Can we deliver ourselves from this state of misery and condemnation?*

We can as little help ourselves, as they could.

131. *And must we therefore forever be lost?*

We must for ever have been lost and condemned sinners with our first parents, if God had not sent a Redeemer into the world.

132. *Who is that Redeemer?*

Jesus Christ, as we are taught in the following article of the christian faith.

THE SECOND ARTICLE OF THE

CHRISTIAN FAITH.

Anfangs-Büchlein,

mit schönen Bildern und deren Namen, nach dem A B C, um den Kindern das Buchstabiren leichter zu machen.

Von Ambrosius Henkel.

Zweite Auflage.

The Henkel Press helped establish New Market as a literate, educational town in early Virginia. The press was established in 1805, producing dynamic and diversified literature having Christian messages, save some broadside advertisements and later publications. The Henkels produced the Shenandoah Valley's and New Market's first newspaper in German. *Der Virginische Volksberichter, und Neumarketer Wochenschrift* was printed weekly from about 1807 to 1811 and gave little local information and mostly news of the world's events borrowed from Philadelphia newspapers. This rare children's school primer, published in 1811, was one of the most important books in the American South since it was the first book of its kind printed for children in both English and German. The Henkel Press also incorporated many decorative, fanciful woodcut illustrations in their publications, some crafted by Solon Henkel and other Henkel family members while other decorative ink blocks were imported from the North. (Luray Caverns Corporation.)

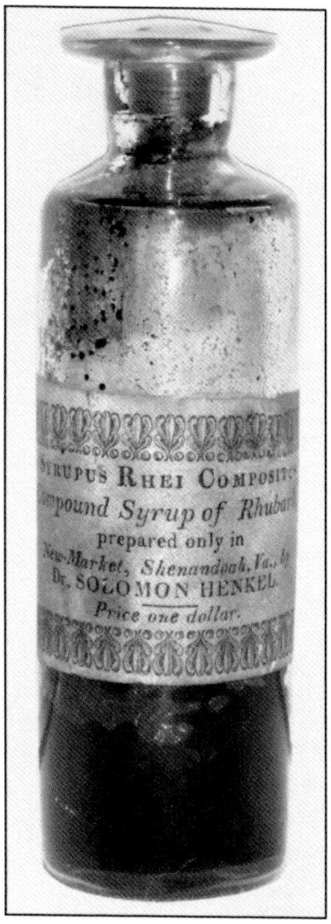

This bottle of rhubarb medicine was prepared by Dr. Solomon Henkel in the very early 1800s. The label reads, "Syrupus Rhei Compound / Compound Syrup of Rhubarb / prepared only in / New Market, Shenandoah, Virginia by / Dr. Solomon Henkel / Price one dollar." This hand-blown bottle has a pontil mark on the bottom, stands four inches high, and is about one and a half inches in diameter. Considering the times, $1 seems a high price. (John D. Crim.)

BOTTOM LEFT: Ambrose Henkel printed this *Confirmations Shein* or Confirmation Certificate broadside in 1827 at the Henkel Press in New Market on the original mahogany rammage press bought from Conrad Zentler, a Philadelphia printer, in 1806. The rare document exposes the artist's great craft in printing and aesthetic arrangement. Many other Henkel books (such as *A Drop Honey from the Dew of Jesus Christ*) and broadsides would use the same prints ordered cleverly in different formats. By the time the Christian Confirmation was signed by Ambrose in 1841, he was no longer a printer but the Lutheran minister in town. Birth and baptismal certificates, or *fraktur*, were also printed at the Henkel Press. The *frakturs* were paint decorated by New Market's first mail carrier and folk artist Peter Bernhart, who was also thought to be a part-time tutor and educator. (Luray Caverns Corporation.)

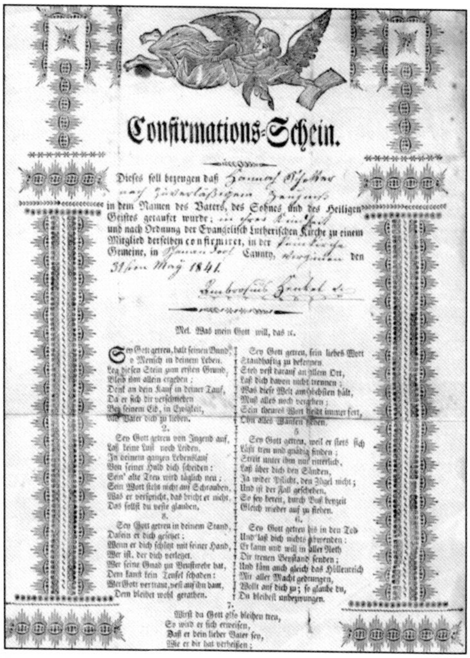

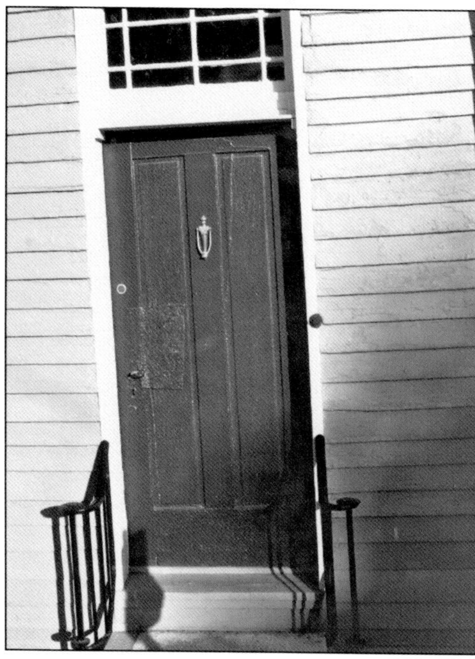

BOTTOM RIGHT: The door of 9417 Congress Street still bears Civil War scars. In 1864, German soldiers with the "damyankees" attempted to gain entry to this house of Dr. and Mrs. Solon Henkel, perhaps seeking medicine and food. Alone Anna Maria Henkel poured chamber pot water on them from an upstairs window, and the enraged mob broke the door down with their rifle butts. The door was repaired with a large iron plate that can still be seen today as the entrance to the New Market Area Library. (John D. Crim.)

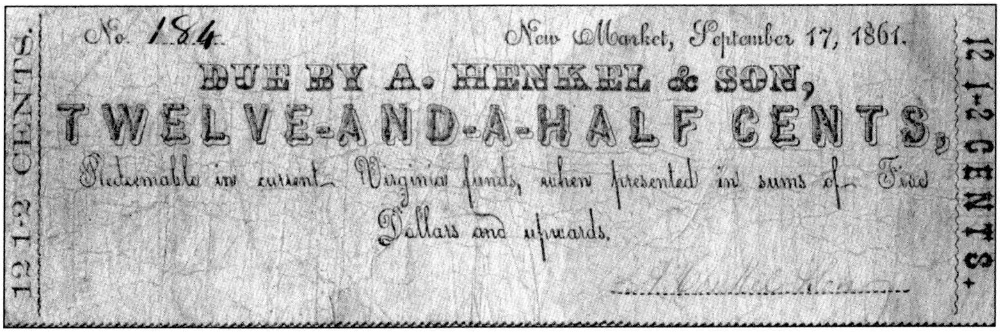

12 1-2 CENTS.

No. 184. New Market, September 17, 1861.

DUE BY A. HENKEL & SON,

TWELVE-AND-A-HALF CENTS,

Redeemable in current Virginia funds, when presented in sums of Five Dollars and upwards.

12 1-2 CENTS.

From the outset and all through the Civil War, New Market was very patriotic toward the Southern cause. The Henkel Press printed this strange denominational note of 12.5¢ in September 1861 and called it "Virginia Funds." Banks in the Confederacy did not regulate currency as the Union government did. This was a hardship for advocates of states' rights in the South as counterfeiters easily reproduced these bills. The U.S. dollar got its name, the greenback, because of the expensive, high grade of green ink, texture, and extra-detailed notes, making them harder to counterfeit. The unified banking system helped give the North an early economic supremacy that contributed greatly to the Confederacy's demise. (Nancy Branner Stewart.)

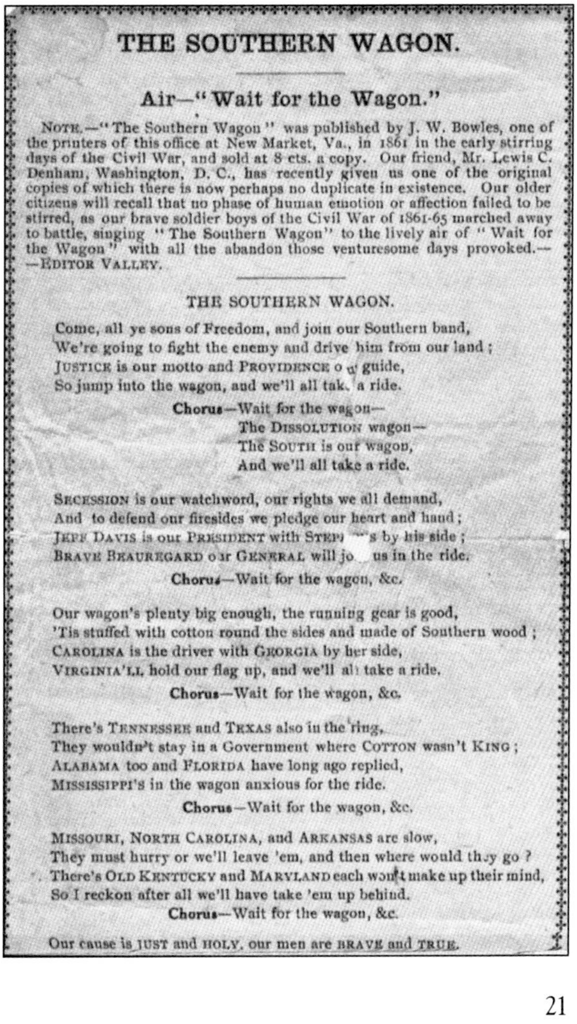

THE SOUTHERN WAGON.

Air—"Wait for the Wagon."

NOTE.—"The Southern Wagon" was published by J. W. Bowles, one of the printers of this office at New Market, Va., in 1861 in the early stirring days of the Civil War, and sold at 8 cts. a copy. Our friend, Mr. Lewis C. Denham, Washington, D. C., has recently given us one of the original copies of which there is now perhaps no duplicate in existence. Our older citizens will recall that no phase of human emotion or affection failed to be stirred, as our brave soldier boys of the Civil War of 1861-65 marched away to battle, singing "The Southern Wagon" to the lively air of "Wait for the Wagon" with all the abandon those venturesome days provoked.—EDITOR VALLEY.

THE SOUTHERN WAGON.

Come, all ye sons of Freedom, and join our Southern band,
We're going to fight the enemy and drive him from our land;
JUSTICE is our motto and PROVIDENCE o[illegible] guide,
So jump into the wagon, and we'll all tak[illegible] a ride.
Chorus—Wait for the wagon—
The DISSOLUTION wagon—
The SOUTH is our wagon,
And we'll all take a ride.

SECESSION is our watchword, our rights we all demand,
And to defend our firesides we pledge our heart and hand;
JEFF DAVIS is our PRESIDENT with STEP[illegible]s by his side;
BRAVE BEAUREGARD o[illegible]r GENERAL will jo[illegible] us in the ride.
Chorus—Wait for the wagon, &c.

Our wagon's plenty big enough, the running gear is good,
'Tis stuffed with cotton round the sides and made of Southern wood;
CAROLINA is the driver with GEORGIA by her side,
VIRGINIA'LL hold our flag up, and we'll al[illegible] take a ride.
Chorus—Wait for the wagon, &c.

There's TENNESSEE and TEXAS also in the ring,
They wouldn't stay in a Government where COTTON wasn't KING;
ALABAMA too and FLORIDA have long ago replied,
MISSISSIPPI'S in the wagon anxious for the ride.
Chorus—Wait for the wagon, &c.

MISSOURI, NORTH CAROLINA, and ARKANSAS are slow,
They must hurry or we'll leave 'em, and then where would th[illegible]y go?
There's OLD KENTUCKY and MARYLAND each won't make up their mind,
So I reckon after all we'll have take 'em up behind.
Chorus—Wait for the wagon, &c.

Our cause is JUST and HOLY, our men are BRAVE and TRUE.

A reprint Henkel Press musical broadside was originally produced in 1861. In this broadside is a patriotic sonnet about joining the Southern army. The stanzas express the sympathy with the Southern cause and states' rights. Metaphorically the "Southern Wagon" symbolized the new Confederate nation and the call to join the fight. Very few documents were produced by the Henkel Press during the Civil War due to rag and pulp shortages. Most citizens' basic needs were supplied to fight a war. The people of the Shenandoah Valley gave a remarkable effort for that cause. It would be difficult for a modern American to contemplate their sacrifice learned from the early pioneer days. (Dr. John Stewart.)

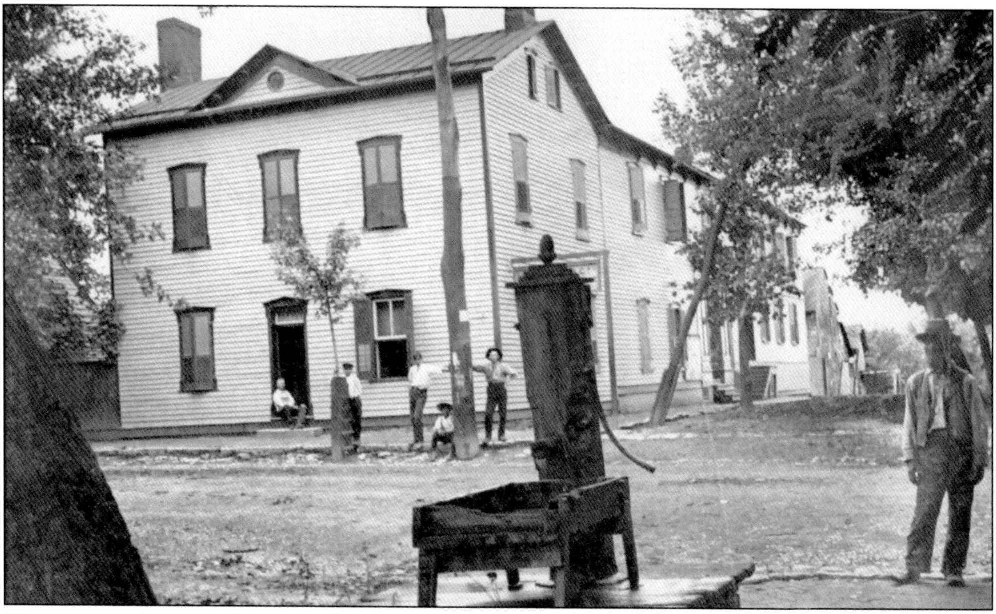

The grace and simple lifestyle of early New Market life abounds in this *c.* 1890 tintype image of the Elon Henkel House on Congress Street. Still standing, this home is located almost directly across the street of the original town pump. Trees still command the vision as they did, rambling beautifully down the Congress Street as a truly fine feature of the town. The young man sitting inside the doorway is Elon Henkel, one of the last of the family to be associated with the Henkel Press and one of the town's beloved citizens. (Dr. Gene Comstock.)

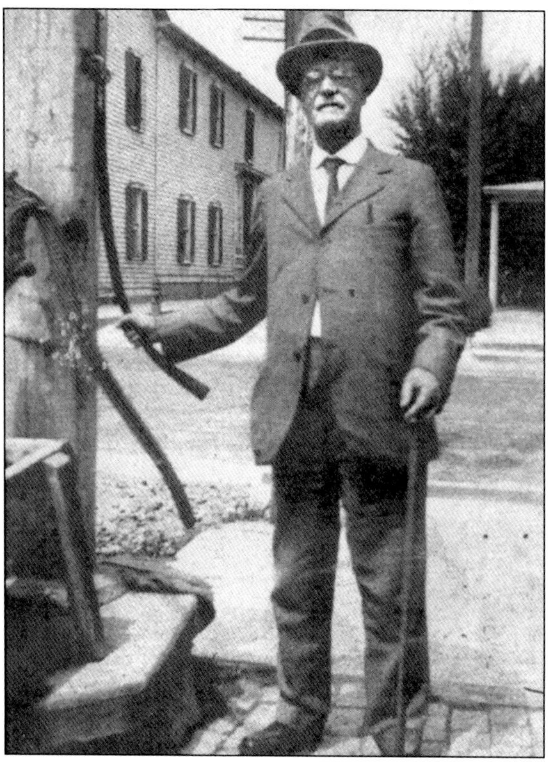

Elon Henkel stands at one of the town pumps on Congress Street. His house is visible across the street over his right shoulder. He and his brother, Ambrose, ran Henkel Printing until Ambrose passed away early in life. Elon then ran the business for many years before poor health forced him to sell the business to Dr. C. O. Miller. (Nancy Branner Stewart.)

A rare, scrap test print from the early Henkel Press illustrating the town pump is one of the earliest views. This print is likely one of the original Henkel woodcuts produced by the Henkel family in about 1815. The authors feel this is the first representation of the original well pump in the town. Well pumps with quality water played an important roll in the story of New Market and why it was chosen as a town site. (Luray Caverns Corporation.)

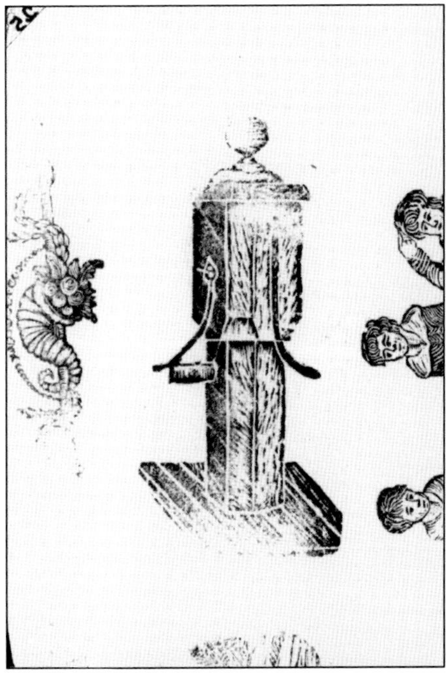

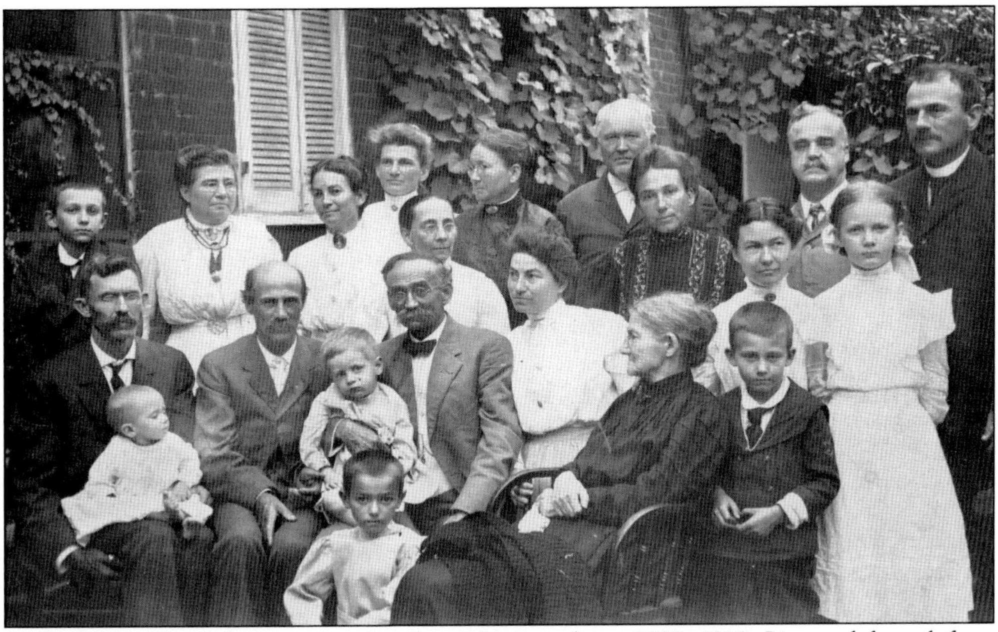

Anna Maria Henkel chairs her family gathering about 1909–1910. Pictured from left to right are (first row) Rev. Dr. Wylie Washington Josephus Ritchie with Miller Ritchie, Matthias Henkel, Fred Ritchie (on the ground), Dr. Miller Henkel with George Miller Fetzer, Julia (Mrs. Elon) Henkel, Anna Maria (Miller) Henkel, Annie Wornam, Charles Ritchie (in front), and Martha K. Moore; (second row) unidentified boy, Emily Fisher (Mrs. Matthias) Henkel (behind Dr. Henkel), and Anna Maria (Mrs. Wylie W. J.) Ritchie (behind Anna Maria Henkel); (third row) Rebecca (Mrs. Isaiah) Funkhouser, Gertrude Huffard, Martha Henkel, Josephine (Mrs. Newton) Moore, Newton Moore, Elon O. Henkel, and Dr. Alfred Henkel, M.D. (Nancy Branner Stewart.)

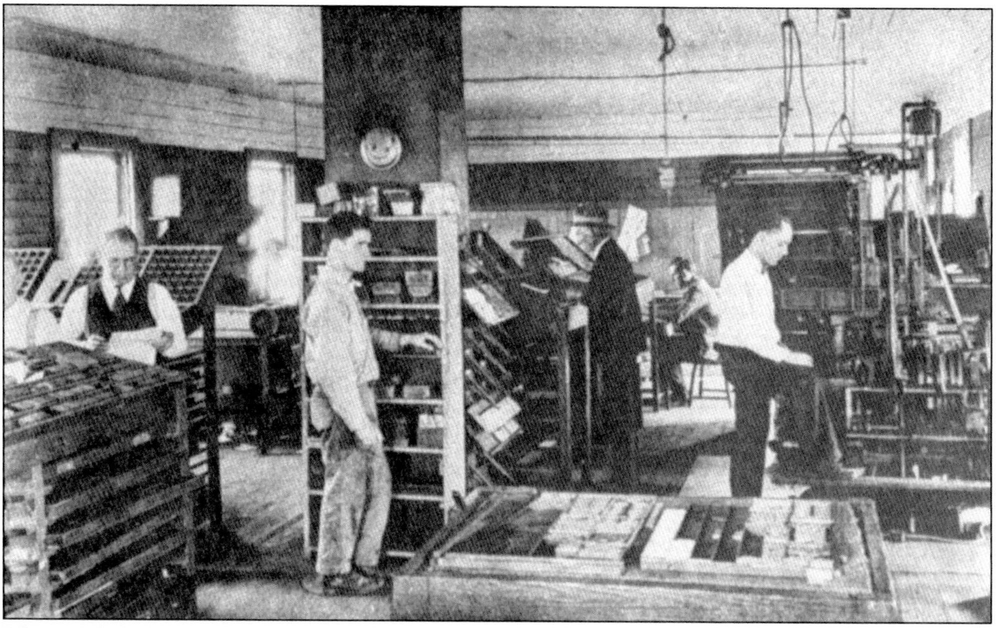

The Henkel Printing office, shown about 1921, was located directly behind Elon Henkel's house. Pictured from left to right are employees L. Benton Baker; Richard Zirkle; Charles "Cooney" Long (with his ever-present hat); editor John G. Miller, son of Dr. C. O. Miller (seated at a table in the back); and Herman Olinger, the linotype operator. (Nancy Branner Stewart.)

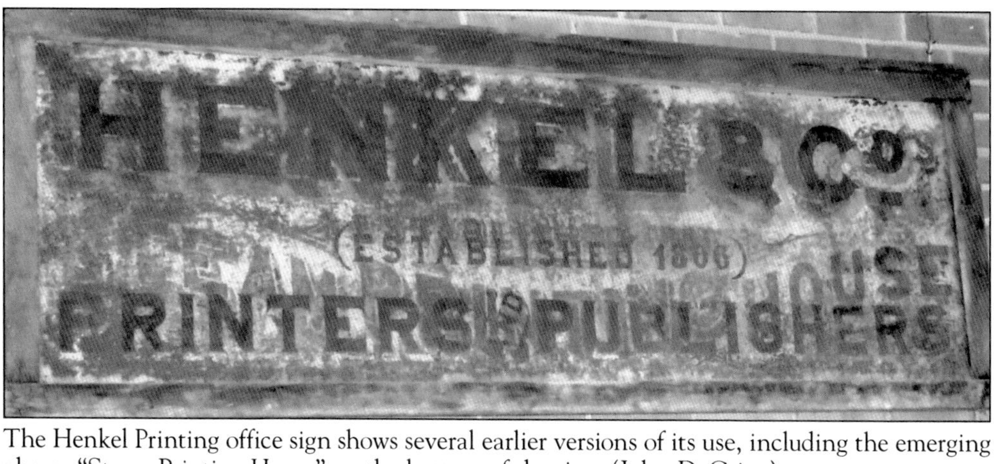

The Henkel Printing office sign shows several earlier versions of its use, including the emerging phrase "Steam Printing House" on the bottom of the sign. (John D. Crim.)

Three

CIVIL WAR AND "THE BATTLE"

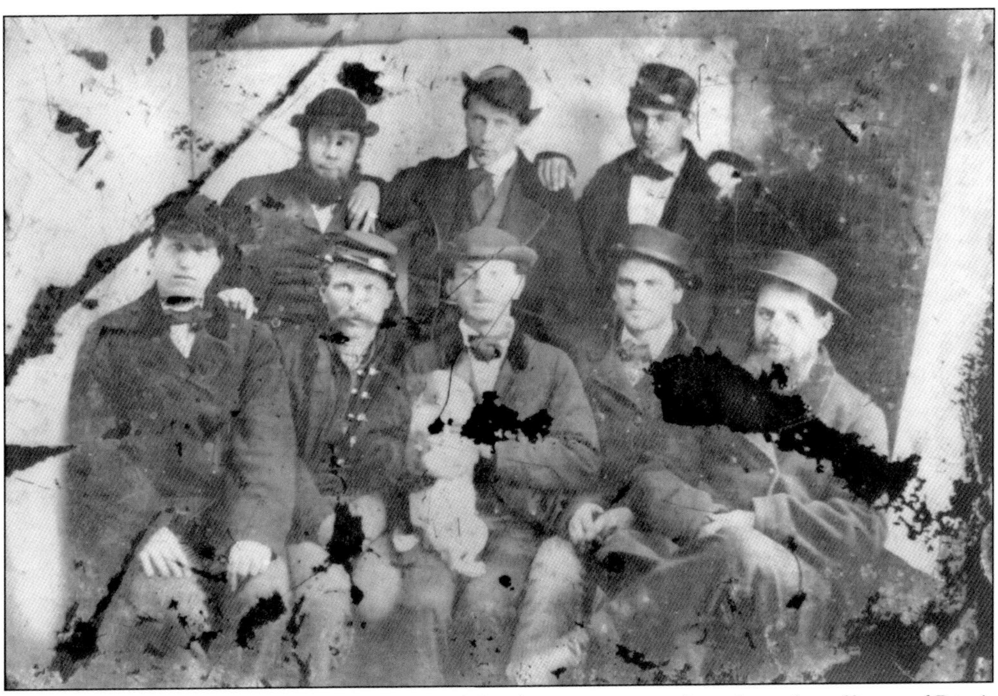

A group of local Confederate soldiers posed for the camera are thought to be officers of Rice's Battery. The young man in the center of the first row is identified as Capt. Billy Rice of New Market's Rice's Battery. Captain Rice is holding his favorite companion for the image. (John D. Crim.)

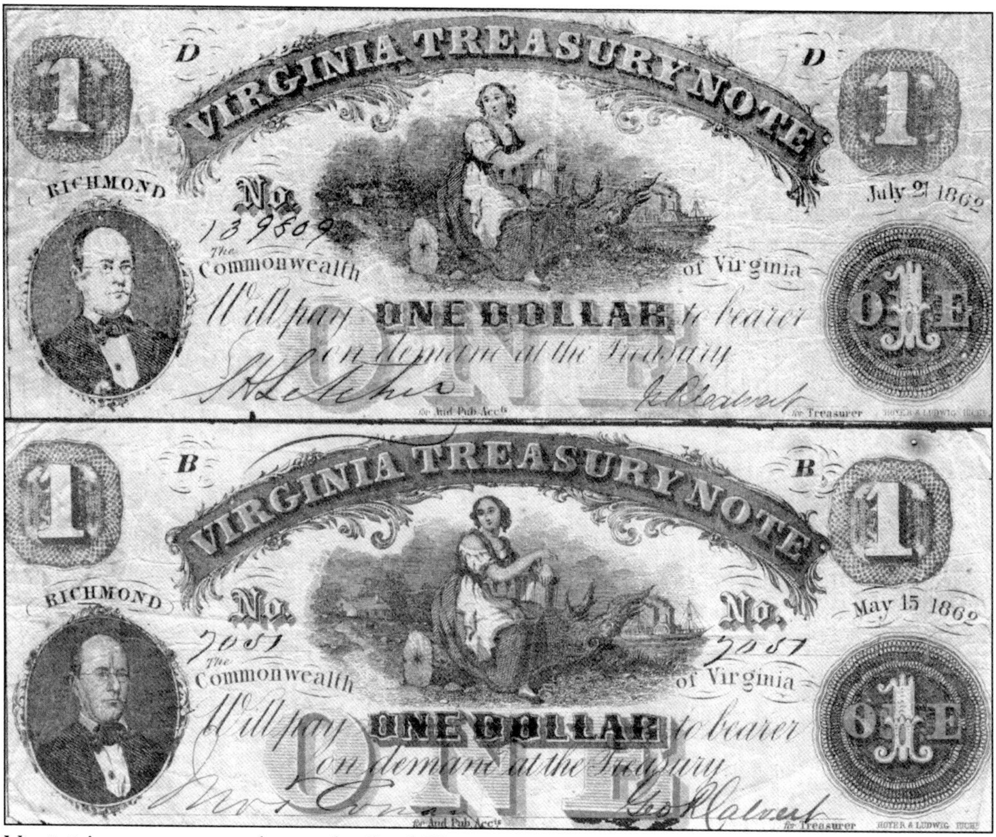

Virginia's state treasurer during the Civil War, New Market native John S. Calvert, authorized his son, Judge George R. Calvert, to also sign Virginia's treasury notes during the war. George married Annie Clinedinst, the sister of Eliza (Clinedinst) Crim and John W. "Johnny-Go" Clinedinst, the carriage maker. (John D. Crim.)

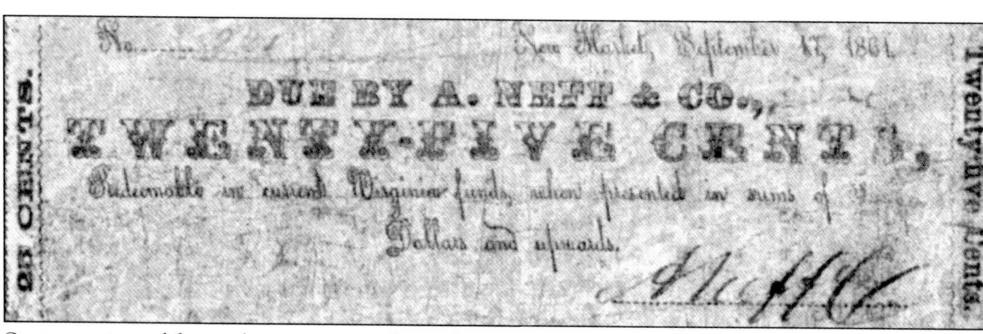

Scrip was issued for trade purposes early in the Civil War by Abraham Neff for use at his store in the stone building at the town crossroads (see page 2). Other merchants issued similar scrip for their own commercial operations. (John Bracken.)

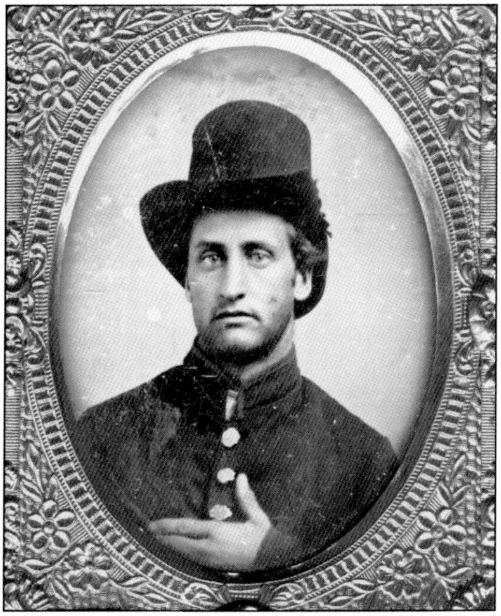

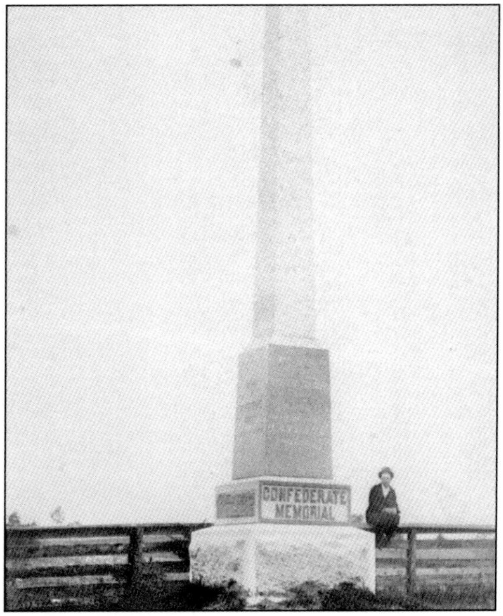

LEFT: In this early 1861 image, Casper Branner poses with his regulation Hardy hat in Forestville. He was a member of the 7th Virginia Cavalry, Company K with his brother, Phillip. He got his degree at Mossy Creek Academy under the famous Jedediah Hotchkiss before the war. Hotchkiss was Stonewall Jackson's mapmaker during the Valley Campaign. (Nancy Branner Stewart.)
RIGHT: The Women's Memorial Society for the Lost Cause dedicated this obelisk on May 12, 1898. The monument was dedicated to all Confederate veterans. The society was founded in 1867 in New Market. It was dedicated to the memories of Southern soldiers and the Virginia Military Institute (VMI) cadets. John S. Wise, New Market cadet, spoke at the dedication ceremony. (New Market Battlefield.)

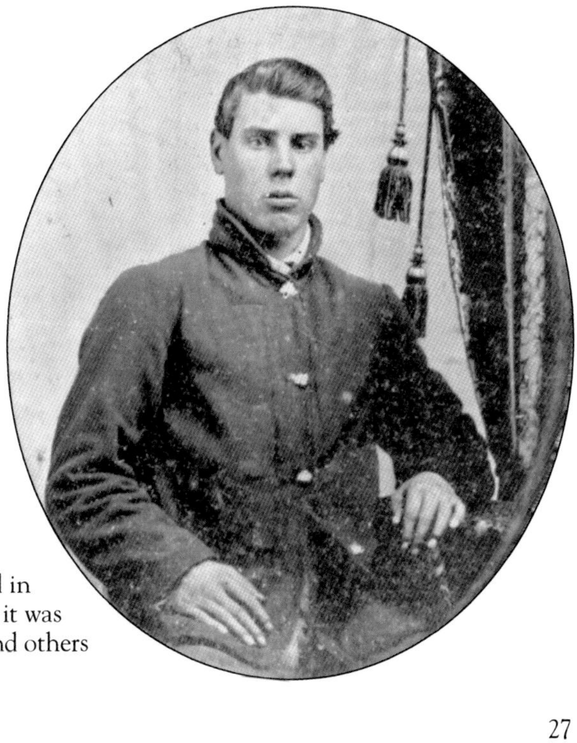

Phillip Branner was born December 2, 1836. He would have been 25 when he enlisted in the 7th Virginia Cavalry, Company K, CSA, when the Civil War broke out. He took leave during the struggle to wed Mary Estep in January 1864 in Forestville. This image may have been taken shortly after that event. He stated in a letter to his brother, Josiah, "I tell you it was awful to be in a battle to see men fall and others hollering." (Nancy Branner Stewart.)

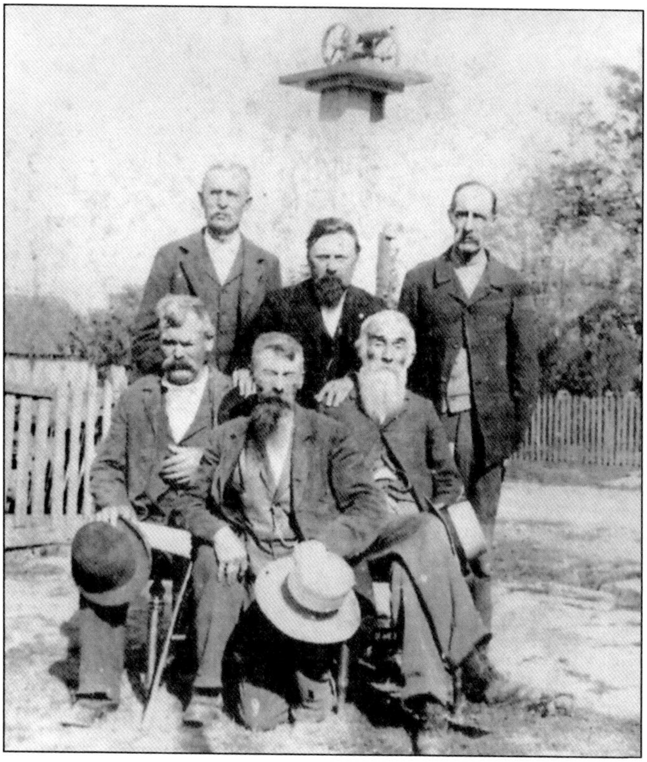

Years after the Civil War, probably on a May 15 in the late 1880s, a group of local veterans gathered at the shell-struck post in front of St. Matthew's Lutheran Church. Pictured from left to right are (seated) Henry Theis, Gustavus Wickes, and George Neese; (standing) George Kennedy, J. T. Neff, and John Shaffer [*sic*]. (John D. Crim.)

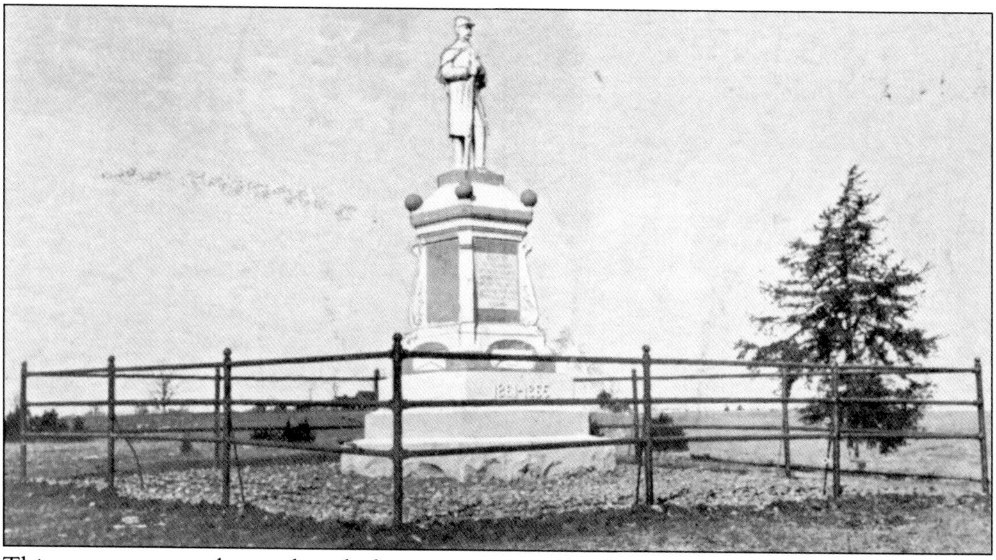

This monument on the north end of town was erected by the veterans of the 54th Pennsylvania Infantry who participated in the May 1864 battle. For their valor and sacrifice in the New Market fight, the old Union veterans were especially touched that the townspeople would let them make this tribute to a former enemy. It was a sincere gesture by the citizens of New Market to share in their loss. This warm extension to their Pennsylvania brethren would later bear fruit, as it helped with generally improved relations and tourism of Northerners seeking to understand the battle long after the dedication in 1906. This monument is now protected by the Shenandoah Valley Battlefields Foundation. (Nancy Branner Stewart.)

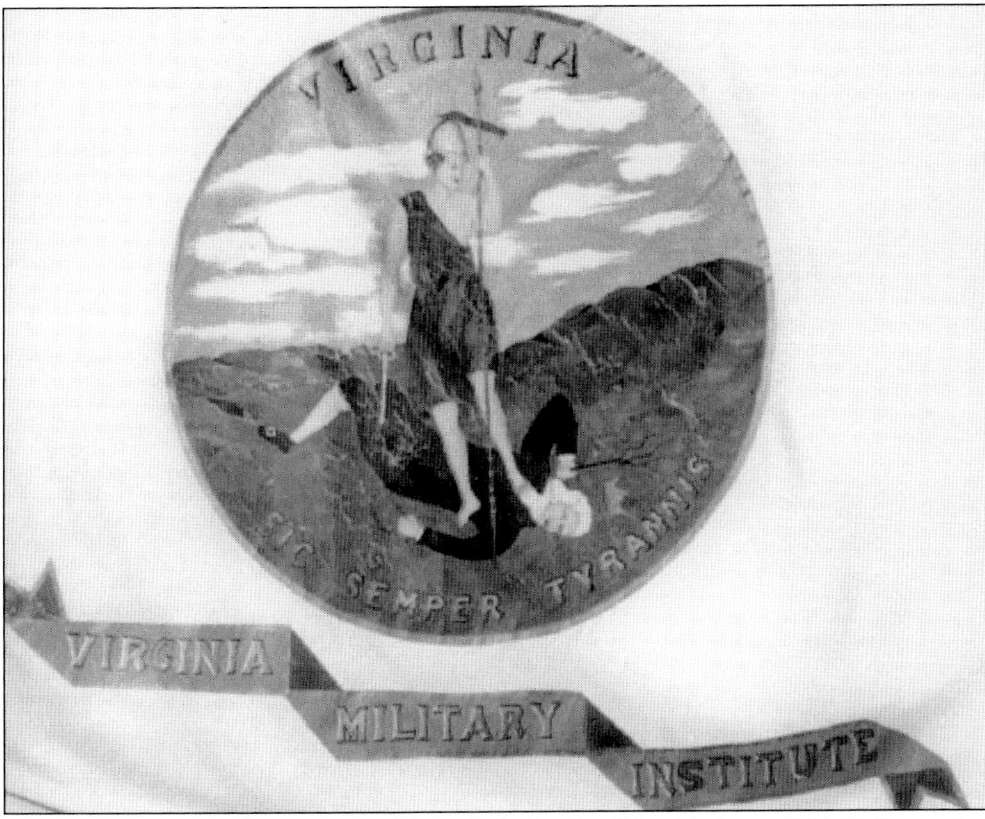

The flag of the VMI cadets was carried through the Battle of New Market in 1864. VMI's standard bearer was Cadet Rusty Evans in the heroic charge of the cadets. Evans stood atop the Union battery waving the banner to encourage his comrades up the muddy hill. (VMI Archives.)

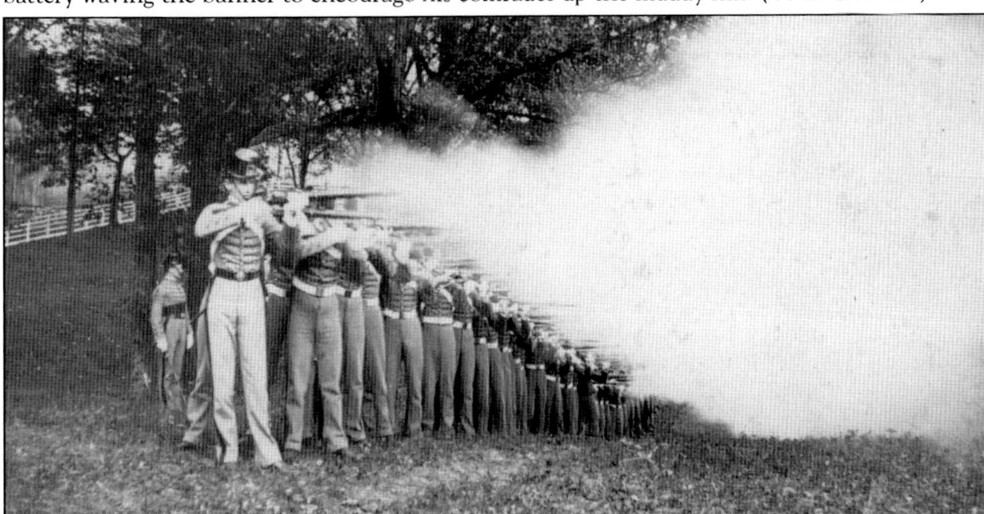
On May 15, 1900, a VMI cadet squad fired a volley in salute at the New Market Cadet Cemetery. The annual ceremony, which continues today, honored the 10 cadets killed in the Battle of New Market on May 15, 1864. The cadet cemetery, established in 1878 in the northwest corner of the VMI Parade Ground, allowed New Market cadet burials until 1912. (VMI Archives.)

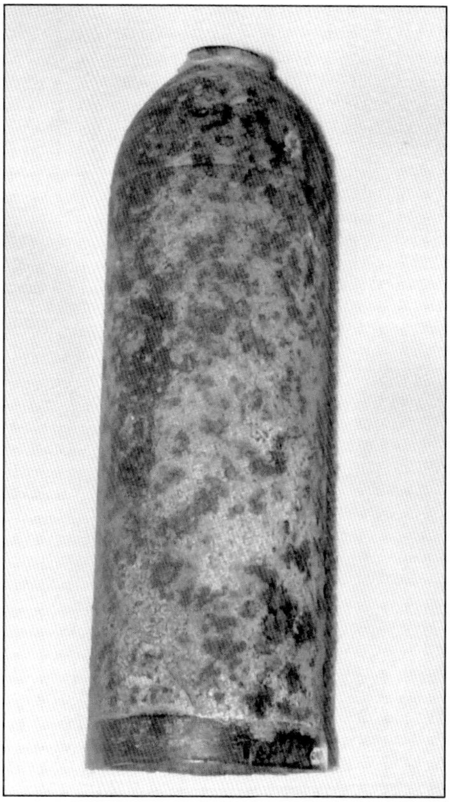

On the second day of fighting in the Battle of New Market, there was a fruitless yet active artillery duel between the North and South into the night before the VMI cadets arrived in town. In the 20th century, an elderly farmer in New Market plowed this Parrott cannon shell on Shirley's Hill where the Confederate artillery was generally located during the fight. Stonewall Jackson had been killed earlier in the war, but his valley army still survived. In 1864, there had only ever been one Parrott rifle cannon in the valley army. The Parrot cannon shell was given to John Bracken (a New Market Civil War historian and collector) for his well-known Civil War museum on Shirley's Hill. (John Bracken.)

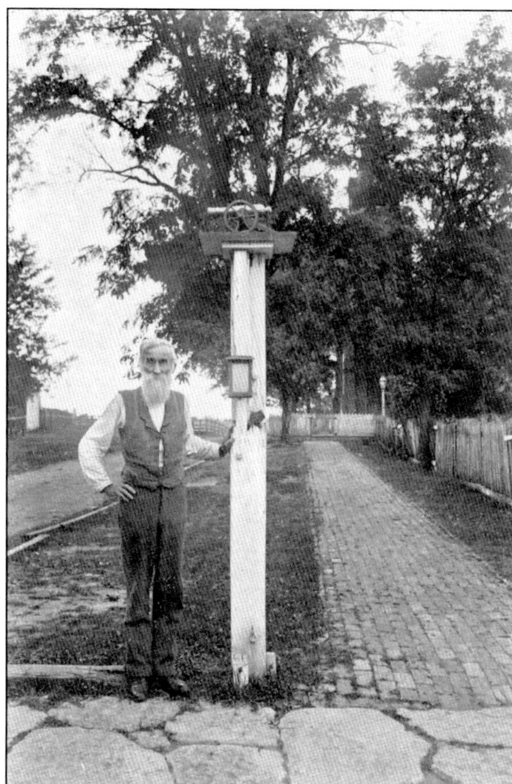

Confederate veteran George Neese, who published his Civil War diary as a book, *Three Years in the Confederate Horse Artillery*, stands beside the shell-struck post in the latter 1890s. He is standing in front of St. Matthew's Lutheran Church on Congress Street. (Fritzi Orebaugh.)

This portrait of young Thomas Garland Jefferson, great-grandnephew of Pres. Thomas Jefferson, was probably painted at the family home of Winterham in Amelia Court House, some 30 miles west of Richmond. One of 14 children, he grew up on a plantation that grew tobacco and cotton. (VMI Archives.)

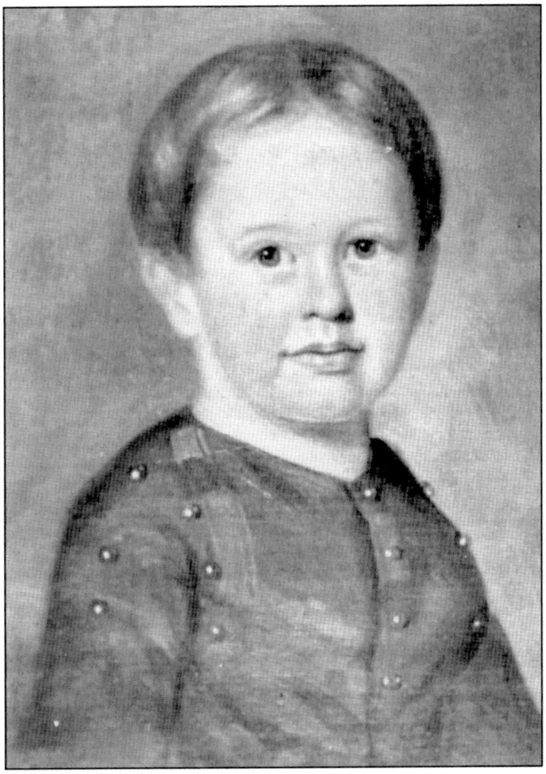

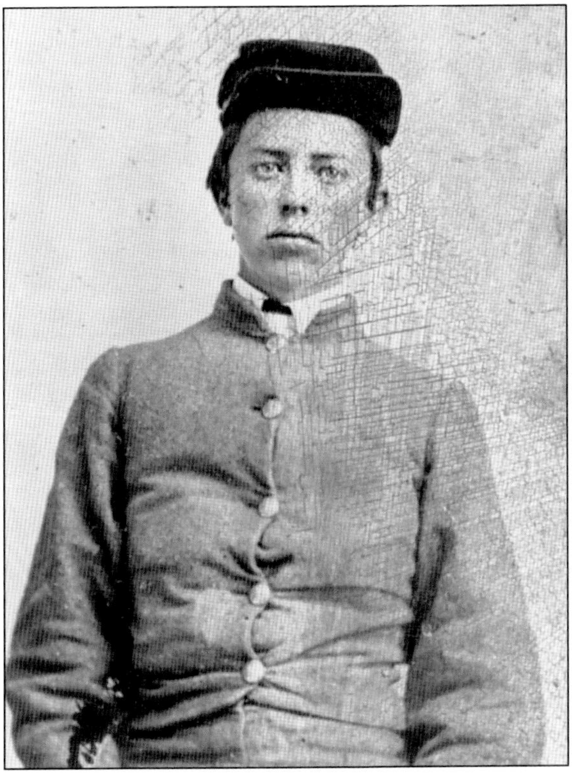

Thomas Garland Jefferson is pictured as a freshman cadet at the Virginia Military Institute. He was mortally wounded at the Battle of New Market, dying two days later in the home of Eliza Clinedinst. By his side was friend Moses Ezekiel, VMI's first Jewish cadet, reading from John 14 of the New Testament. After his death, Eliza remained close with the Jefferson family until her death in 1931. (VMI Archives.)

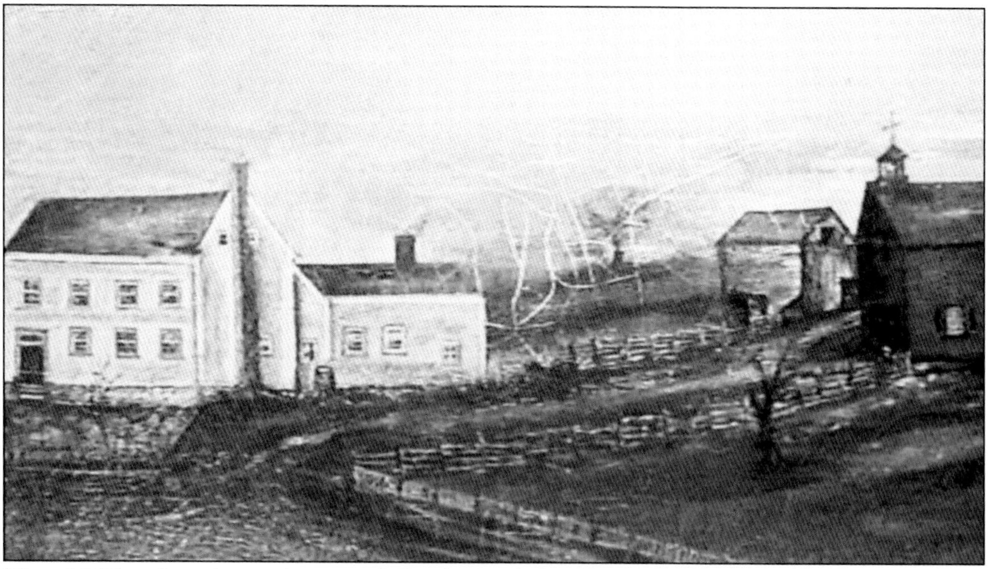

The old Clinedinst home, barn, and Smith Creek Baptist Church along Seminary Lane were painted from memory by Jacob R. Clinedinst Jr. in the 1890s. After the battle, the wounded cadet Jefferson was carried here from the Lightfoot farm north of town. The home was replaced in 1882 by the present house at 9349 Congress Street. Jacob was a brother of Eliza (Clinedinst) Crim and John W. Clinedinst, the carriage maker. (New Market Battlefield.)

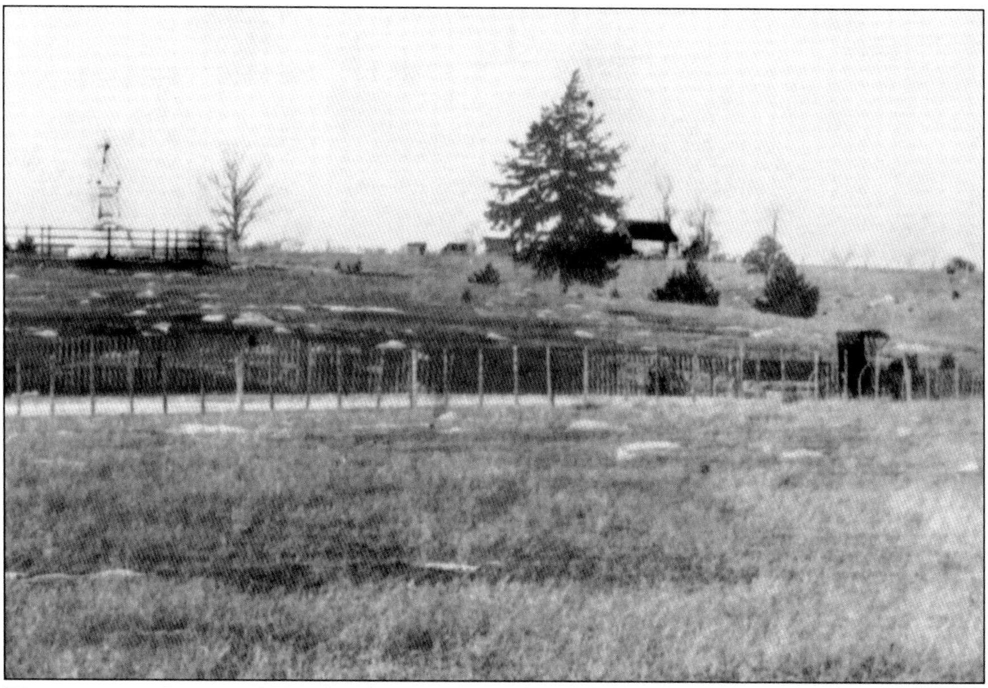

The writing on Branson O'Roark's photograph of the battlefield near New Market, Virginia, reads, "showing the Federal monument, [and] the Lightfoot household [in the background at right] used as a hospital, also hollow where Federals were buried." The Clinedinst family and Moses Ezekiel carried the wounded cadet Jefferson from the farmhouse, where he lay on the cold stone hearth, back to their home. (John D. Crim.)

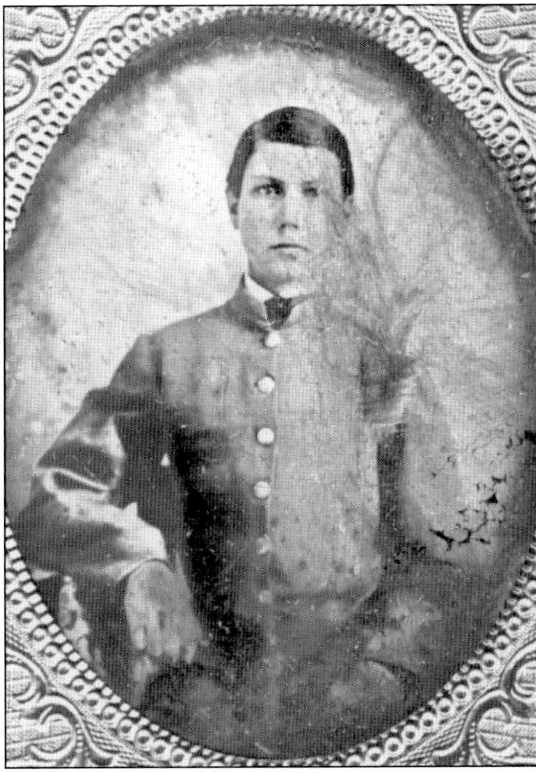

Shown in his new cadet uniform, Cadet William H. McDowell of Orange, Virginia, posed for this image for his mother in Lexington, Virginia, at the Virginia Military Institute about 1863. Rebecca McDowell, his mother, was quoted in a letter from October 3: "Should any misfortune misfall him I would like some likeness of him." His mother's premonition came to bear as her son fell mortally wounded at New Market. Federal troops commanded the hill, and the young men were ordered to advance with the 58th Virginia Infantry to take Shirley's Hill from the Union infantry on Mother's Day 1864. He is re-created in the title role of *The Ghost Cadet*, a popular fictional children's story that used him as the main character. McDowell was one of 10 cadets "Fallen on the field of Honor." Later Confederate president Jefferson Davis lamented their death, stating, "The cadets were the seed corn of the Confederacy." (VMI Archives.)

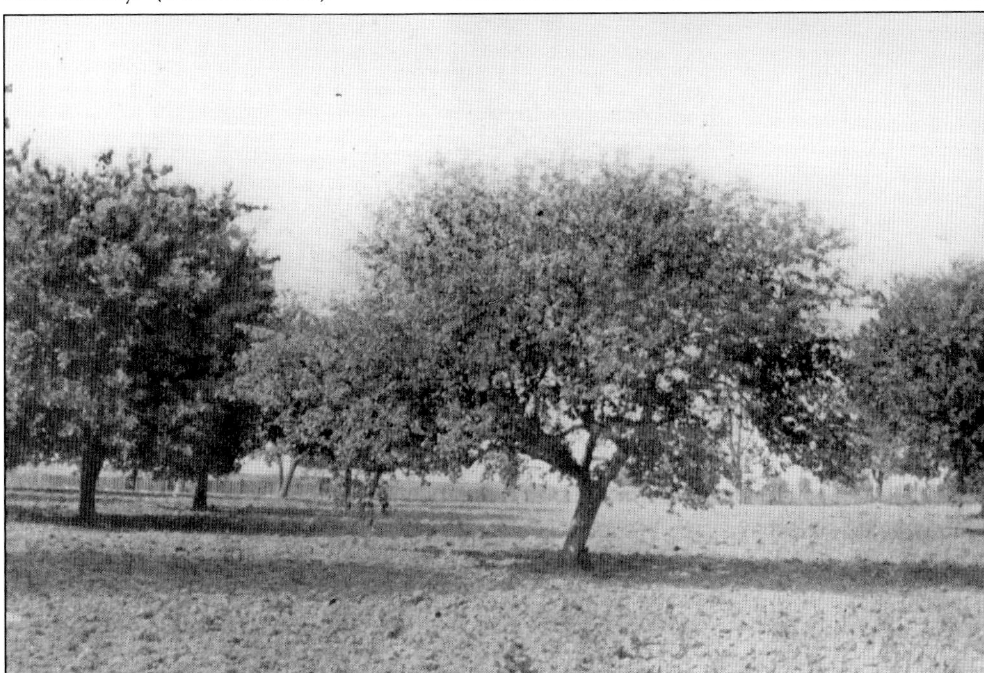

The apple orchard located behind the Bushong house was used by Union and Confederate forces as cover as the fighting ebbed and flowed around the house. The fence in the background replaced the original split rail fence used for cover by both sides during the battle. (New Market Battlefield.)

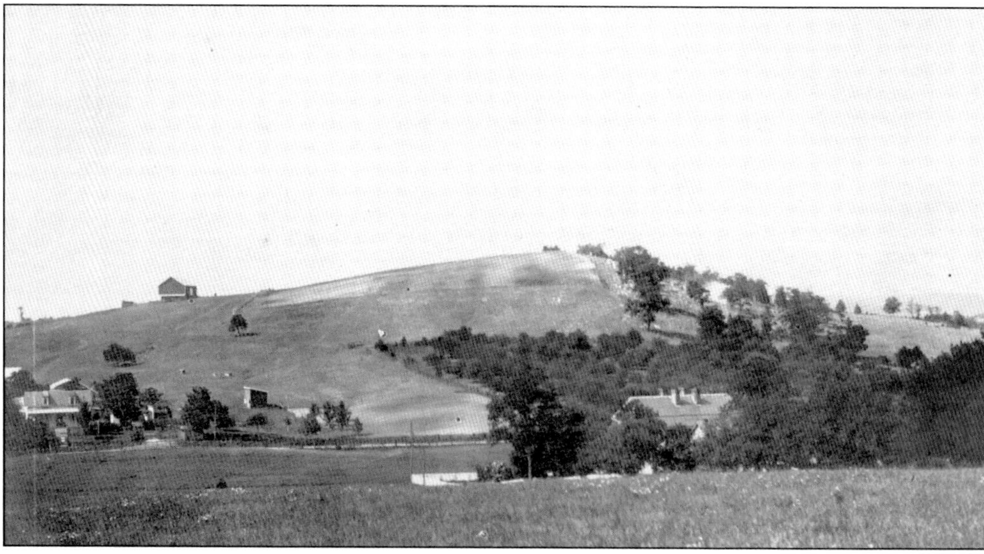

At the start of the battle, Confederate forces were massed behind the crest of the hill. Given the order to advance under heavy artillery fire, the 62nd Virginia Infantry rushed down the slope to the bottom, while the VMI cadets marched down the hill in parade formation. The cadets sustained their first casualties during the cannonade. (New Market Battlefield.)

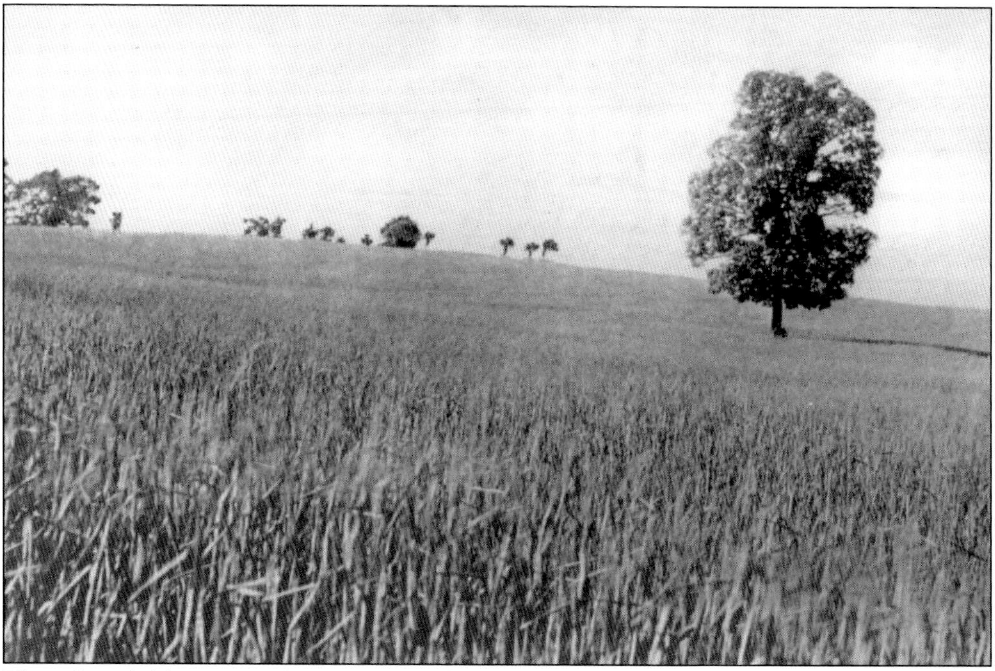

This wheat field was once the scene of hardened Confederate veterans and the VMI cadets. At the top of the hill, Federal artillery were in place with positions of Sigel Union soldiers holding a relatively strong position except for a cliff at the Federal rear with not much diversion. This field was saturated with a cold rain that caused great muddy areas on the battlefield. As they commenced their charge, the cadets' shoes were sucked off them by the wet red clay, dubbing the area "the field of lost shoes." With all these hardships, the Union position was still captured by the brave young boys from VMI. (New Market Battlefield.)

Seen in his 1863 VMI cadet fatigues, Jacqueline Beverly "Bev" Stanard posed for the camera. This is the only known likeness of the boy. Stanard was a member of the class of 1867 at the elite military school of Virginia Military Institute, called "the West Point of the South." The young lad hailed from Orange, Virginia, but he would never see the place again, as he died at the Battle of New Market at the tender age of 18. He was only supposed to be on wagon detail during the fight, but he voluntarily exchanged his duty for action. Prior to his death, he was confirmed in church after having many premonitions of his mortality. His body was buried in New Market and later was reburied back home in Orange at the Graham Cemetery. (VMI Archives.)

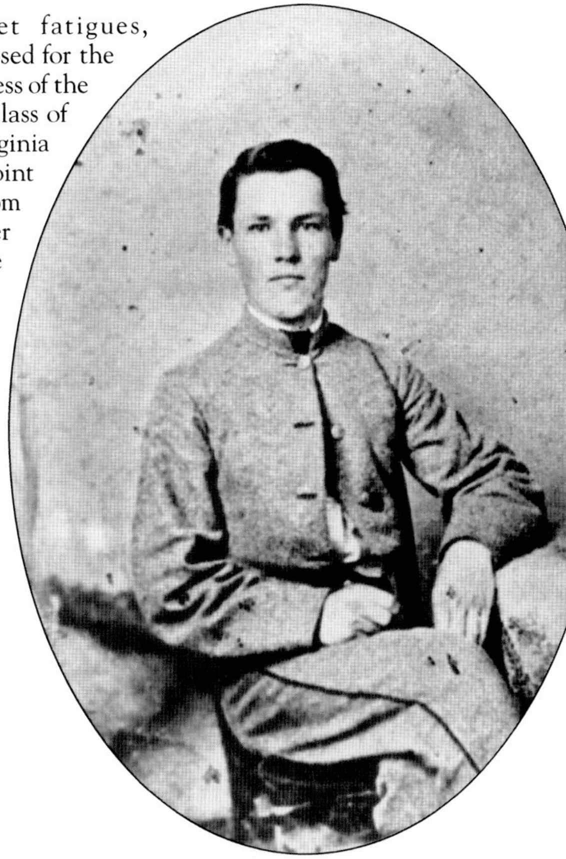

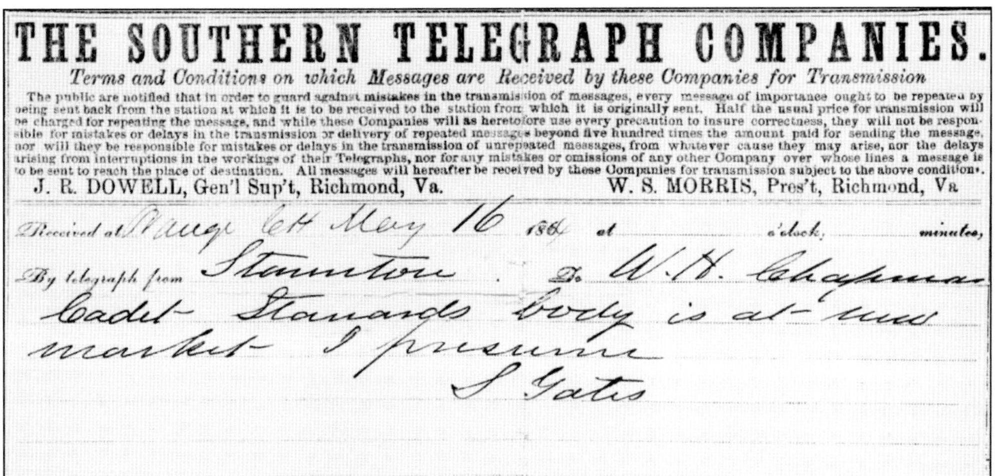

THE SOUTHERN TELEGRAPH COMPANIES.

Terms and Conditions on which Messages are Received by these Companies for Transmission

The public are notified that in order to guard against mistakes in the transmission of messages, every message of importance ought to be repeated by being sent back from the station at which it is to be received to the station from which it is originally sent. Half the usual price for transmission will be charged for repeating the message, and while these Companies will as heretofore use every precaution to insure correctness, they will not be responsible for mistakes or delays in the transmission or delivery of repeated messages beyond five hundred times the amount paid for sending the message, nor will they be responsible for mistakes or delays in the transmission of unrepeated messages, from whatever cause they may arise, nor the delays arising from interruptions in the workings of their Telegraphs, nor for any mistakes or omissions of any other Company over whose lines a message is to be sent to reach the place of destination. All messages will hereafter be received by these Companies for transmission subject to the above conditions.

J. R. DOWELL, Gen'l Sup't, Richmond, Va. W. S. MORRIS, Pres't, Richmond, Va

Received at Orange CH May 16 186[4] at o'clock, minutes,

By telegraph from Staunton. To W. H. Chapman

Cadet Stanards body is at new market I presume

S Gates

News of VMI cadet Bev Stanard's death on the killing fields of New Market reached the Confederate telegraph office in Staunton, Virginia, May 16, 1864. It was just one day after he perished that the sad news was broadcast. The telegram stated "Cadet Stanard's body is in New Market." The death notice was received by William H. Chapman, second in command of the famous 43rd Battalion, 1st Virginia Cavalry, otherwise known as Mosby's Rangers. Chapman was also a native of neighboring Luray, Virginia. (VMI Archives.)

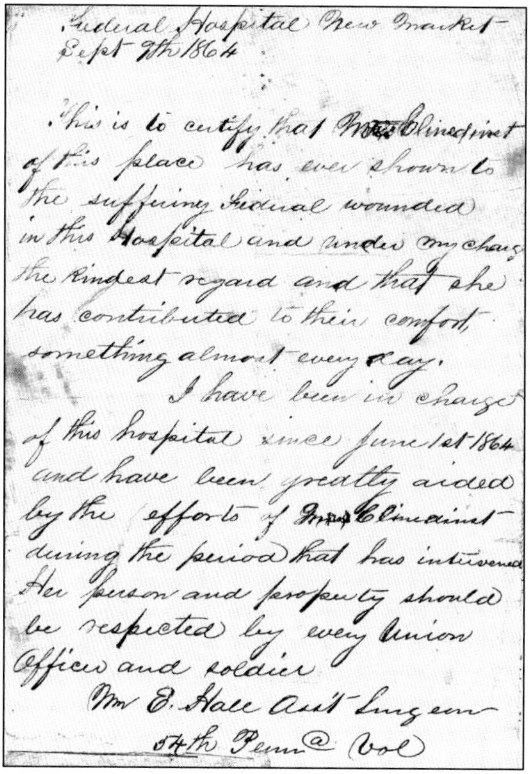
Federal Hospital New Market
Sept 9th 1864

This is to certify that Mrs Clinedinst of this place has ever shown to the suffering Federal wounded in this Hospital and under my charge the kindest regard and that she has contributed to their comfort something almost every day.

I have been in charge of this hospital since June 1st 1864 and have been greatly aided by the efforts of Mrs Clinedinst during the period that has intervened. Her person and property should be respected by every Union Officer and soldier

Wm E. Hall Ass't Surgeon
54th Penna Vol

Eliza Clinedinst was issued this handwritten certification for her assistance from June 1 through September 9, 1864, acknowledging that her tireless efforts for the suffering Federal wounded "has contributed to their comfort something almost every day" and that "Her person and property should be respected by every Union Officer and soldier." The certification was signed by William E. Hall, assistant surgeon, 54th Pennsylvania Volunteers. (John D. Crim.)

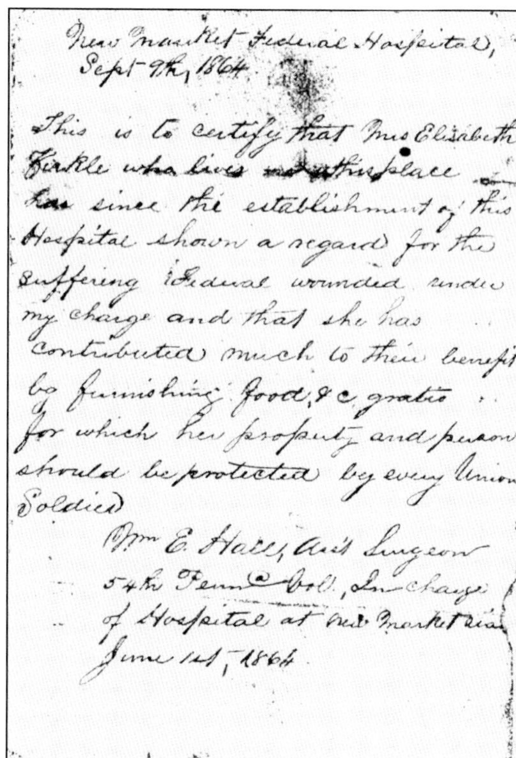
New Market Federal Hospital,
Sept 9th, 1864.

This is to certify that Mrs Elizabeth Zirkle who lives in this place has since the establishment of this Hospital shown a regard for the suffering Federal wounded under my charge and that she has contributed much to their benefit by furnishing food, &c. gratis for which her property and person should be protected by every Union Soldier

Wm E. Hall, Ass't Surgeon
54th Penna Vol, In charge of Hospital at New Market Va
June 1st, 1864.

Elizabeth Zirkle was issued this handwritten certification for her assistance from June 1 through September 9, 1864, acknowledging her effort and "regard for the suffering Federal wounded under my charge and that she has contributed much to their benefit by furnishing food, etc. gratis for which her property and person should be protected by every Union soldier." The certification was also signed by William E. Hall, assistant surgeon, 54th Pennsylvania Volunteers. (*Divine Destiny* by Elder Richard Harris.)

Twenty-six-year-old Eliza C. Crim cared for the wounded of both armies. She gave special attention to the mortally wounded cadet Thomas Garland Jefferson, traveling to his home in Amelia Court House to return his final effects. Though small in stature, she was large in heart and a fervent booster of all things Virginia while she drew breath. In 1941, the VMI Board of Visitors named her "Mother of the VMI Cadets." (VMI Archives.)

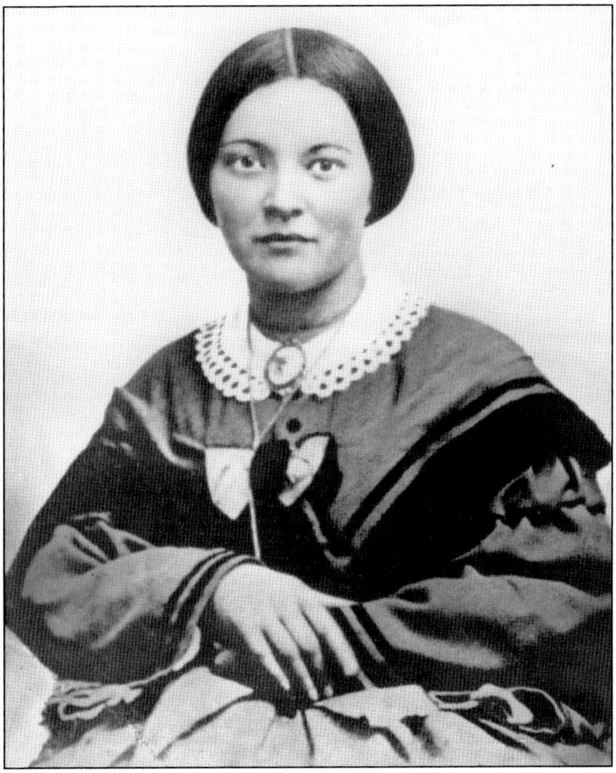

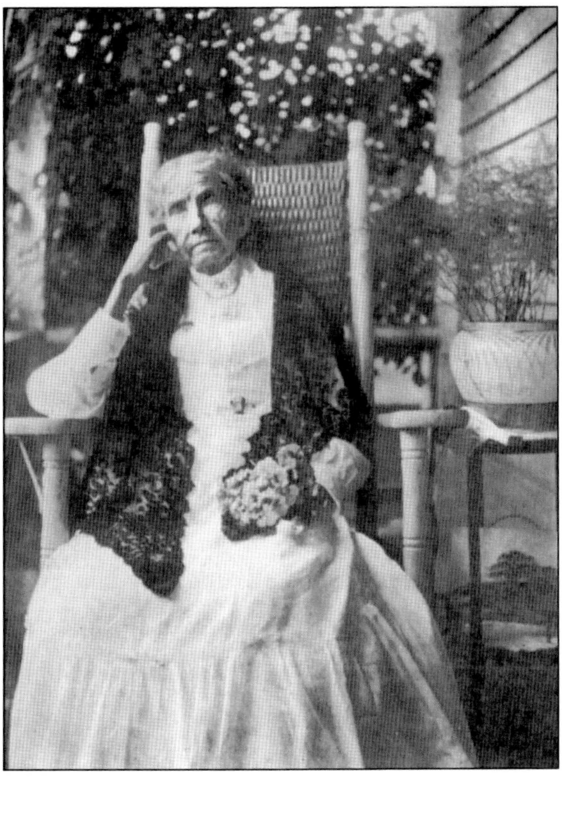

Pictured as an elderly lady at her New Market home is Jessie Rupert. "Miss Jessie," as she was called, was the heroine of the 54th Massachusetts Infantry for her care of their wounded Union soldiers after the battle. She was vilified by the townspeople for nursing Union soldiers in her home. New Market was one big hospital after the May 15 fight. Prior to the war, she taught African American children how to read and write with her friend Thomas "Stonewall" Jackson, who later came to her aid in New Market regarding the townspeople. She would remain steadfast in her beliefs, starting one of the first known mixed-race and unfortunate children schools in the South. She and Eliza Crim were friends, both respecting each other until their deaths. (Nancy Branner Stewart.)

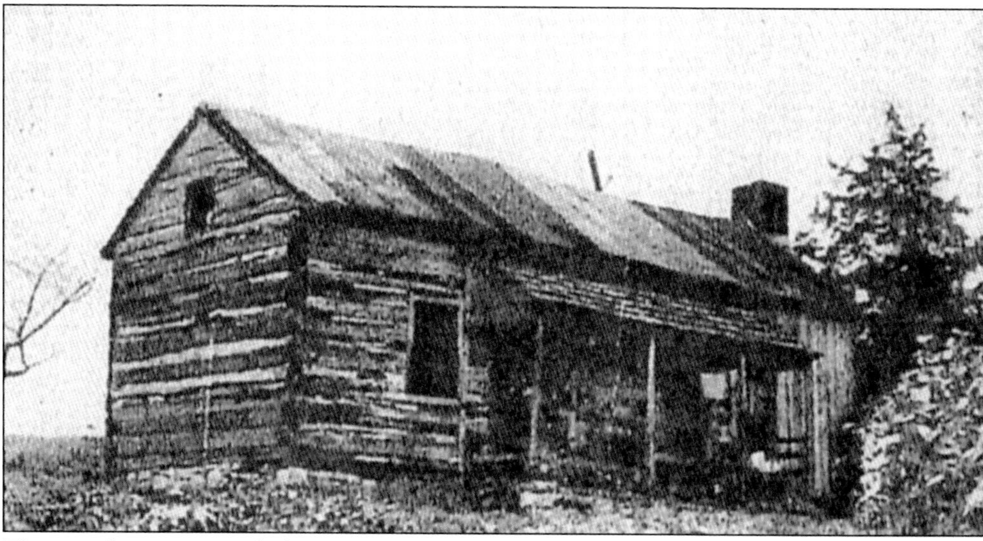

This mundane yet typical "dog trot " (two-bay) log house was the site of one of the many hospitals in New Market. As casualties filled the town to capacity, residents were simply not prepared for the gruesome detail of tending the wounded and cleaning up the carnage. The townspeople were kind, resilient, and hospitable to the soldiers' tragic conditions. It is unknown of the house's exact location, but it no longer stands. It may have been at the Lightfoot Farm, north on the Valley Pike just beyond the town. (Nancy Branner Stewart.)

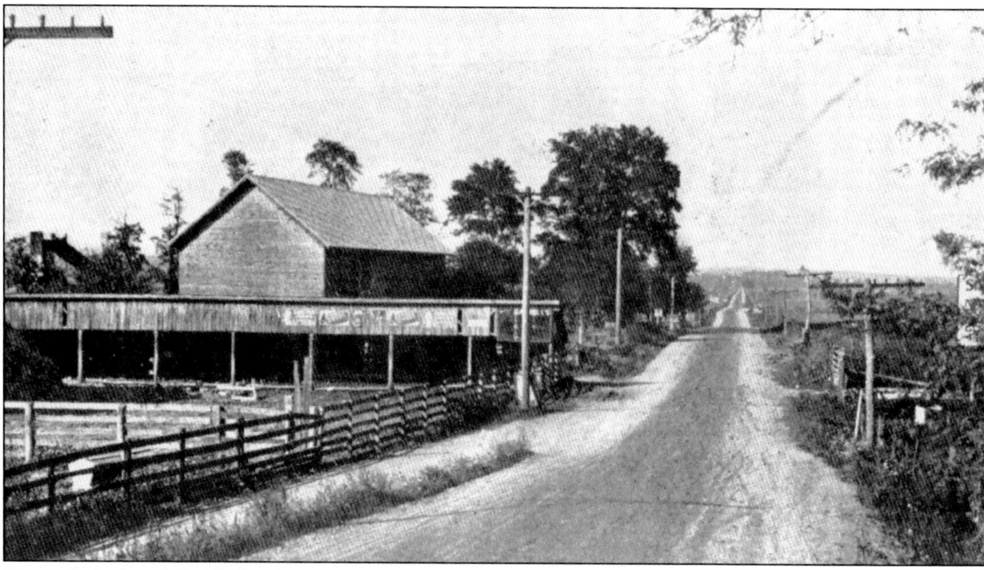

Beyond the battlefield, the defeated Union troops rapidly retreated down the Valley Pike (Route 11). They barely escaped capture by crossing the burning bridge at Meems Bottom along the Shenandoah River, reaching safety in Mount Jackson. One Union soldier committed suicide en route after being exposed to the horrors of the battle. This 1920s photograph of the old road is virtually unchanged at this vantage point of the Rude family barn. Rudes Hill was the site of much camping and campaigning during the war. Shortly after the war, two former Confederates were executed without trial for the supposed stealing of Union horses. They were Capt. George Summers and Sgt. Newton Koontz, both from the Luray Valley in Page County. A monument to this travesty is near this location. (New Market Battlefield.)

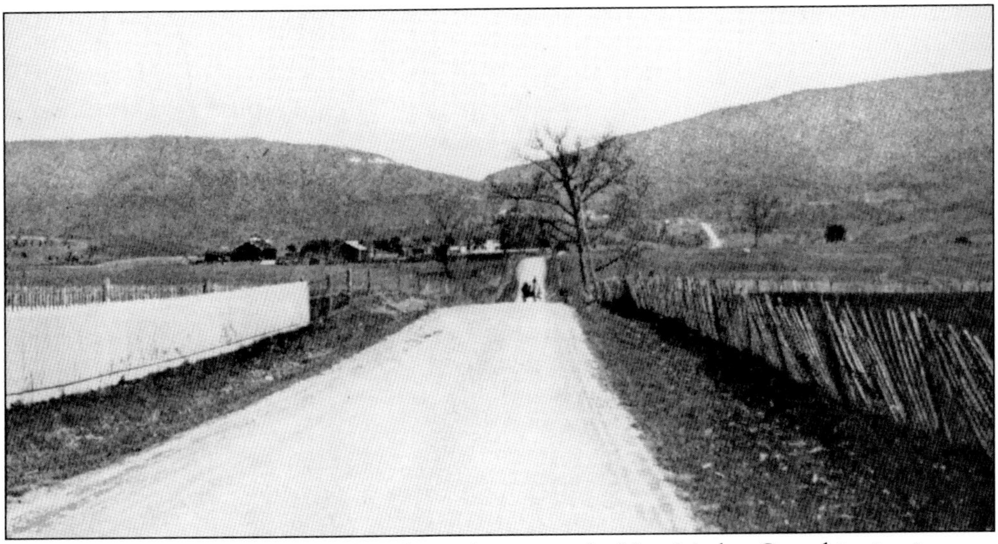

Looking at the old Massanutten Gap, better known as the New Market Gap, this view is a rare sight in a developing valley being yet unchanged in character since the Civil War. During the four years of war, as valley historian Dr. Wayland mentioned in his many scholarly histories, this mountain saw much activity. The famed Wheat's Tigers from Louisiana, in their pantalooned Zouave-styled uniforms, crossed this mountain to join other Confederate forces en route to join Jackson days before his mortal wounding at Chancellorsville. On the other side lies Luray in the Page Valley. On May 15, 1864, many of the Luray residents there thought they heard spring thunder across the mountain, but instead it was the fury of opposing cannons dueling in a terrible battle at New Market. (Nancy Branner Stewart.)

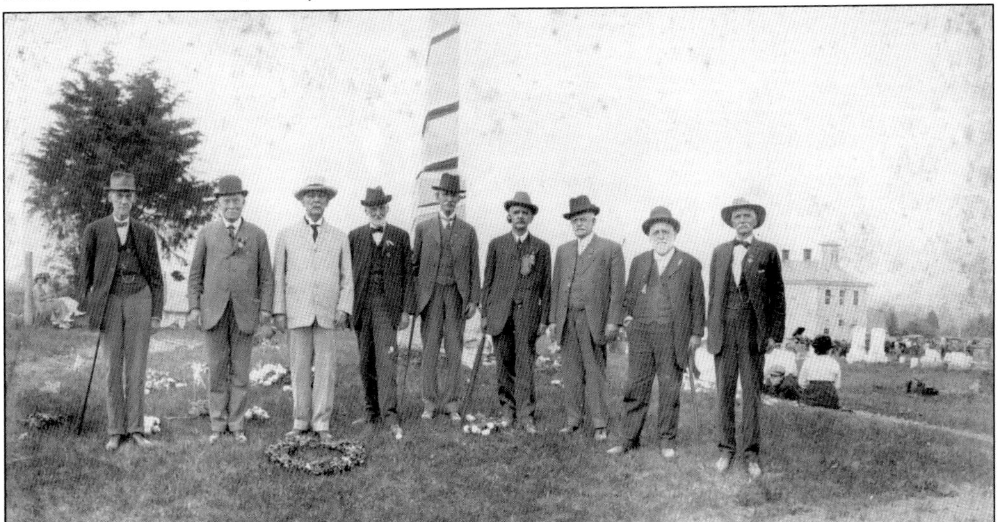

These Confederate veterans of the Battle for New Market proudly stand near the Civil War Monument behind the Lutheran church on May 15, 1914. The decorated monument behind them was dedicated on May 12, 1893. Pictured from left to right are J. P. Clarkson, Scott Shipp, John Bagnall, James Harvie, Francis Lee, Robert Cabell, Benjamin Colonna, and Henry Bowen. Very early reunions took place in the town, and one of the earliest mock battles in the country, now termed as reenactments, was held here and helped the town's growing tourism. It also served as a sobering reminder of how the town was irrevocably changed by war. (VMI Archives.)

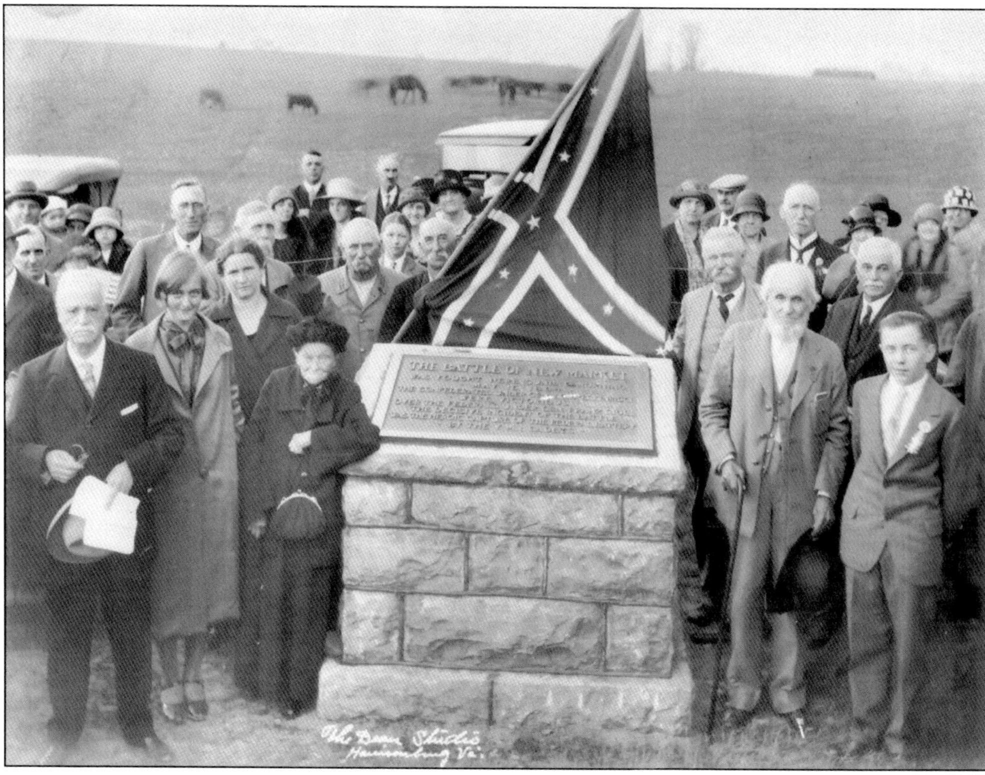

The New Market Battlefield Marker was unveiled on May 15, 1926. Erected by citizens and the State Battlefield Marker Association, the plaque is mounted on stone salvaged from the nearby Rice's barn demolition. Two cannons were added later by Rep. T. W. Harrison from the Watervliet Arsenal in New York. The marker was relocated to the battlefield in May 1986. Those who are tentatively identified below by Barbara Blakey are as follows: 1. Elon Henkel, 2. Catherine Crim, 3. Eliza "Mother" Crim, 4. Behethland Crim, 5. Dr. John W. Wayland, 6. Squire Thomas Williamson, 7. Minnie Snapp, 8. Emily Snapp, 9. Abe Zirkle, 10. William Foltz, 11. Bracky Theis, 12. Pauline Theis, 13. Mrs. Robert L. O'Roark ("Aunt Nan"), 14. Harry Smucker, 15. Martha Williamson, 16. Myrtle Moffitt Wunder, 17. Rev. J. C. Hooks, 18. Noah Zirkle, 19. Dr. C. O. Miller, 20. John G. Miller, 21. William Keyser Price Jr., and 22. John D. Miller. (John D. Crim, Barbara Blakey.)

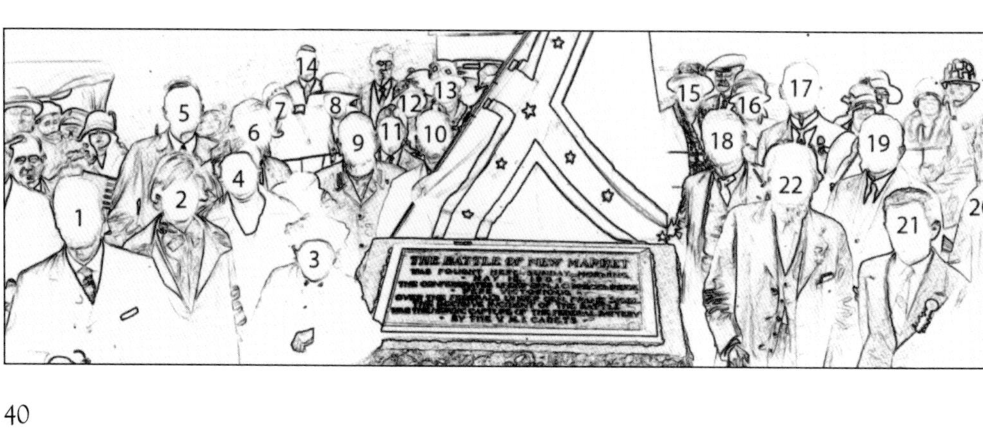

Luther M. Henkel was a Civil War veteran who is wearing the badge of the Neff-Rice Camp No. 1194 (see below). This photograph was possibly taken while he attended the United Confederate Veterans Reunion held in Houston, Texas, from October 4 through October 9, 1920. Similar Union veterans reunions were also held around the country by the Grand Army of the Republic (GAR). Veterans from both sides were warmly welcomed at all reunions. (John Bracken.)

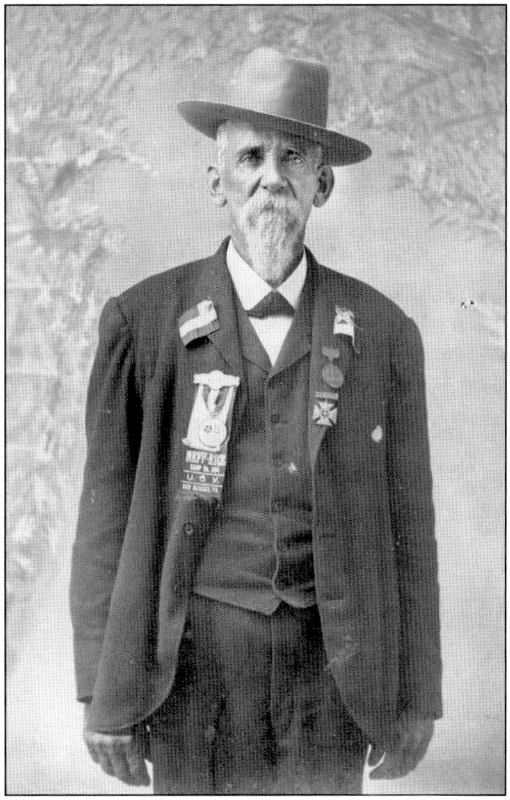

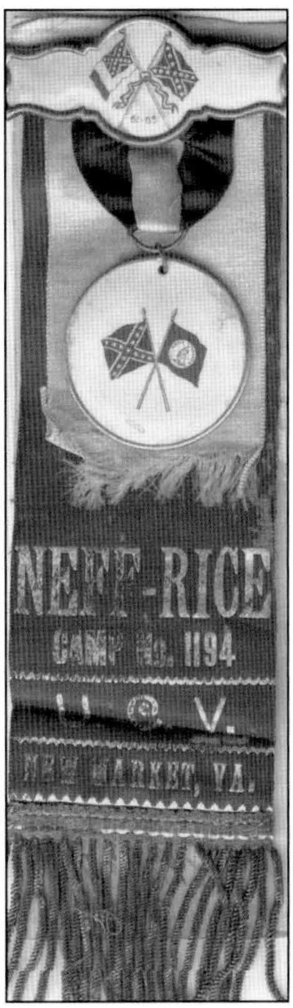

The note accompanying the Neff-Rice badge shown reads: "I borrowed this from my old friend Capt. John W. Clinedinst and wore to the Re-union of the Old Confederate Veterans held in Houston, Texas, on Oct 4th to 9th 1920. Leaving home Woodstock Oct 1st I arrived in Houston Monday evening Oct 4th 1920. Never enjoyed myself better. The people & the ladies especially could not do enough to make you feel at home. G. W. Koontz." (John D. Crim.)

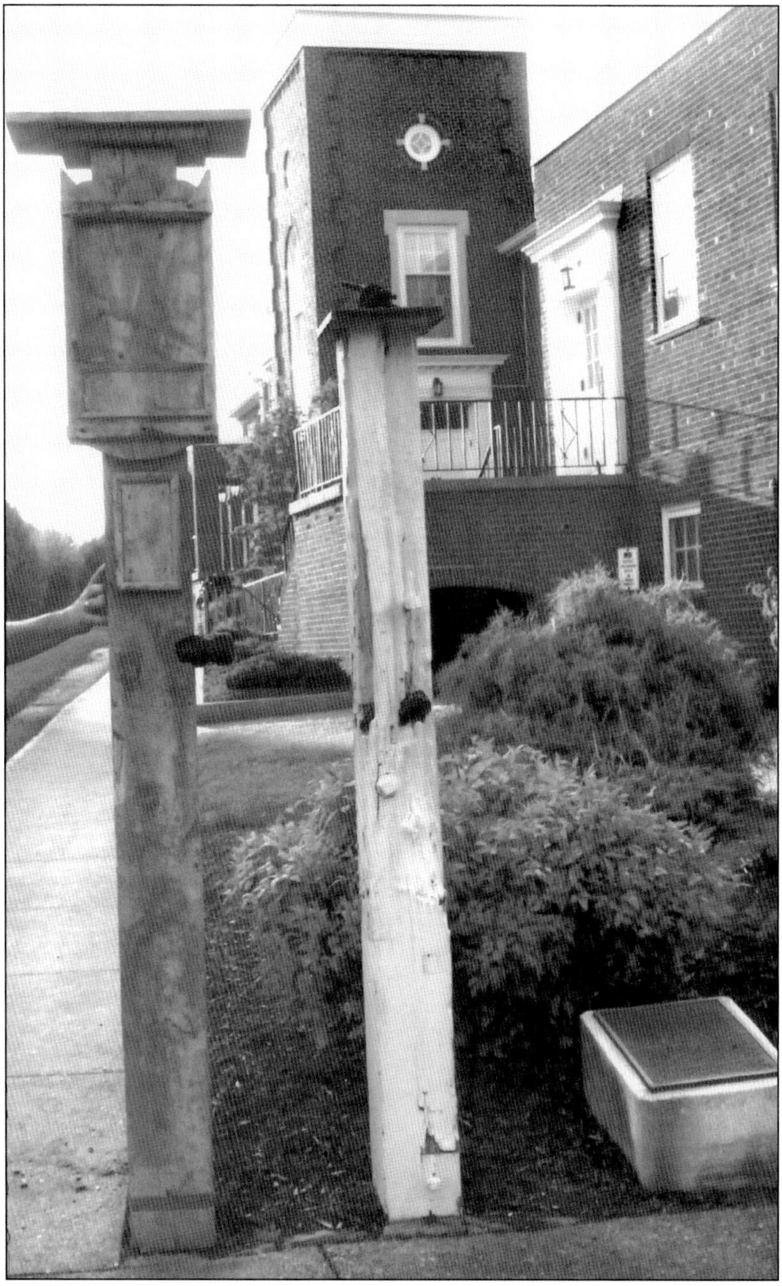

Here is a mystery from more than a century ago. For decades, local lore has held that the post (at right) in front of the Lutheran church is the one struck by a 3-inch Hotchkiss shell with Gen. John Breckinridge nearby during the battle. The shell did not explode. In 2004, the Crims' old, timber-frame barn at 9349 Congress Street was being dismantled. In the attached buggy shed, the post at left was found, having apparently been there for many years. The hole in this post perfectly fits a 3-inch Hotchkiss shell (shown at center), and the top platform indicates screw holes that could have held the model of a cannon. Asked about the possible fate of the original post, local historian Bracky Theis is said to have responded, "The Crims have it." So which one is the real post? (John D. Crim.)

Four

Sporting and Hunting

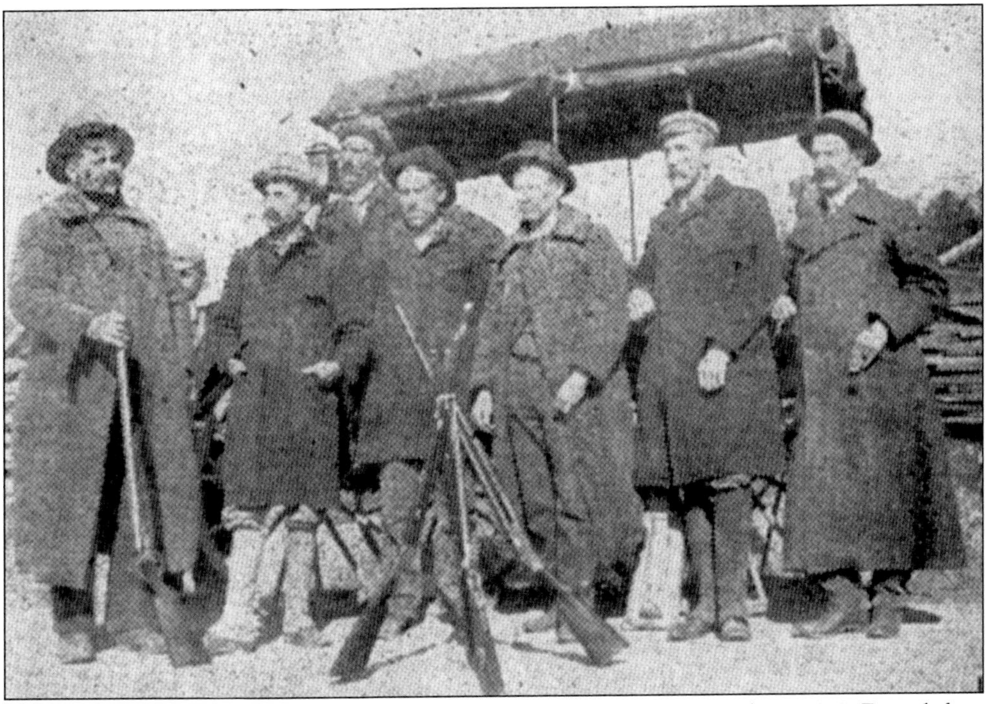

These rough-and-tumble New Market hunters posed by a jitney wagon about 1910. From left to right are Mark Minnick, "Bush" Kagey, E. M. Rice, G. A. "Dutch" Tidler, E. R. "Raz" Bowman, Walter Kingan, Tom Rice, and Charles Ruff. (Dr. John Stewart.)

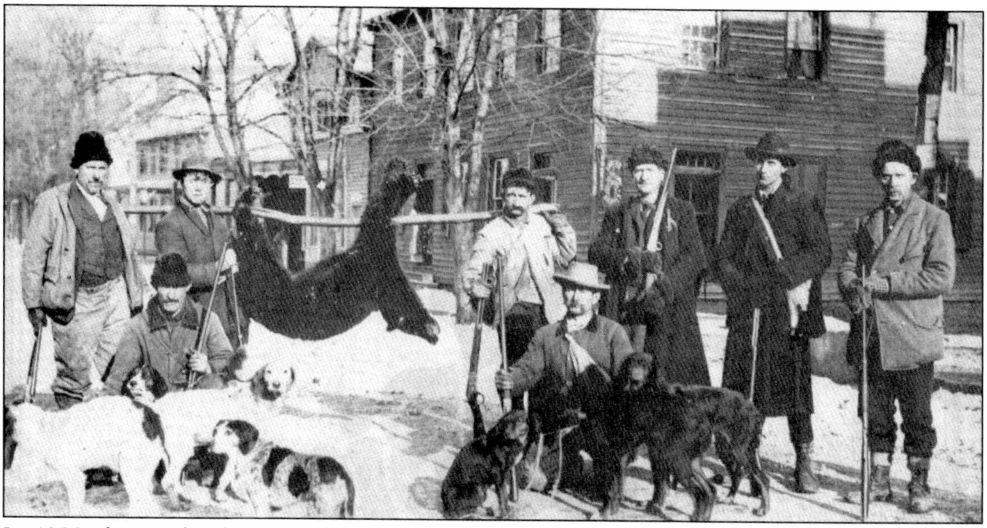

In 1909, the result of a winter bear hunt is displayed at the Crossroads. From left to right are E. R. "Raz" Bowman, John Webster (kneeling), Asa O. Murphy, Robert L. O'Roark, John Buhl (kneeling), Miller A. Price, unidentified, and Pete Minnick. The bear was shot by Miller A. Price. (Nancy Branner Stewart.)

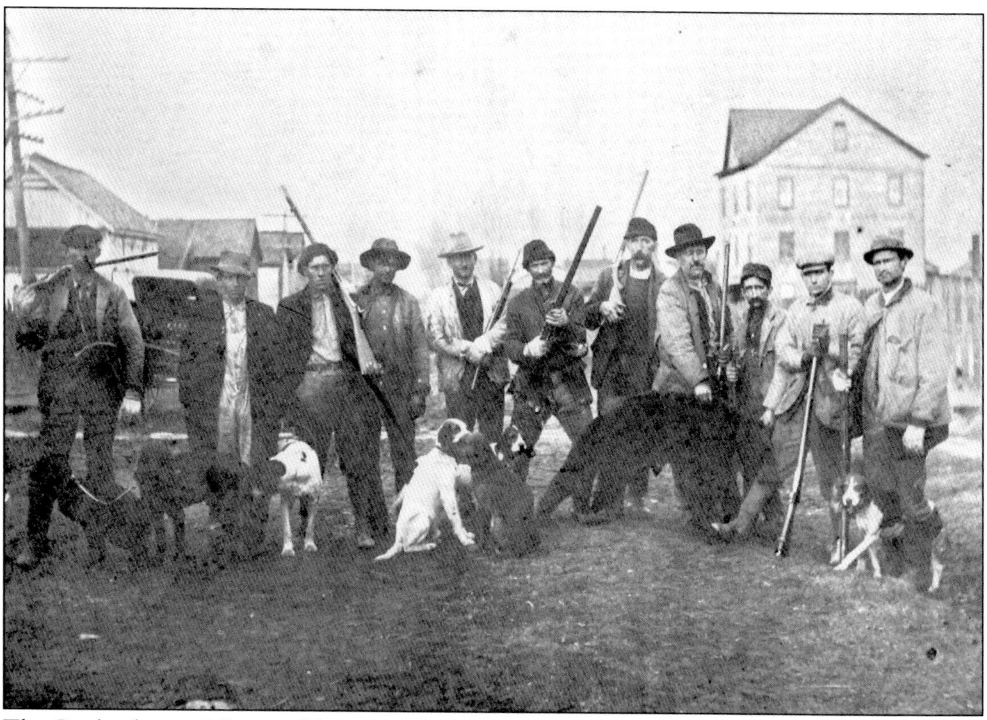

The Crickenbergers' flour mill looms in the background of these local hunters in the early 1900s. Many times, city men would pay New Market men for a valley hunt. This group appears to be local hunters who bagged a black bear. Note a few of the men are brandishing early Kentucky-style rifles and powder horns. (Nancy Branner Stewart.)

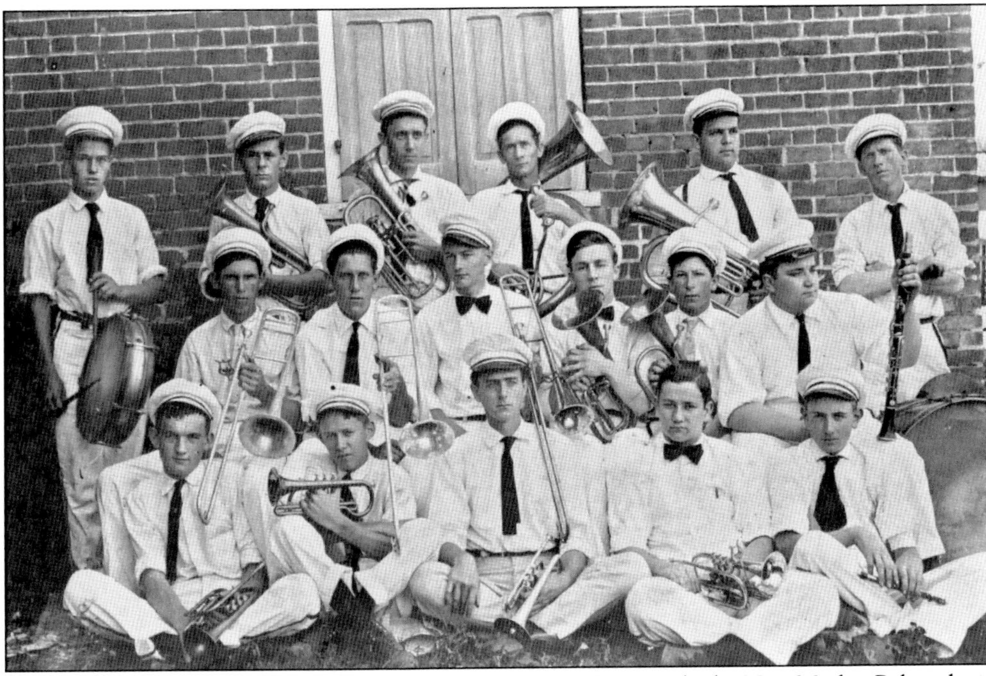

Members of the Shenandoah Valley Band take a rest in 1909 outside the New Market Polytechnic Institute. The institute was located on what is now the Municipal Parking Lot on the southeast corner of Lee Street and John Sevier Road. (Nancy Branner Stewart.)

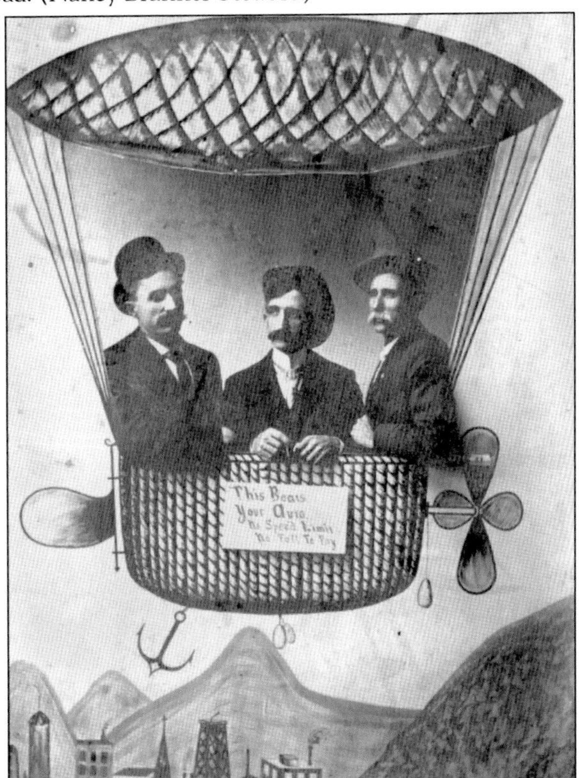

Three friends sit for a fun photograph, perhaps in the early 1900s. The man at right is thought to be Branson B. O'Roark, New Market photographer, and the man in the middle may be Robert L. O'Roark. The basket sign brags "This Beats Your Auto, No Speed Limits, No Tolls to Pay." (Nancy Branner Stewart.)

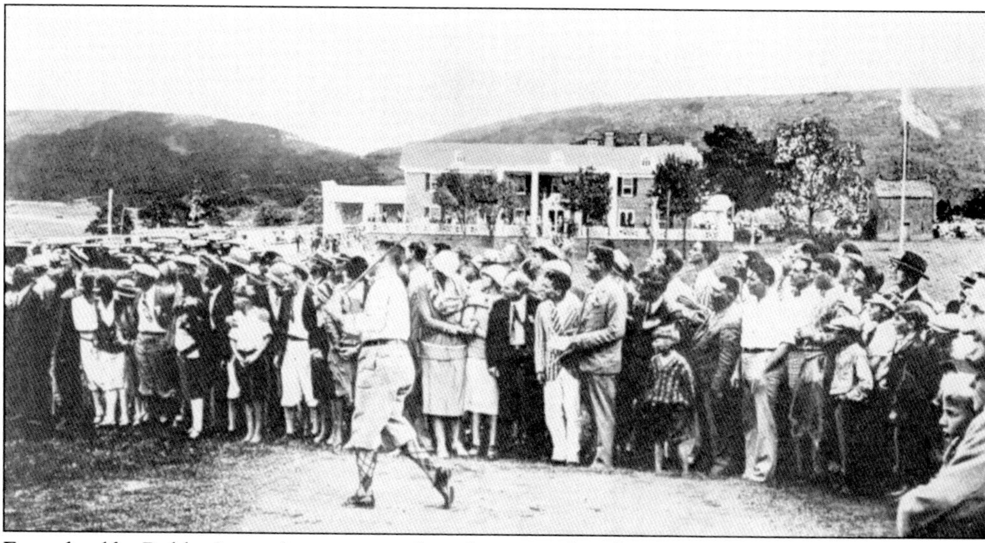

Famed golfer Bobby Jones demonstrates his championship form at the Shenvalee Country Club in the summer of 1927. The tall gentleman facing left and holding the paper to the right of the photograph's center is John G. Miller, editor of the *Shenandoah Valley*. The young boy behind him is Lefty Lindamood, while the stout gentleman at Lefty's left shoulder may be Roland Hill, the country club's developer. (Nancy Branner Stewart.)

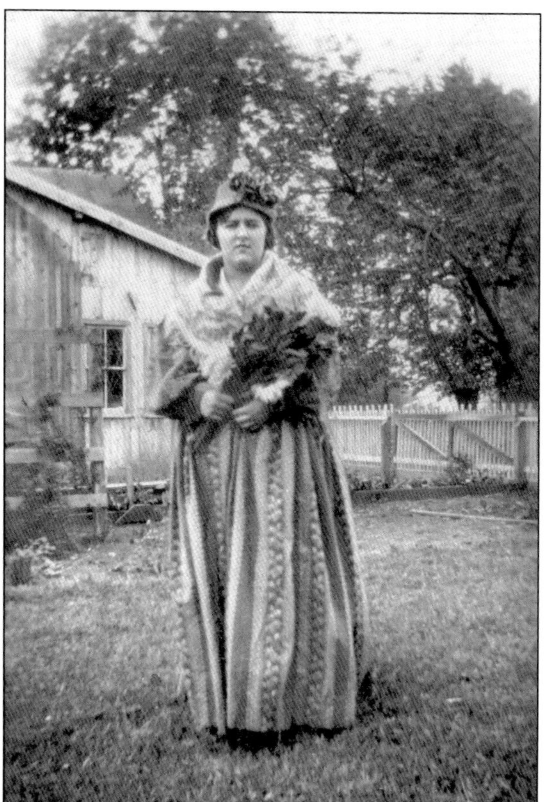

In 1927, Mande Hopeworth was a member of New Market's Old Maid's Club, which celebrated their situation of no matrimony as an orchestra club. (Nancy Branner Stewart.)

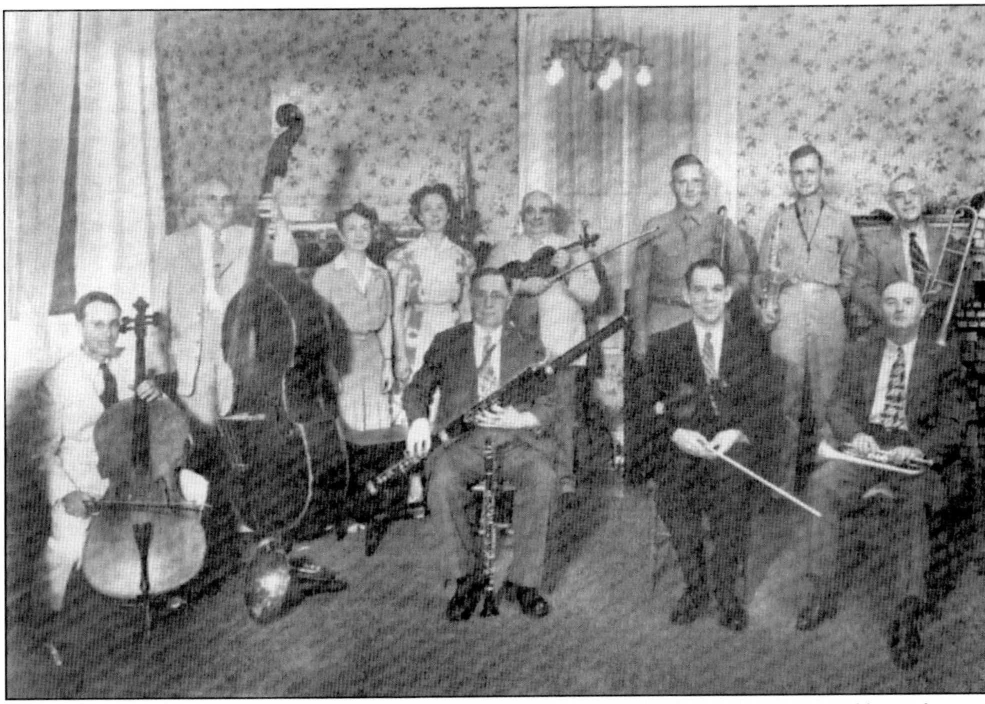

Dr. W. C. Shirley's parlor orchestra was evening entertainment before television, and here they are practicing in his home. The two men in army uniforms date the photograph to about 1943–1944. Pictured from left to right are (seated) James Farrow, Adolph Torovski, Frank Hartman, and W. B. Wickes; (standing) Dr. W. B. Fahrney, Madge Ring, Shirley Miller, Dr. Shirley, Rosie Orebaugh, Jake Crim, and Lupton Kaylor. (John D. Crim.)

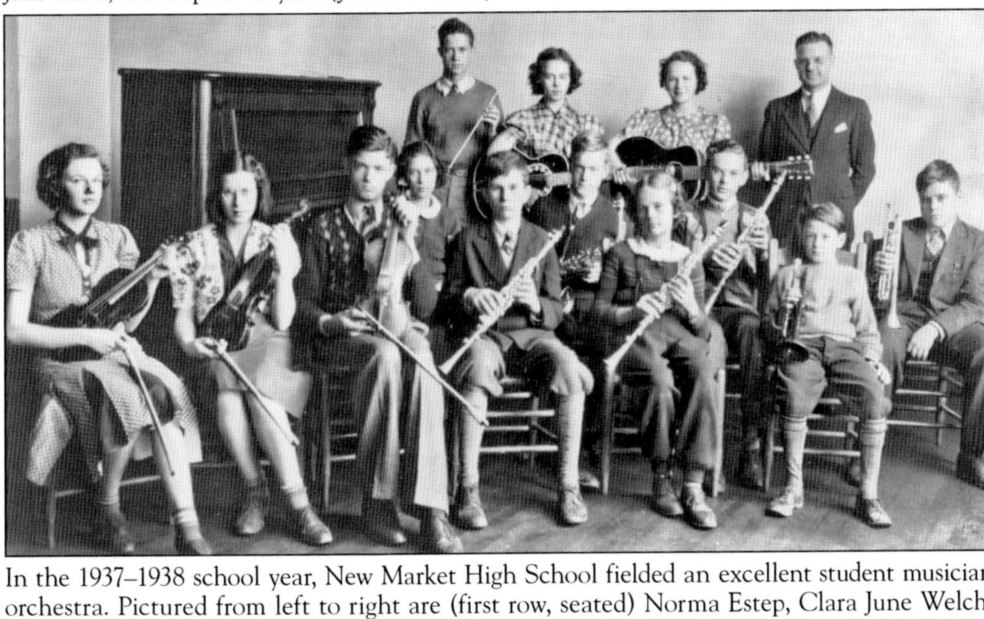

In the 1937–1938 school year, New Market High School fielded an excellent student musician orchestra. Pictured from left to right are (first row, seated) Norma Estep, Clara June Welch, Franklin Zirkle, G. B. Lohr Jr., Janice Lohr, and Nelson French; (second row, seated) Ruth Riley Rice, Jake Crim, Phillip Mims, and Mike Crim; (third row, standing) Roland Tankersley, Ruth Lynch, Gladys Effler, and director Gilbert Curtis. (John D. Crim.)

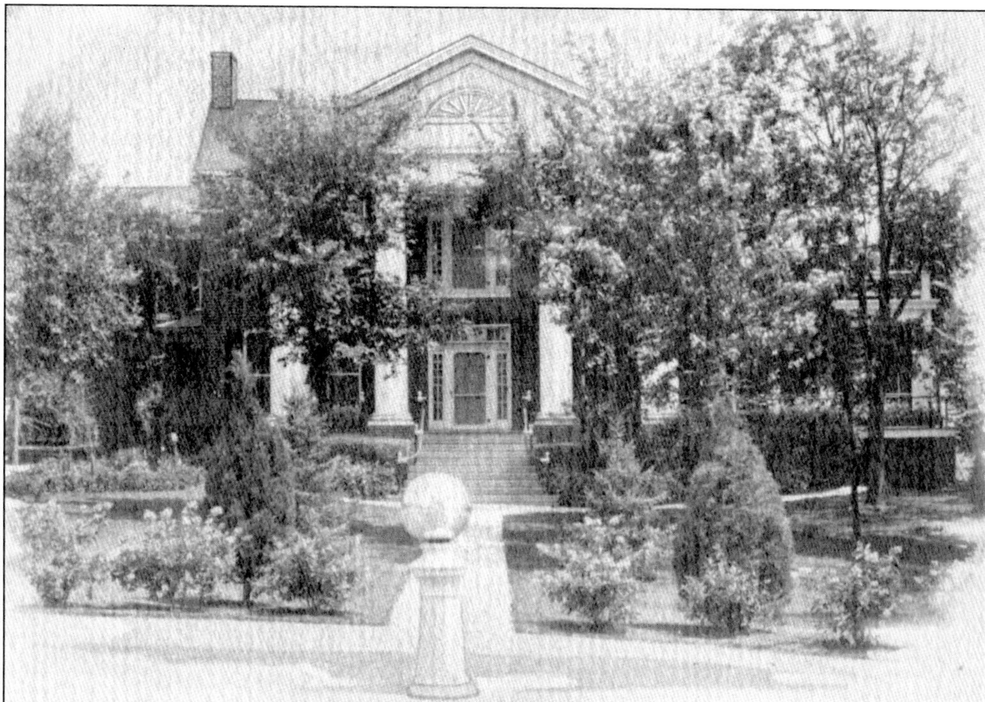

MANOR HOUSE - COURT MANOR

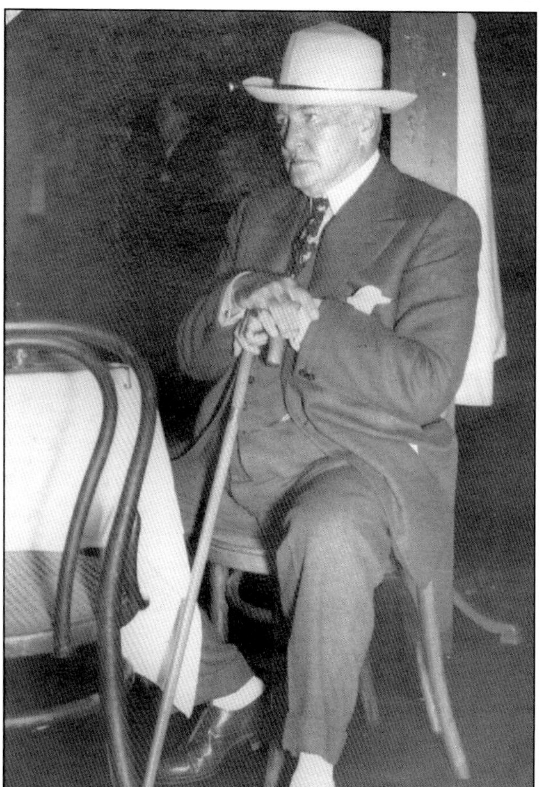

Located on Route 11, Court Manor was one of the homes of millionaire Willis Sharpe Kilmer. Originally built by the Moore family in 1838, it was later remodeled by Kilmer and transformed into a horse breeding farm. Mrs. Kilmer was known to love trees, and the large trees that line Route 11 on both sides near Court Manor were planted in her honor. A former employee of Court Manor stated, "There was no finer lady anywhere." (James R. Graves, Katie Terry.)

In the 1930s, Willis Sharpe Kilmer was the owner of Court Manor Farm, where he bred racing horses. Kilmer made some of his millions with a wildly popular cure-all called Swamp Root, which was introduced during Prohibition and contained alcohol. Known for his curtness, Kilmer was once asked what the tonic was good for. He replied, "It is good for a quarter million a year!" Swamp Root was eventually exposed for its dubious health benefits toward the end of Prohibition. (James R. Graves, Katie Terry.)

Bred, owned, and raced by a proud Willis Sharpe Kilmer, Sun Beau poses in this photograph with his owner in 1931, the year of his retirement from racing. Foaled on May 11, 1925, in Court Manor, Sun Beau was sired by the famous Sun Briar, the two-year-old champion in 1917, and Beautiful Lady. Sun Beau was considered the greatest money-winning horse in history until 1940, when he was passed in winnings by Seabiscuit. In his racing career, Sun Beau started 74 times, won 33 races, was in second place 12 times, and 10 times in third. (James R. Graves, Katie Terry.)

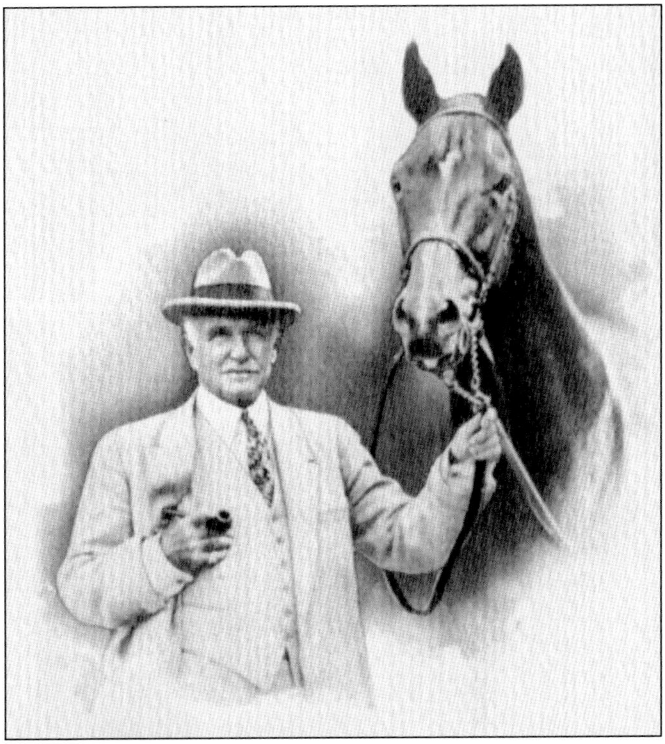

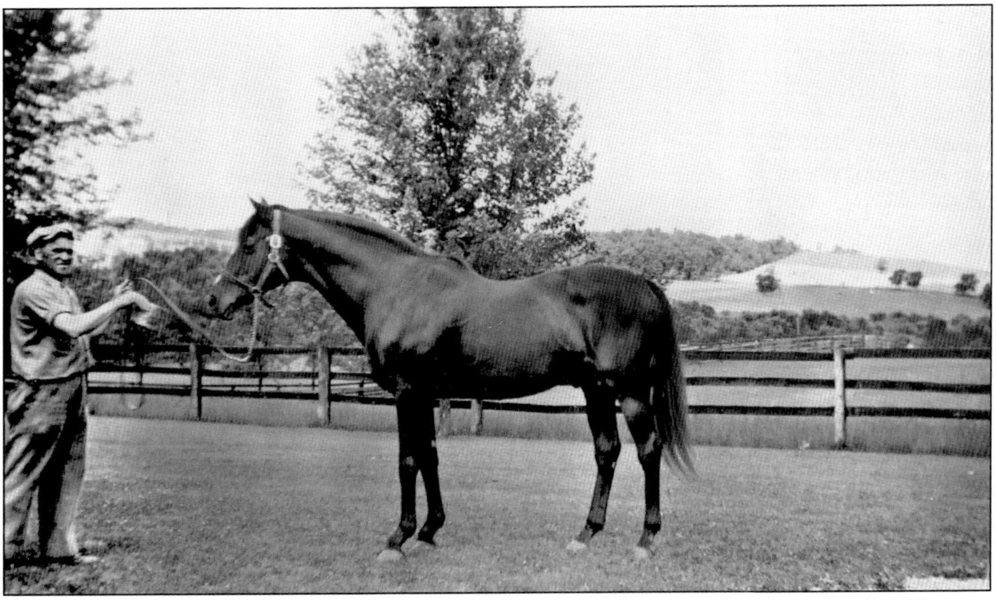

In this 1930s picture, "grand old" Sun Briar is held by Mike Terry, his caretaker for 25 years. Born in France in 1915, Sun Briar was considered one of the fastest Thoroughbreds on the turf and, together with Man O'War, the greatest American sire. He was the apple of Willis Sharpe Kilmer's eye but was retired from racing in 1919 and spent a lot of his retirement years in Court Manor siring other champions. He died in July 1940 in Binghamton, New York, on the day of the anniversary of his owner's death, leaving his stable-mate Exterminator in the loving care of Mike Terry. (James R. Graves, Katie Terry.)

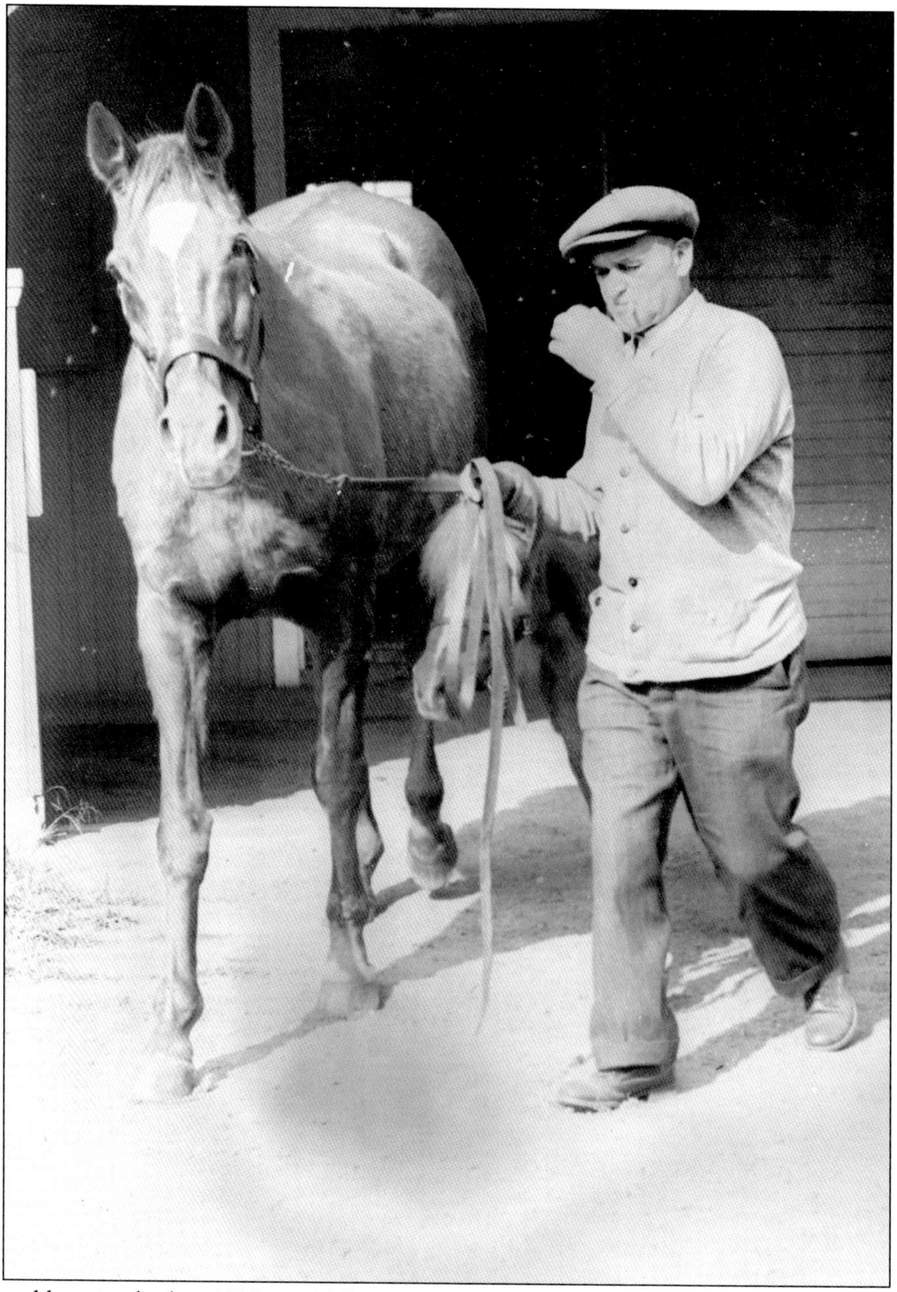

Pictured here in the late 1930s is old Exterminator with caretaker Mike Terry and buddy pony Peanuts. An awkward, bony gelding, Exterminator was bought just to help Kilmer's Derby hopeful, Sun Briar, in his workouts, but he ended up winning the 1918 Kentucky Derby himself. He was affectionately known as "Old Bones" and the "Racing Hat Rack." Mike and his wife, Katie, said, he was the most intelligent horse they had ever known. He spent many years of his long retirement at Court Manor and was later moved to Binghamton, New York, with Sun Briar. Every year, his birthday was celebrated with a carrot and mash cake by Mrs. Kilmer and the neighborhood children, whom he loved. Exterminator is buried Binghamton beside his stall-mate, Sun Briar. (James R. Graves, Katie Terry.)

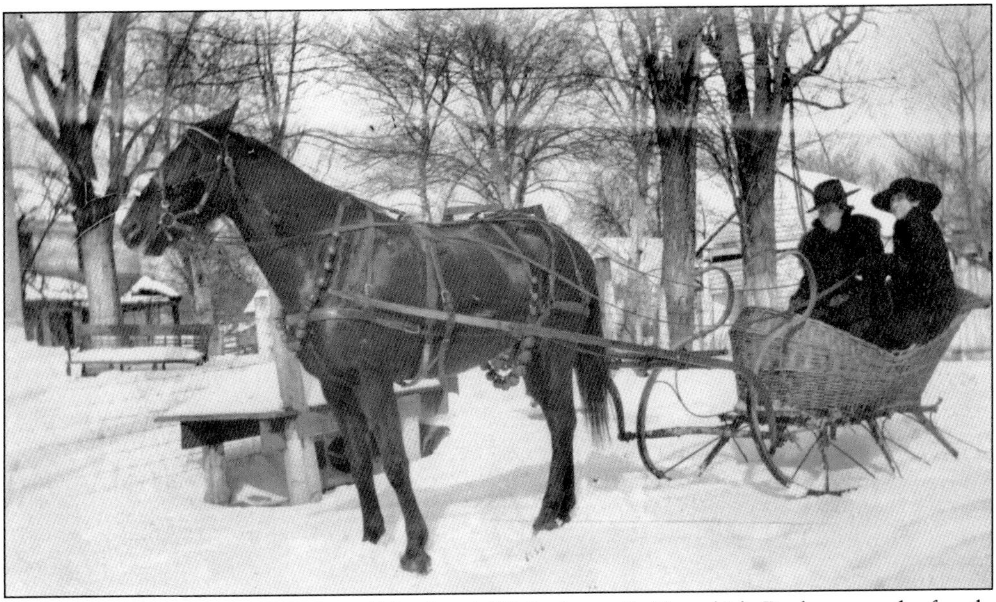

It's a 1920s snow journey for Emma (Mrs. Jacob E.) Bushong (left) and Ida Bushong on the family wicker-style sleigh sporting red and green hand-painted decorations. The front rails were turned up into hand-carved swan heads that pointed the way. The sleigh survives in the care of the New Market Battlefield Museum. (New Market Battlefield.)

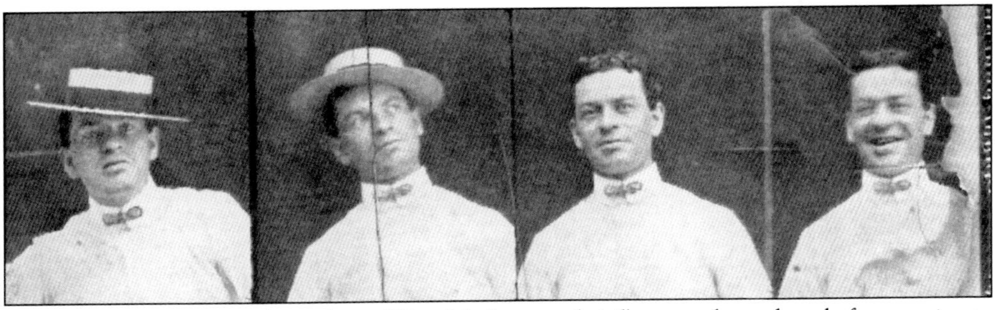

Emmanuel Sherry, a Jewish resident of New Market, was briefly a merchant there before moving to Luray, Virginia. Known for his comedic and even temperament, he was a popular man about town. Sherry is viewed here from a film clip at the Happy Land Picture Show in a silent film at the old theater in New Market. He would participate in many plays and theatrical acts in New Market. The old theater still survives in a wonderful state of repair and is an architectural icon in the town. It is hoped by some that the New Market Theater can return to its glory days as the grand center of entertainment of downtown Congress Street. (Betty Booten Grubbs.)

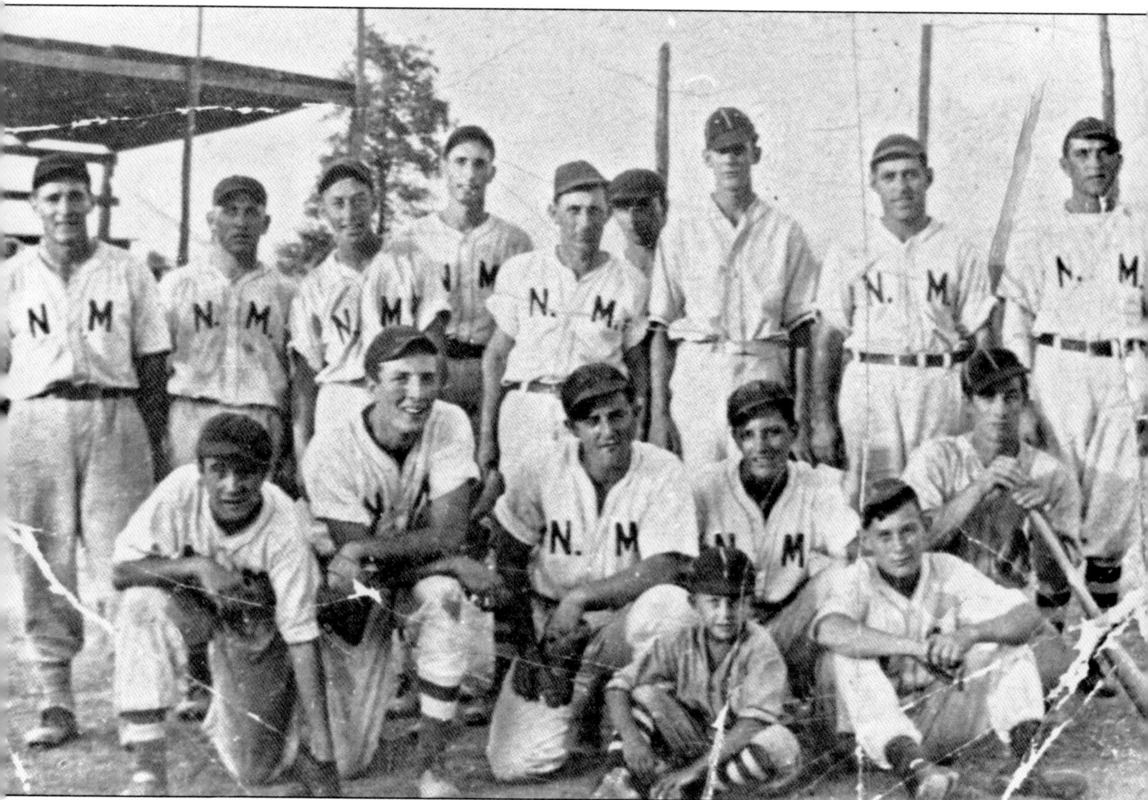

In 1937, the New Market Rebels tapped New Market High School talent to cover the bases. Pictured from left to right are (first row, seated) Wayne Weaver and C. Holt Maloney; (second row, kneeling) Frank "Slicky" Neofotis, Frank Moyers, Pat Emswiler, Byno Rhodes, and Lawrence "Benji" Phillips; (third row, standing) Earl "Skinny" May, Hugh Good, Dick Weaver, Jim Moyers, Everette Driver, Edgar "Jim" Zirkle, Robert Perry, Louie Weaver, and Morrel "Snuffy" Helvey. (New Market Rebels Baseball Team.)

Five

Worship and a Hickory Stick

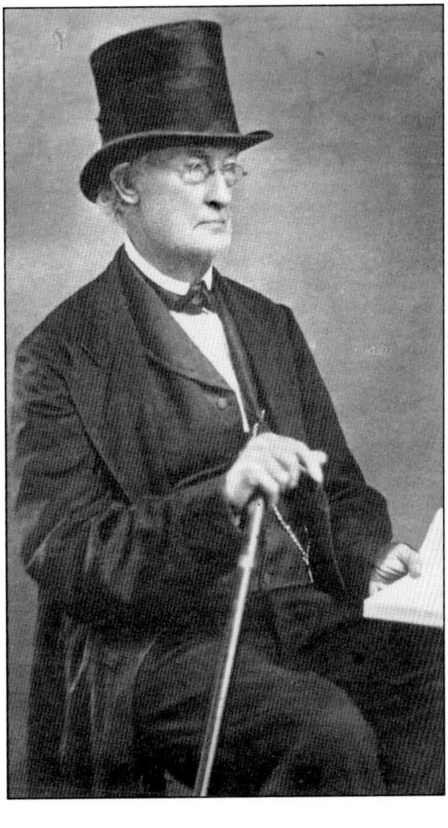

Prof. Joseph Salyards was the preeminent educator of the New Market area from 1846, when he headed the New Market Academy, until his death in 1886. He was born in 1808 near Front Royal, Virginia. Taking advantage of what schools were available for the time, he read books so prodigiously that by an early age he had completely mastered English, geography, and mathematics as well as six or seven languages. On September 5, 1870, he was one of the two principals who opened the New Market Polytechnic Institute, which strove to provide a college-level education to many New Market and county residents. The institute was the predecessor for New Market High School, which offered a stable education for area residents. Not content with education, he made significant contributions to the Lutheran Church. Early on, he assisted with the Henkel Press's monumental publication of *The Christian Book of Concord*, which, even with his assistance, took over seven years to translate from the original German. Salyards was the most fondly remembered instructor and advisor by many in the community. He lived for education and only slowed down in the 1880s when his sight began to fail. This photograph is believed to date from the late 1870s. (John D. Crim.)

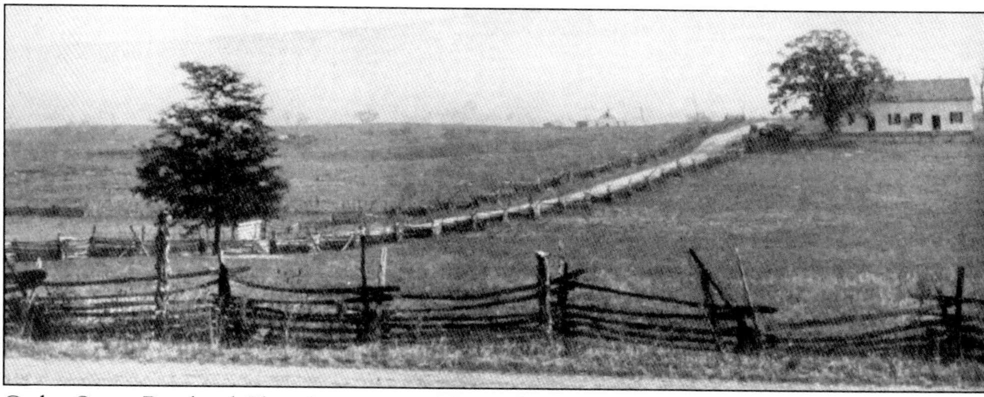

Cedar Grove Dunkard Church was one of the earliest settlements, once known as Hupp's Shop (Rude's Hill). This community, according to historian John Wayland, moved most of the houses because better wells were at the Crossroads. The church remained and has now been rebuilt. Chestnut split-rail fences ramble along the old Valley Pike in front where these people worshipped in the simple meeting house. They were formally called Brethren Dunkards or *Tunker* (German meaning to dunk for the baptismal Christian tradition) appearing much as the Mennonites do today. The old church was the site during the Battle of New Market where Union commander Franz Von Sigel briefly reorganized his fleeing Union army from the Confederate route. Ironically the Dunkard faith strictly forbade war and slavery. (Nancy Branner Stewart.)

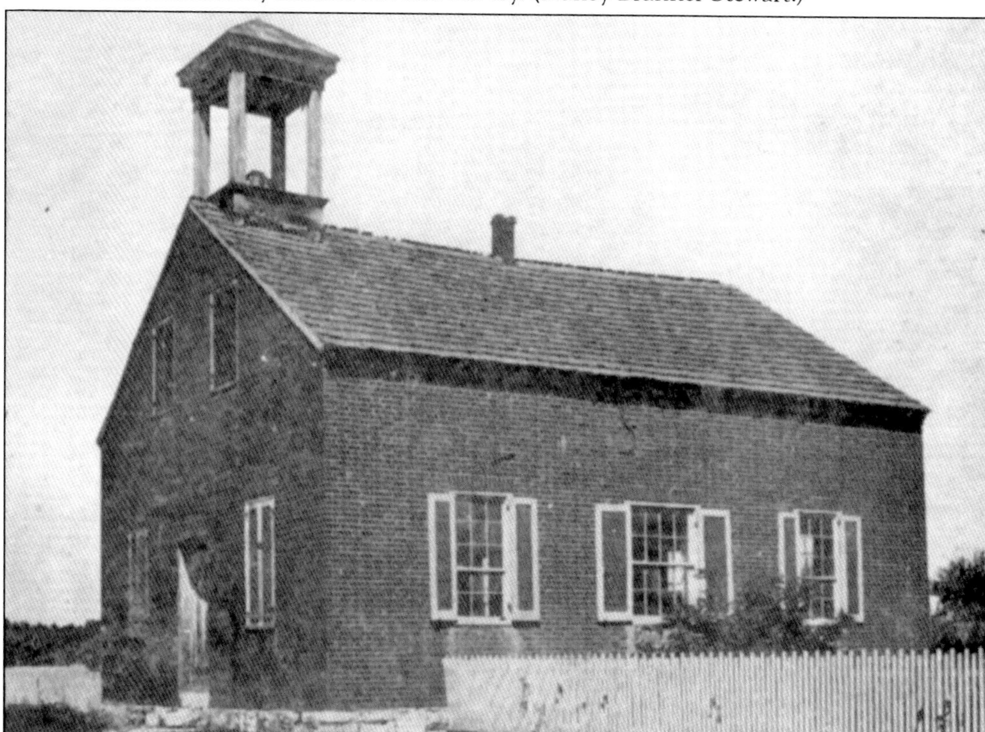

Here is the Smith Creek Baptist Church on Seminary Lane as it looked in the early 1900s. The church replaced the original log meeting house (which may yet exist) and was built on land originally set aside for the Baptist Society according to Jacob Rinker's 1805 town plat. The building was torn down in the second decade of the 20th century and the bricks reused in the Driver house foundation and walls at 9335 Congress Street. (Elder Richard Harris.)

St. Matthew's Lutheran Church, in this 1910 view, replaced the Davidsburg Lutheran Church after a serious fire. St. Matthew's was in turn replaced in 1955 with the current Reformation Lutheran Church. In the right foreground stands a wooden post that has a Civil War shell embedded in it. Local lore has it that during the 1864 battle, Confederate general John C. Breckinridge was on horseback nearby when this 3-inch Hotchkiss shell struck the post but didn't explode, sparing his life and saving the Confederate victory. (John D. Crim.)

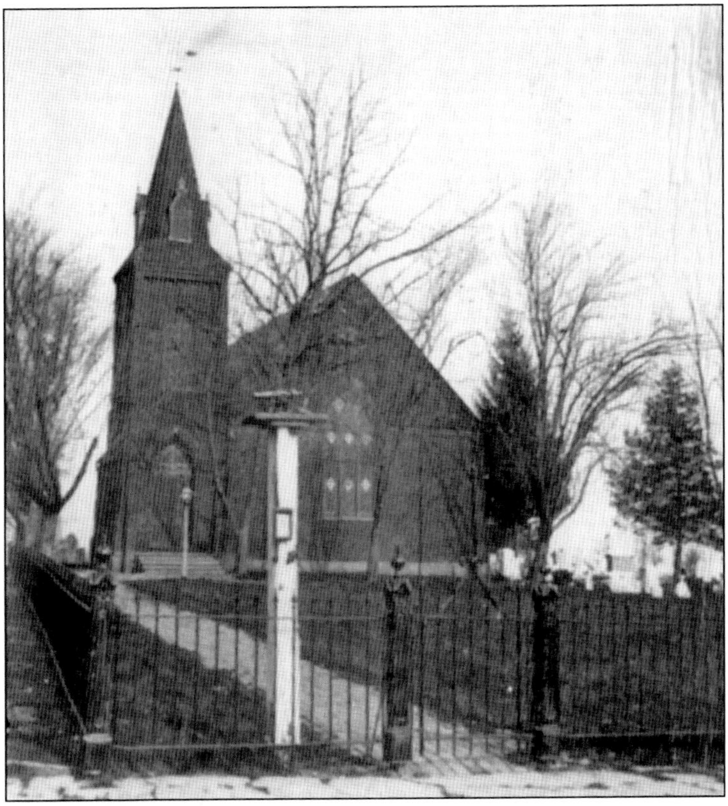

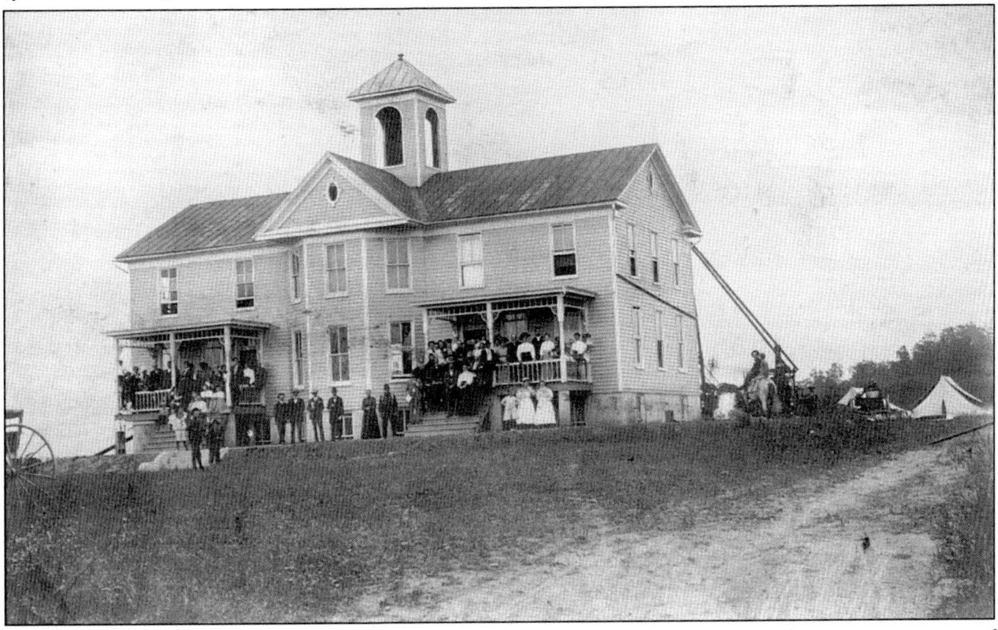

The original, 24-room Shenandoah Valley Academy school building opened in 1908 just west of town. The 42 acres of land for the school was bequeathed by Charles D. Zirkle on his deathbed at his father's farm. At the right-hand side of the building, workmen appear to be drilling a new well for the new school building. (Elder Richard Harris.)

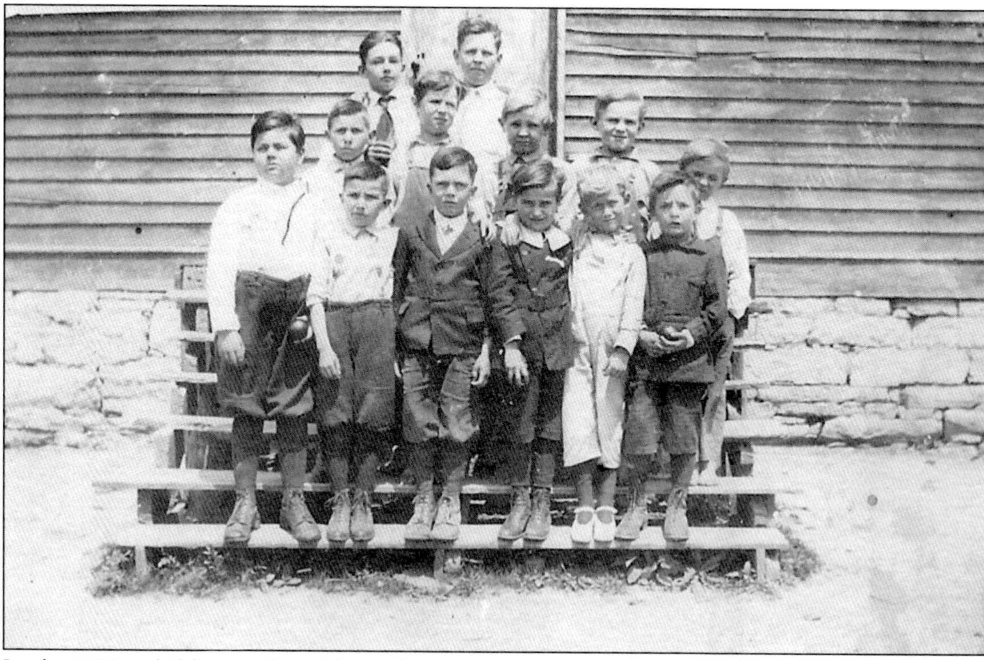

In the 1880s, children gathered for a photo opportunity on the steps of a one-room school near New Market. There were a number of such schools in and around town, bringing education to the rural community. Teachers were required to instruct every grade level in that one room. (Edward "Casey" Billhimer.)

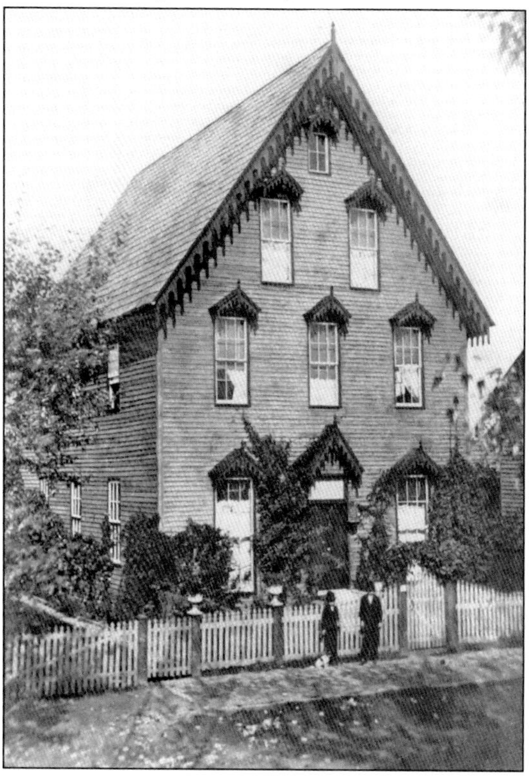

The Cottage Institute was founded in New Market by Jessie Hainning Rupert after the Civil War and provided education to a number of its citizens. The building exists today at 9401 Congress Street, still serving the community as a doctor's office. (Nancy Branner Stewart.)

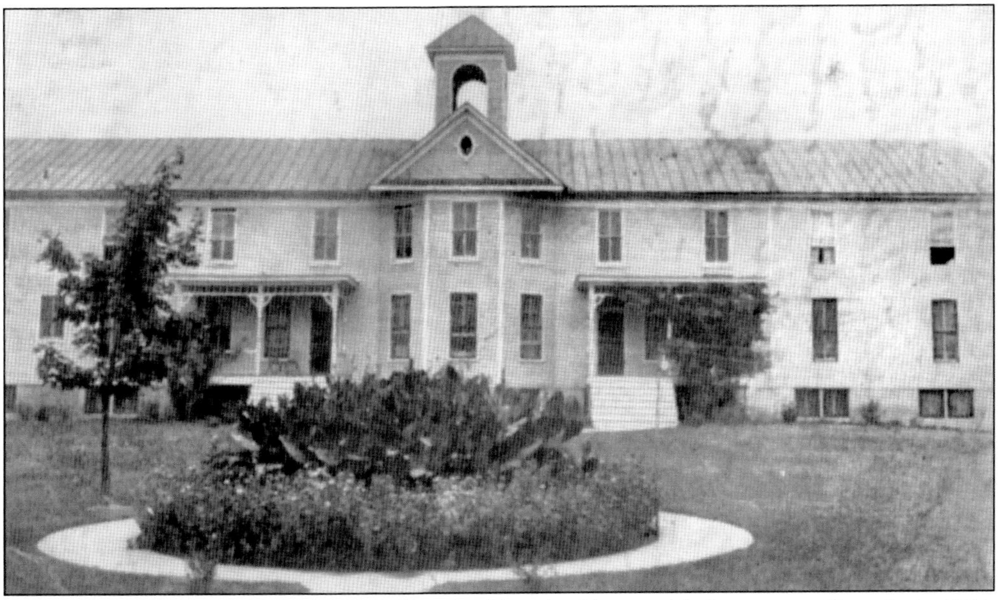

The original Shenandoah Valley Academy building had been added on to significantly in 1924, accommodating more classes, resident students, teachers, and staff. (Edward "Casey" Billhimer.)

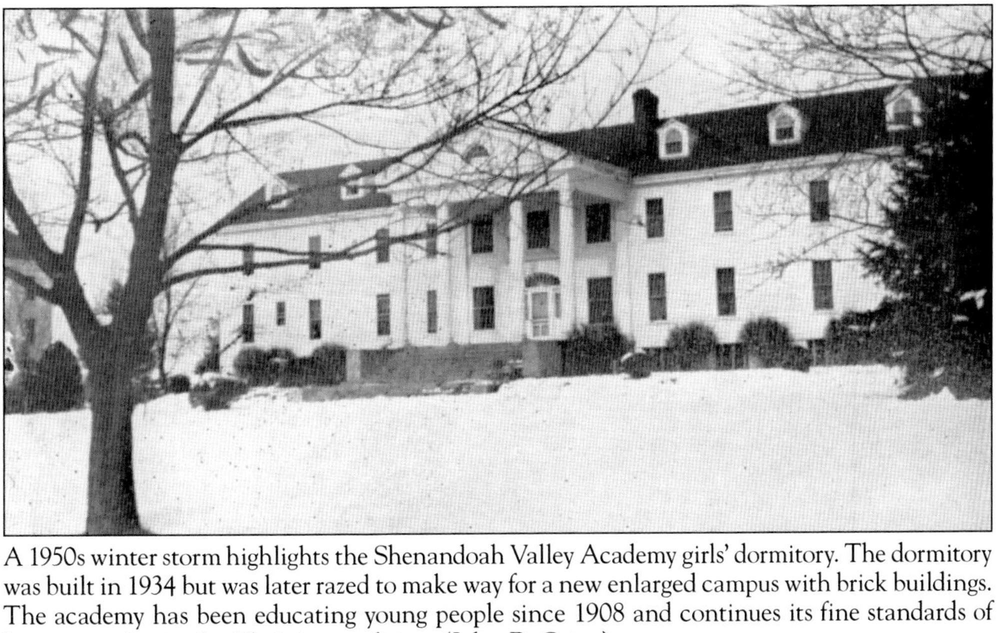

A 1950s winter storm highlights the Shenandoah Valley Academy girls' dormitory. The dormitory was built in 1934 but was later razed to make way for a new enlarged campus with brick buildings. The academy has been educating young people since 1908 and continues its fine standards of learning today in the Christian tradition. (John D. Crim.)

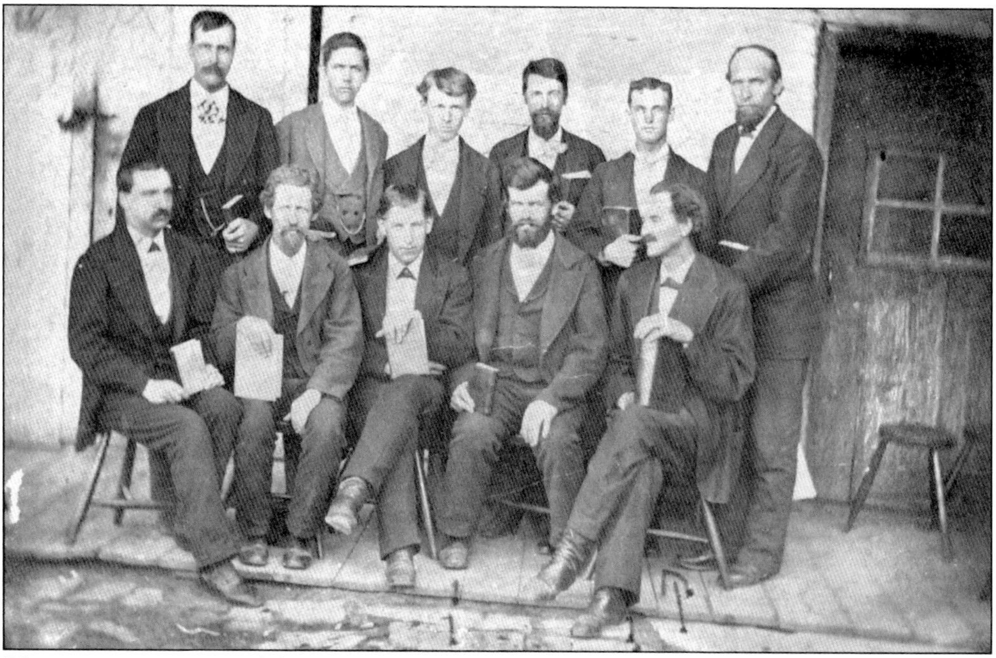

These men are a part of the men's Bible class of St. Matthew's Lutheran Church. They are posed *c.* 1870 in what is believed to be the early whitewashed New Market Academy, part of the New Market Polytechnic Institute located on the southeast corner of Lee Street and John Sevier Road. Christian Theis (standing far right) and Henry Theis (seated second from right) holding their Bibles were both teachers in town. Also seen in the photograph (seated far right) is a man thought to be Prof. Benjamin Hyde Benton of the New Market Polytechnic Institute. (Nancy Branner Stewart.)

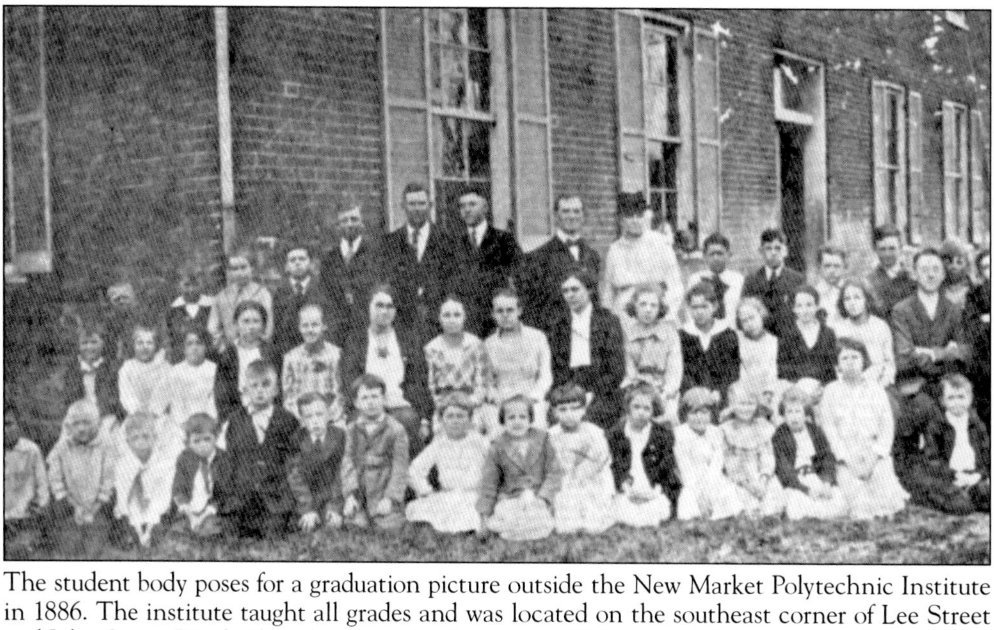

The student body poses for a graduation picture outside the New Market Polytechnic Institute in 1886. The institute taught all grades and was located on the southeast corner of Lee Street and John Sevier Road. The school remained in use until the early 1900s when the New Market High School opened. (Nancy Branner Stewart.)

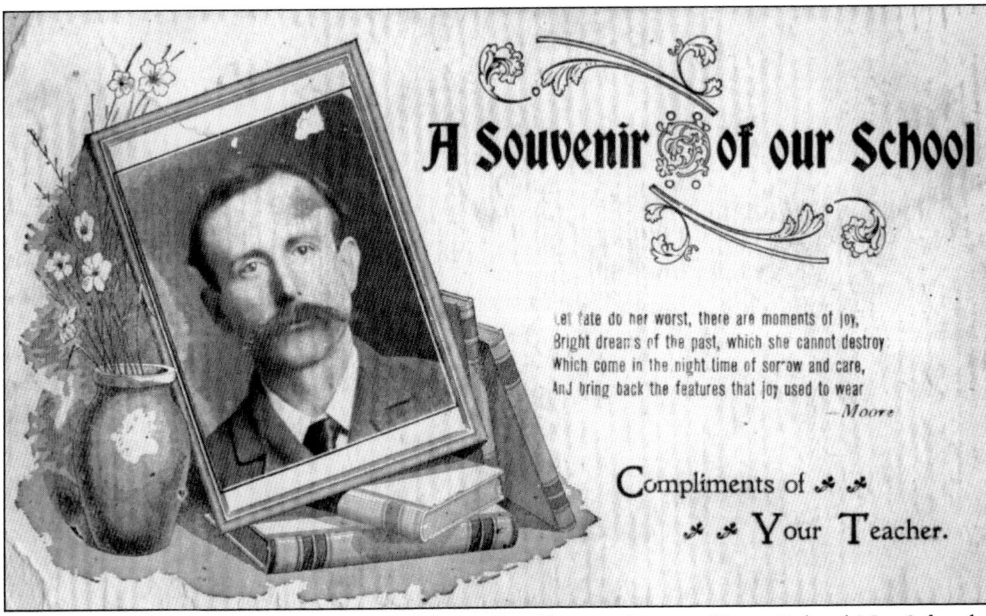

John L. Zirkle, teacher, prepared a card for each of his students at Kipps School No. 8 for the 1901–1902 school year. Kipps School was a small, one-room school serving a predominantly rural area near New Market. (Nancy Branner Stewart.)

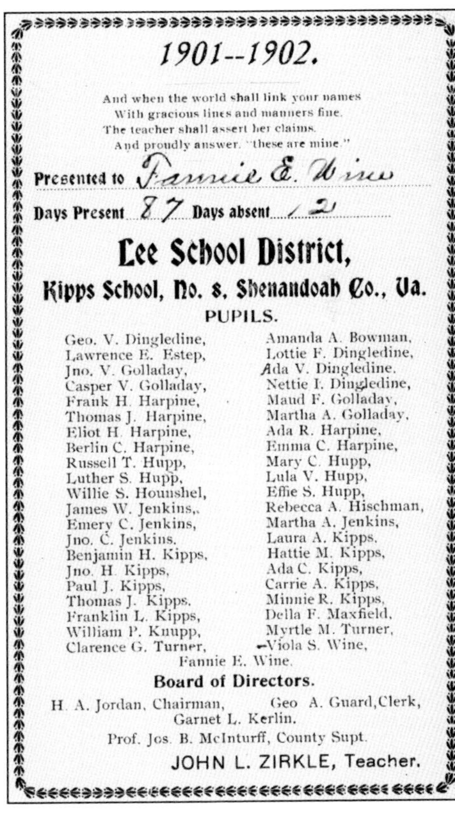

1901--1902.

And when the world shall link your names
With gracious lines and manners fine,
The teacher shall assert her claims,
And proudly answer, "these are mine."

Presented to Fannie E. Wine

Days Present 87 Days absent 12

Lee School District,

Kipps School, No. 8, Shenandoah Co., Va.

PUPILS.

Geo. V. Dingledine, Amanda A. Bowman,
Lawrence E. Estep, Lottie F. Dingledine,
Jno. V. Golladay, Ada V. Dingledine.
Casper V. Golladay, Nettie I. Dingledine,
Frank H. Harpine, Maud F. Golladay,
Thomas J. Harpine, Martha A. Golladay,
Eliot H. Harpine, Ada R. Harpine,
Berlin C. Harpine, Emma C. Harpine,
Russell T. Hupp, Mary C. Hupp,
Luther S. Hupp, Lula V. Hupp,
Willie S. Hounshel, Effie S. Hupp,
James W. Jenkins, Rebecca A. Hischman,
Emery C. Jenkins, Martha A. Jenkins,
Jno. C. Jenkins. Laura A. Kipps.
Benjamin H. Kipps, Hattie M. Kipps,
Jno. H. Kipps, Ada C. Kipps,
Paul J. Kipps, Carrie A. Kipps,
Thomas J. Kipps. Minnie R. Kipps,
Franklin L. Kipps, Della F. Maxfield,
William P. Knupp, Myrtle M. Turner,
Clarence G. Turner, Viola S. Wine,
Fannie E. Wine.

Board of Directors.

H. A. Jordan, Chairman, Geo A. Guard, Clerk,
Garnet L. Kerlin.

Prof. Jos. B. McInturff, County Supt.

JOHN L. ZIRKLE, Teacher.

The back of Zirkle's student card shows that it was presented to Fannie E. Wine. It lists the students, the County School Board of Directors, and the superintendent for the year. The card summarizes Wine's attendance and was probably intended to be given to her parents for their review and possible action. (Nancy Branner Stewart.)

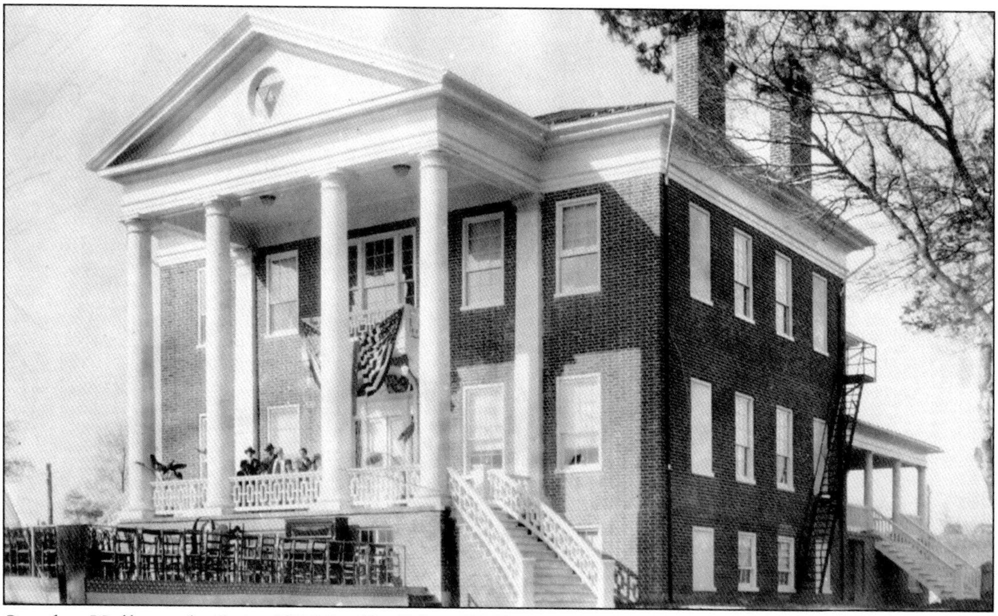

Stanley Hall was built in 1830 by Dr. John W. Rice. Its Greek Revival style was designed by a Philadelphia architect. It remained the Rice home until about 1880. Around 1882–1883, it was known as the "Southern Seminary" by William Stirewalt until it was reorganized and donated to the Emmanuel Lutheran Church as Stanley Hall Female Seminary by a generous gift from the Coiner family. On October 29, 1927, the home was a refuge for abandoned children or orphans called the Hines Memorial Pythian Hall. Oddly enough, Stanley Hall became the Mason and Dixon Terminal Stop for truckers traveling the old Valley Pike with their goods by the 1950s. The home remains standing today. (Edward "Casey" Billhimer.)

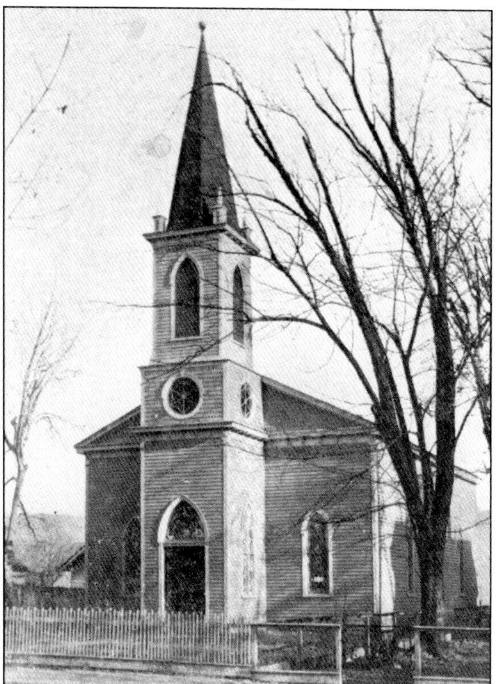

The Methodist Episcopal church (known today as Manor Memorial United Methodist Church) was built *c.* 1845. It was remodeled in 1902. This image was captured for a postcard in 1908. The church was encapsulated in brick and has also a meeting hall addition, but still one can see the same original architectural form. The exquisite porthole windows and adorned spire attest that the congregation had prospered. (Edward "Casey" Billhimer.)

Emmanuel Lutheran Church on Lee Street was built to replace an earlier, smaller structure. The original congregation at Davidsburg Lutheran Church not only split over theological differences; part of the congregation was locked out and refused admittance. The exiled group then built another church on this Lee Street site in 1848, replacing it in 1892 with the one shown. (Edward "Casey" Billhimer.)

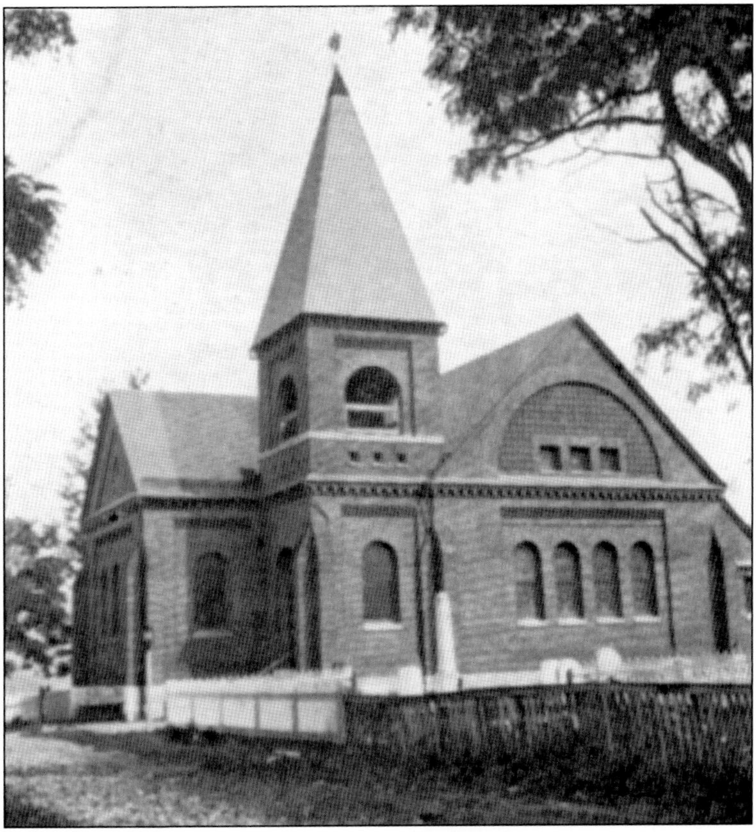

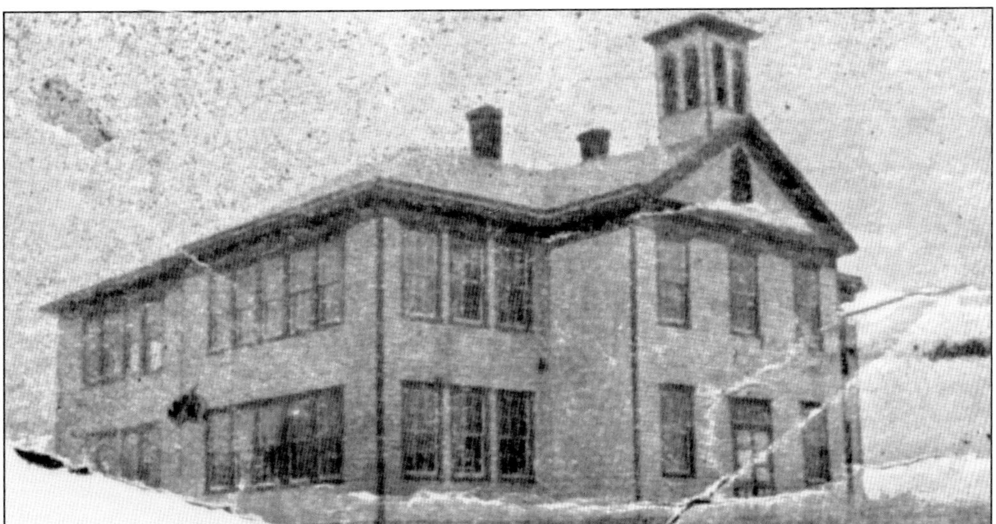

This first version of the New Market High School around the 1920s shows the school still in use. The school was built from atypical construction methods from the Victorian time and was a balloon frame structure built originally about 1894. The school accidentally burned in the late 1920s, leaving a shell. Soon afterward, a new high school was built nearby out of brick and still stands today. (Nancy Branner Stewart.)

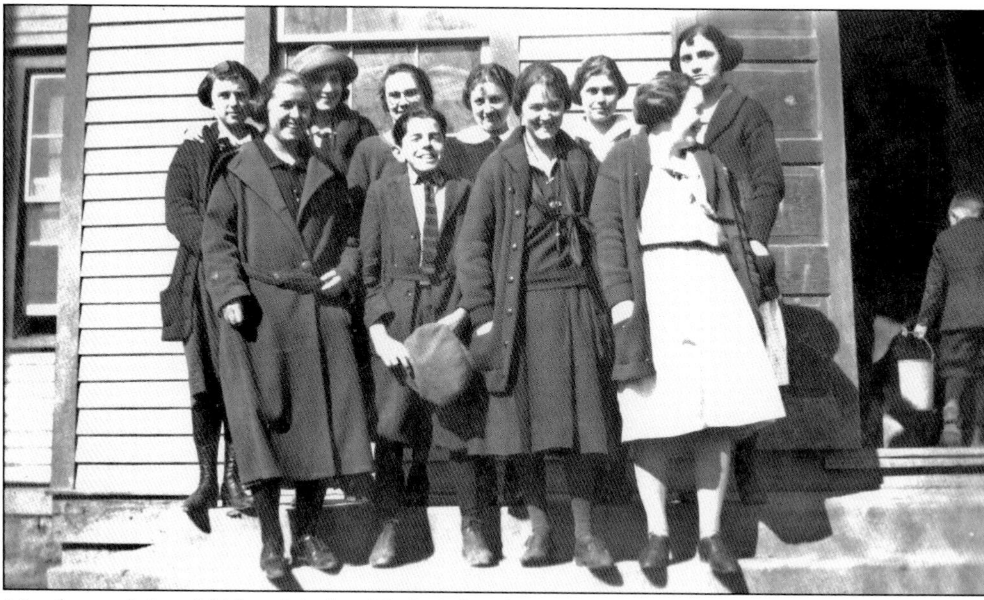

Members of the old New Market High School 1923 junior class take a break on the front steps. From left to right are (first row) Pauline Theis, Everette Zirkle, Virginia Driver, and Naomi Grim; (second row) all unidentified. The old high school stood near 9225 Congress Street. (Nancy Branner Stewart.)

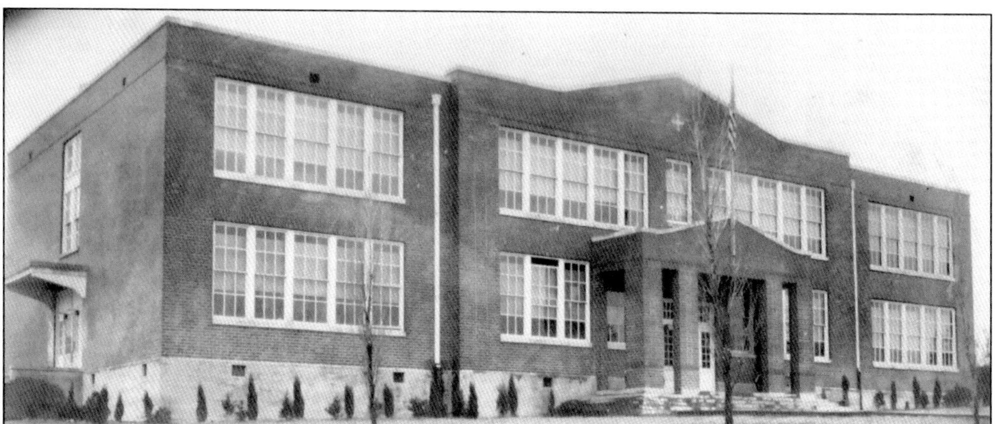

In the early 1930s, New Market High School was a brand-new, brick school in town and was considered to have ushered in the modern age of education for the community. All grades, 1st through 12th, were taught except the 8th. The gymnasium was added a couple of years later when funding became available. It continued as a high school, graduating its last class in 1959. (John D. Crim.)

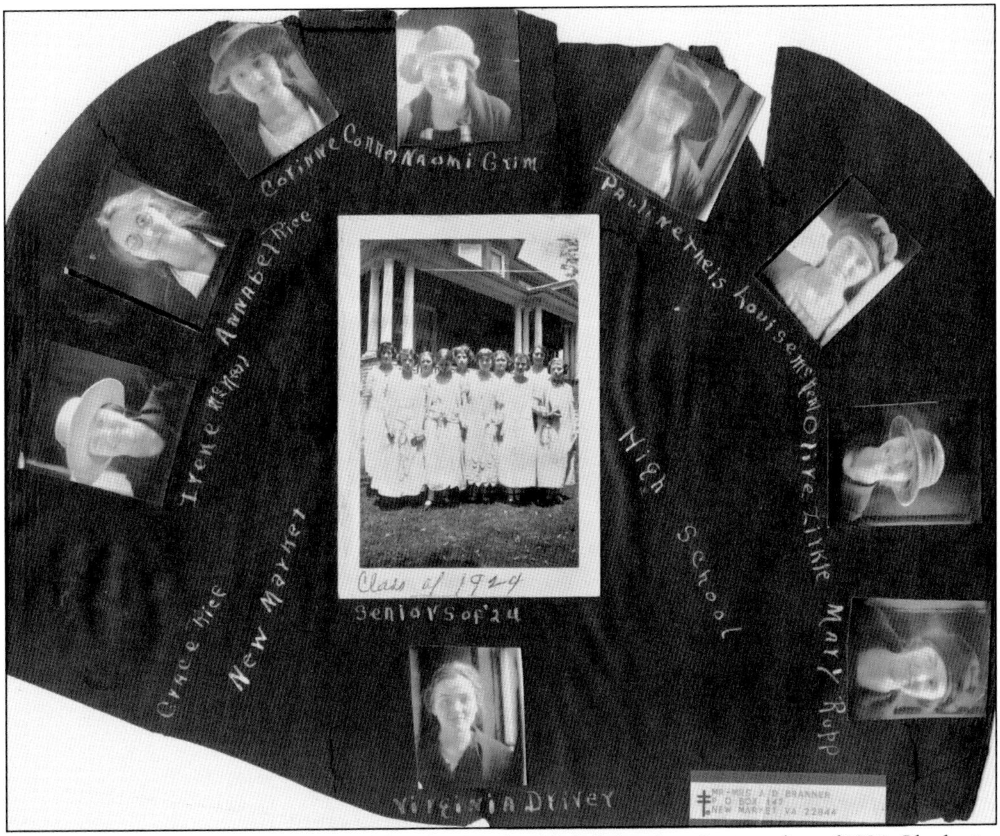

Informal poses surround the women of the New Market High School graduating class of 1924. Clockwise from left are Grace Rice (photograph missing), Irene McNeal, Annabel Rice, Corinne Conner, Naomi Grim, Pauline Theis, Louise McNeal, Olive Zirkle, Mary Rupp, and Virginia Driver (at bottom). The graduates' photograph was taken in the front yard of the Driver house at 9335 Congress Street, probably just prior to baccalaureate services. (Nancy Branner Stewart.)

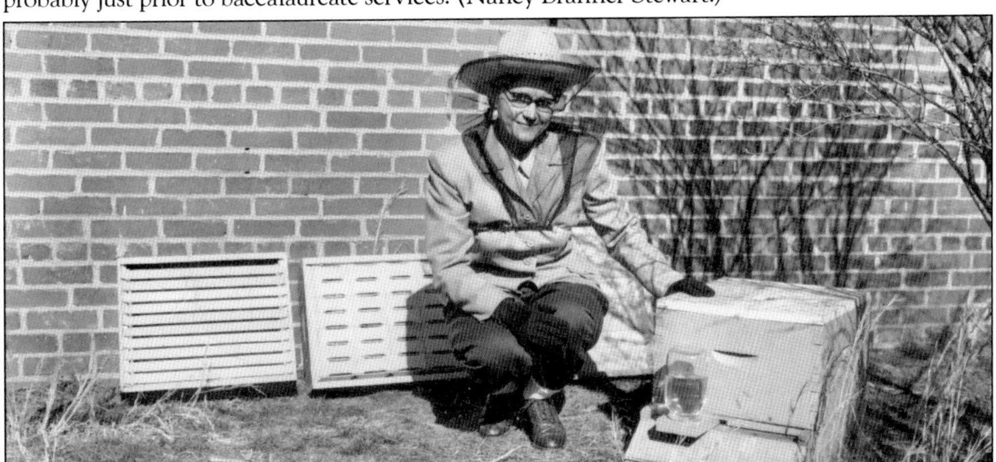

Prof. Samuella H. Crim monitors a beehive used during one of her college classroom research projects. Refused entry to a medical college because of her gender, she went on to attain her Ph.D. in science and biology and taught on a collegiate level for many years. (John D. Crim.)

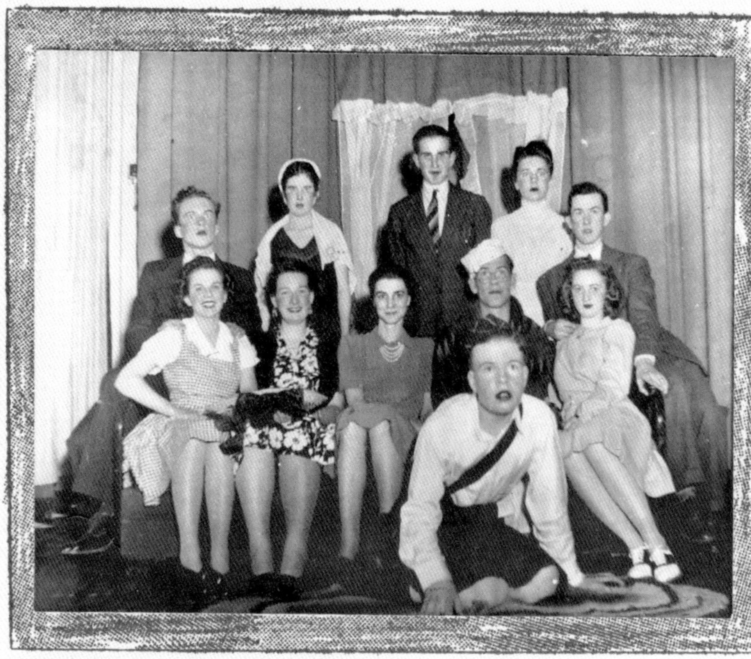

SENIOR PLAY

The seniors selected as their play Grandpa's Twin Sister. It was a farce in three acts by Jean Provence. Grandpa was a cranky old man who was enjoying poor health. He was surrounded by a lot of relatives waiting for his money. Betty, his granddaughter, wanted no money but most of all desired Dr. Wyatts. He was chased by the Widow Williams who desired to marry him. And what of Grandpa's twin sister? You should have seen the play and found out.

CAST OF CHARACTERS

Grandpa Hatcher---a cantankerous old man--------------------Ray Welch
Maggie---his Irish cook-------------------------------Mary Lee Golladay
Louise---his grandniece--------------------------------Patsy Wickes
Betty---his granddaughter--------------------------Shirley Tankersley
Edgar---his grandnephew-------------------------------G.B. Lohr, Jr.
Clara---Edgar's bossy wife------------------------------Virginia Lambert
Ralph Wyatt---a young doctor----------------------------Victor Landis
Henry Collins---a smart lawyer---------------------------David Thornton
The Widow Williams---an undying flame--------------------Suzanne Brown
Adam Mc Pherson---a specialist in saving---------------Bill Rosenberger

This shot of the 1941 New Market High School senior class play depicts a successful production held in the school's auditorium. The old school continues serving the area as the New Market Community Center, located near Rebel Baseball Park. Can you match the pictures of the cast members with the characters they played? (John D. Crim.)

Six

Commerce and Tourism

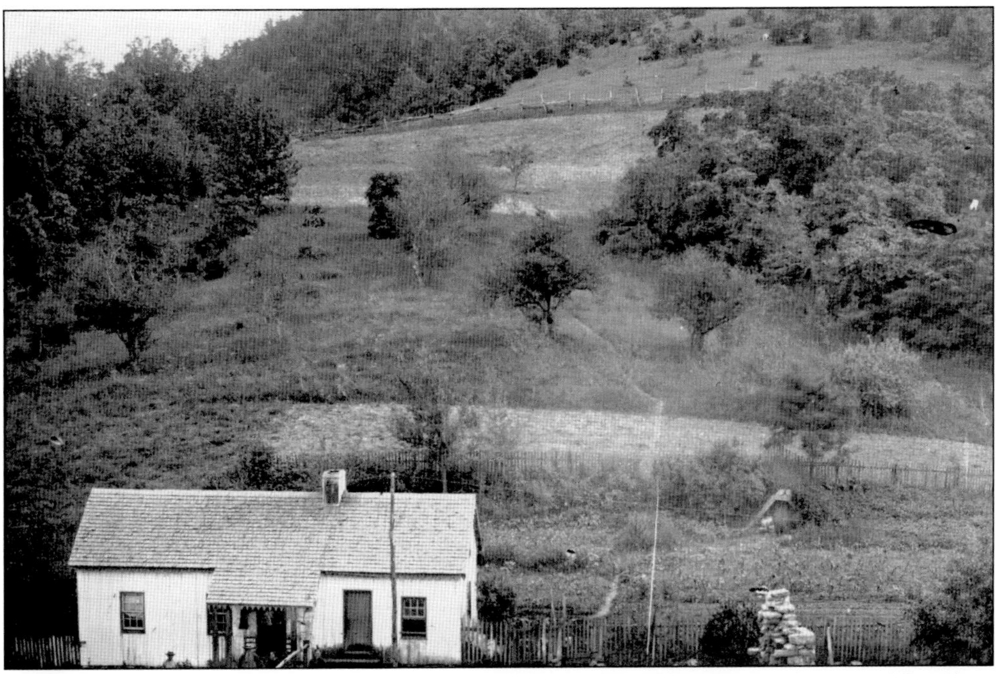

At the top of the Massanutten Mountains, there is a juncture called New Market Gap. This place separates what was once a whole county called Shenandoah County. After 1831, the Luray side of Shenandoah became Page County, named after John Page, a Colonial governor. The cabin to the left of the photograph was not an ordinary mountain home, but the residents collect freight and travel tolls to maintain the New Market and Sperryville Turnpike from Shenandoah and Page to Thornton Gap in Rappahannock County. This was a new public works program that was very successful in turning a bad road into a plank and gravel road project early in the mid-1800s. Although much was done to fix this road, it was spotty at best and was not completed due to lack of funds and the beginning of the Civil War. (Edward "Casey" Billhimer.)

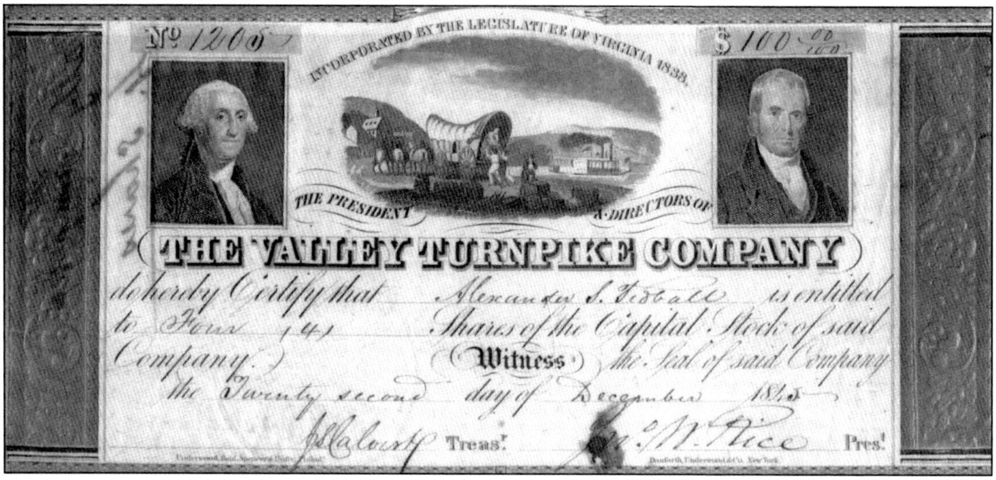

Valley residents took up bonds and donations on March 3, 1843, for a new kind of road that would insure good commerce throughout a prosperous and productive Shenandoah Valley. In 1843, Dr. John Rice of New Market was the president of the Valley Turnpike Company. An Act of Assembly by the State Board of Public Works was to build a new road from Winchester 68 miles south to Harrisonburg, having tolls every 5 miles. The project was held by public stock and state funds jointly. The bonds were illustrated and had a commerce freight wagon scene. It was successful and continued on to Staunton from Harrisonburg. The Civil War was its only interruption, but by 1918, the Valley Turnpike Company, due to its finances, turned its assets over to the Commonwealth. (John Bracken.)

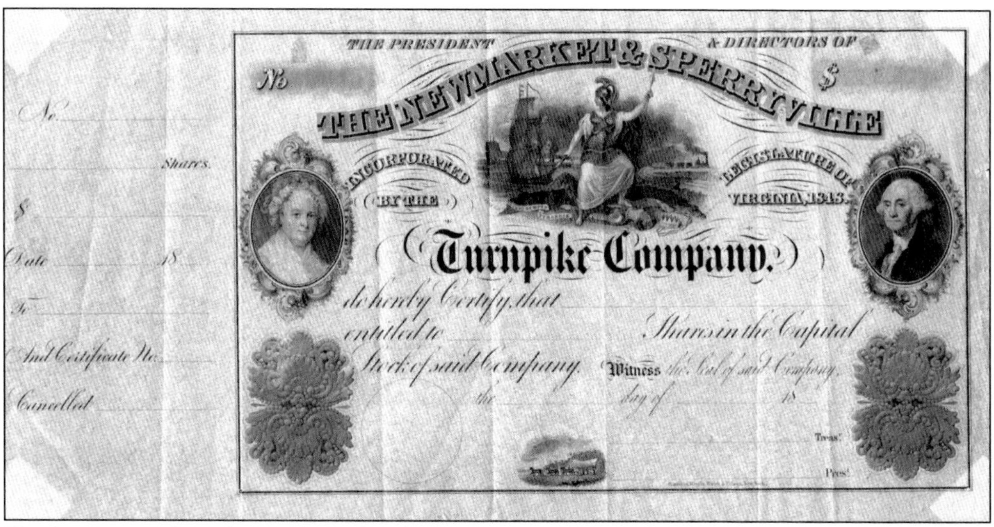

Here's an unused stock certificate for shares in the New Market and Sperryville Turnpike, first chartered by the Virginia General Assembly in 1847. Like many such roads of the day, the route utilized the Massanutten Gap and the Appalachian Mountains' Thornton Gap to connect Sperryville with the Valley Turnpike. Property owners were allowed to charge tolls in exchange for maintaining the roadway adjoining their lands. The turnpike survives as Route 211. (John Bracken.)

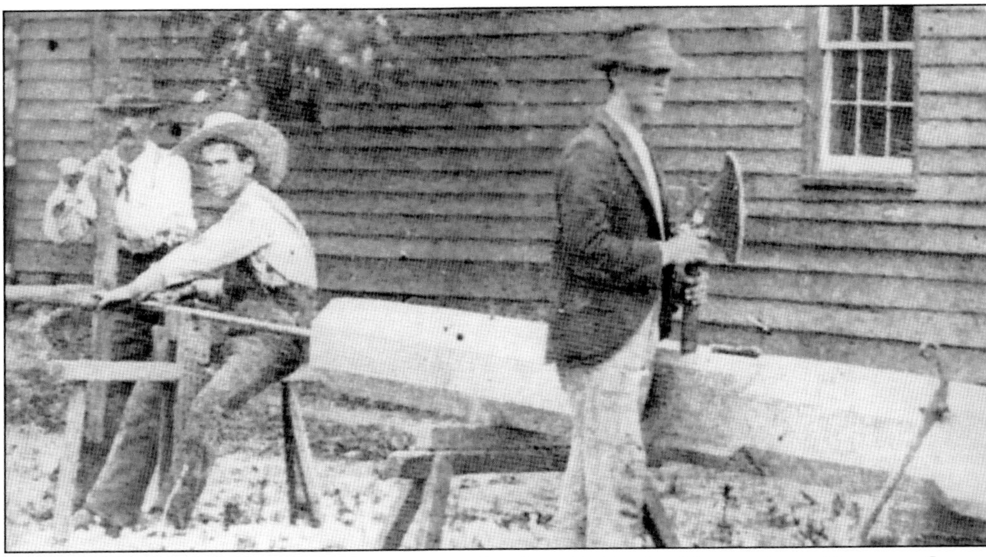

It is likely that these rugged men are posing by the old Henkel House along Congress Street. This remarkable New Market photograph displays the 1854 well pump–making machine that was operated by the Theis family. They made well pumps all over the valley. Boring augers were turned, cutting into large white oak and occasionally yellow heart pine timbers for making the pump device. According to a Theis family member, their earliest ancestor followed this profession just after arriving to Virginia from Germany. This wonderful machine still survives complete today as it was in this c. 1890 photograph. Pictured, from left to right, are Charles O'Roark, Otis Braxton Theis, and Ike Phillips is using the axe. ("Bracky" Theis, Gary Bauserman.)

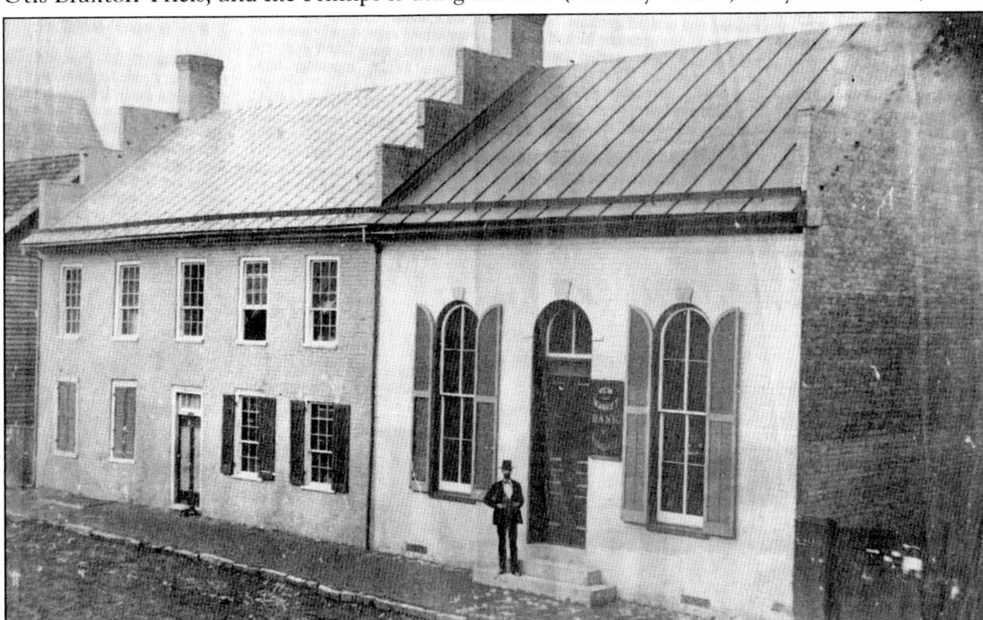

The New Market Bank of Virginia was open and awaiting depositors on this late-1800s morning. The bank building and the Dave Kagey building to the left were remodeled in the mid-1920s into the New Market Department Store. The site remains commercial, serving the community today at 9397 Congress Street as the SunTrust Bank. (New Market Area Library.)

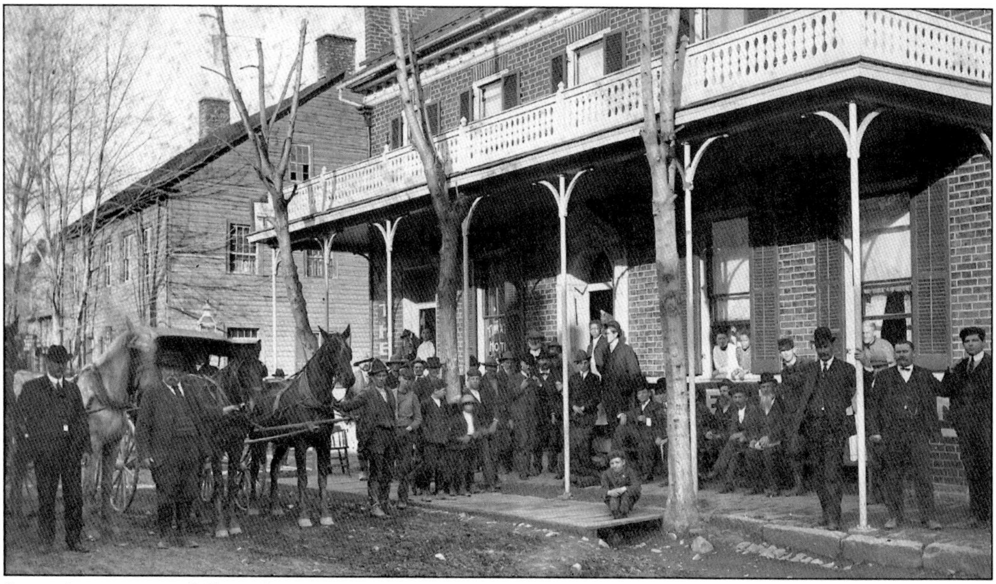

In early spring or fall in the 1900s, a group of men gather with employees of the Thaxton Hotel at the Crossroads to air their opinions in general and the hotel in particular. Perhaps it's Election Day (women were not allowed to vote), the men are returning from the Fire Hall, and the debate continues. Or maybe it's just a Wednesday afternoon when valley towns and businesses slowed or stopped altogether. (New Market Area Library.)

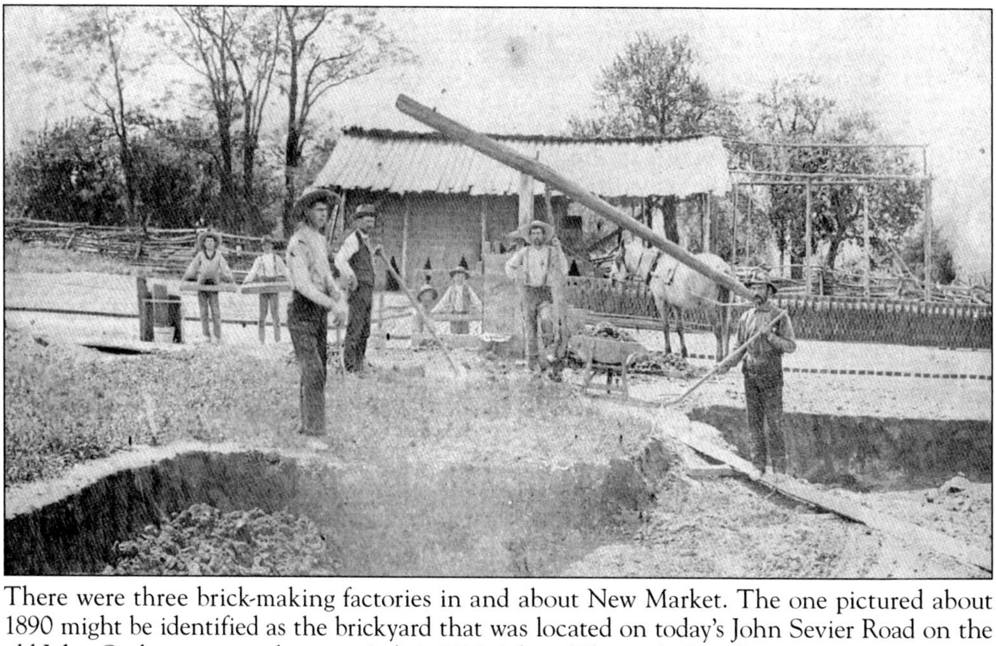

There were three brick-making factories in and about New Market. The one pictured about 1890 might be identified as the brickyard that was located on today's John Sevier Road on the old John Gorley property shown in Lake's 1885 *Atlas of Shenandoah and Page Counties.* The kiln is actively firing brick judging by the smoke from the wood fire. The men are arranging the freshly baked brick in the foreground while posing for the camera. A brick factory owned by Jonas Kennedy employed brothers William and John Watkins, who may be the men pictured above. New Market has about eight buildings still surviving built from brick between 1825 and the 1850s. (Nancy Branner Stewart.)

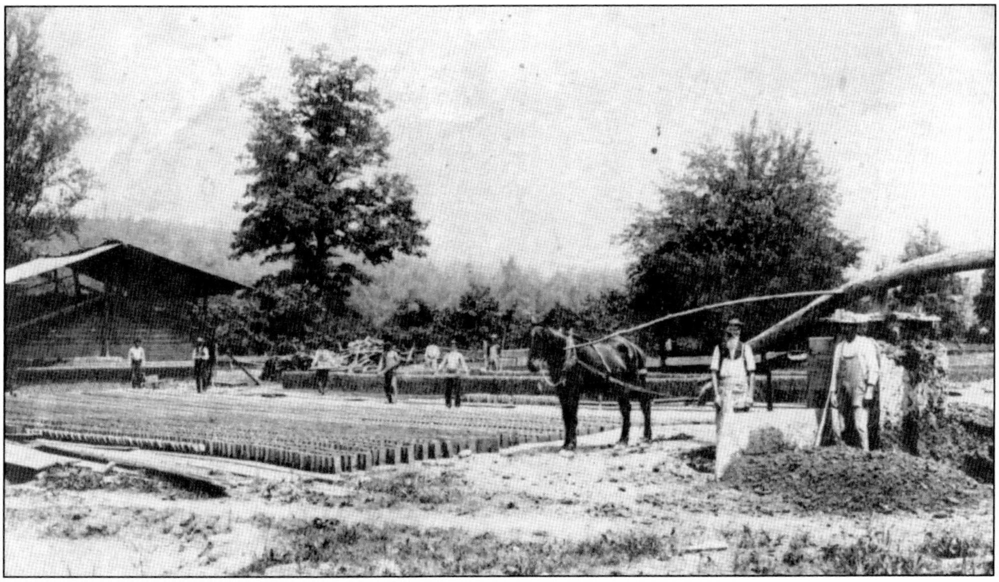

The Sam Wine Brick factory was still a good business in the valley in 1905. However, Valley brick was not known for its high quality as other areas were, such as Orange, Virginia, or Martinsburg, West Virginia. Note the pug mill located in the center, which removed all the impurities out of the red clay to prepare it for firing. The bricks were wood fired in an earthen kiln and then stacked by a brick handler for stack curing as seen above. (Nancy Branner Stewart.)

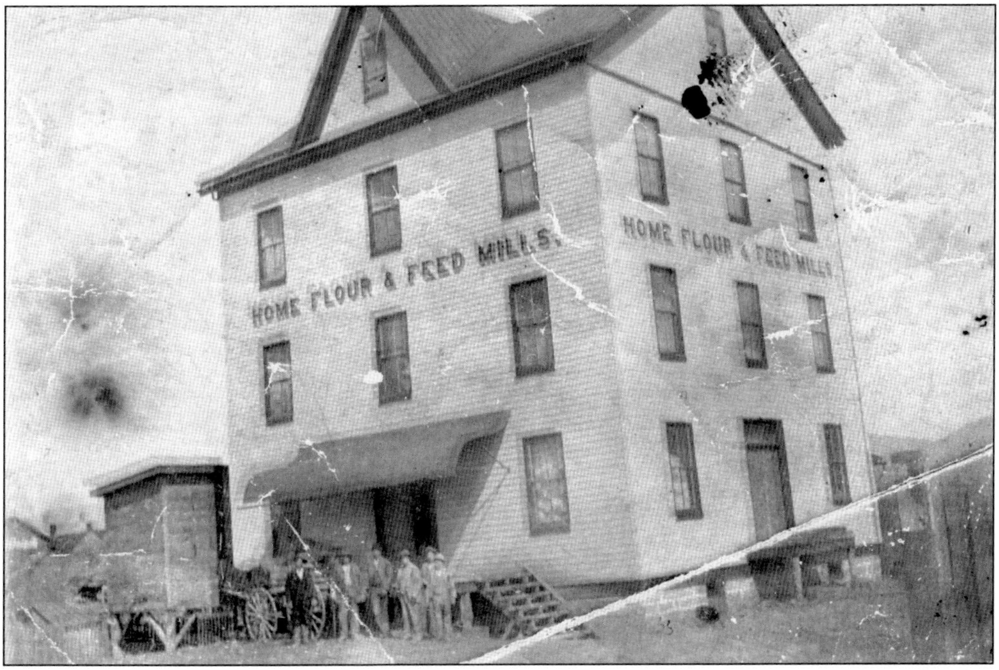

The Home Flour and Feed Mill was also known as the Crickenberger and Hottle Mill. This 1885 image of the mill shows the millers having just loaded a wagon with flour, ground corn, or other feeds for livestock. Every town or village had mills similar to this one at one time to help maintain their families and farms. This mill was listed in operation on the 1915 Sanborn Map of New Market. (Nancy Branner Stewart.)

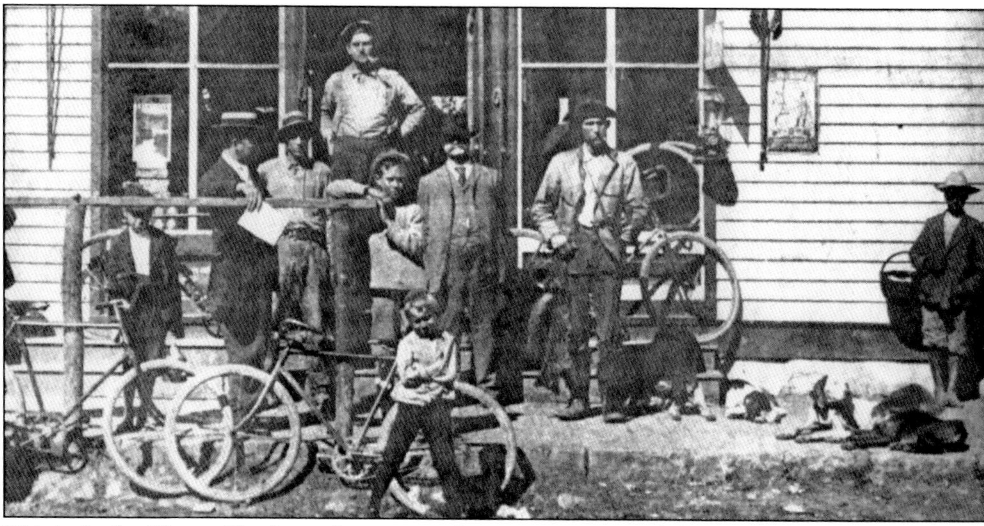

This is the Joe Tusing Hardware Store around noon as it appeared about 1907. Joe Tusing, father of Henry Tusing, appears in the doorway, and the man standing on the sidewalk to his left is believed to be Elon Henkel. Local foxhunter William (Billy) Rice is standing to Elon's left, holding his rifle and carrying a fox, with his hounds awaiting the next chase. (Nancy Branner Stewart.)

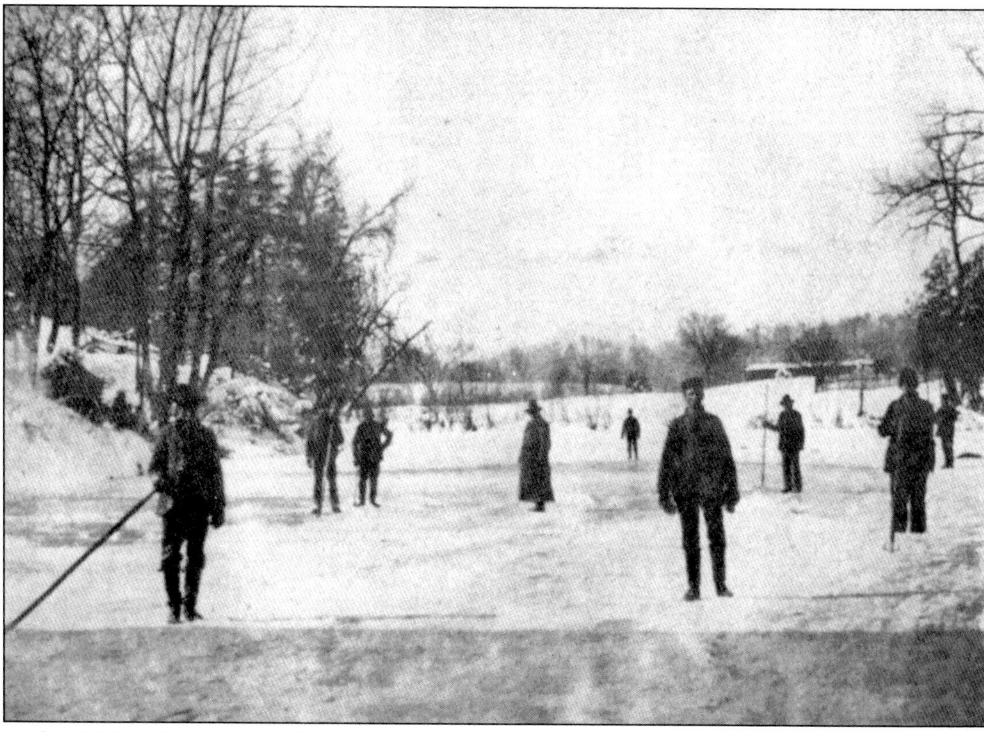

In the 1880s–1890s, a team of men gather on the frozen-over Shenandoah River for the winter job of cutting out 30-pound blocks of ice and hauling them to commercial ice houses in New Market. The ice houses stored the blocks indoors in piles of sawdust, insulating them for later sale during the warmer months. Ice houses continued operation until the availability of household refrigeration made them obsolete. (James R. Graves.)

In the 1920s, an early morning photograph catches proprietor Tom Funkhouser (right) with an unidentified helper getting ready to start the day. The ramp at left was used to skid 300-pound ice blocks to and from the wagons as the season progressed. This last ice house was located at the southwest corner of John Sevier Road and Stonewall Street and was still standing in the early 1960s. (Pat Funkhouser Vaughan.)

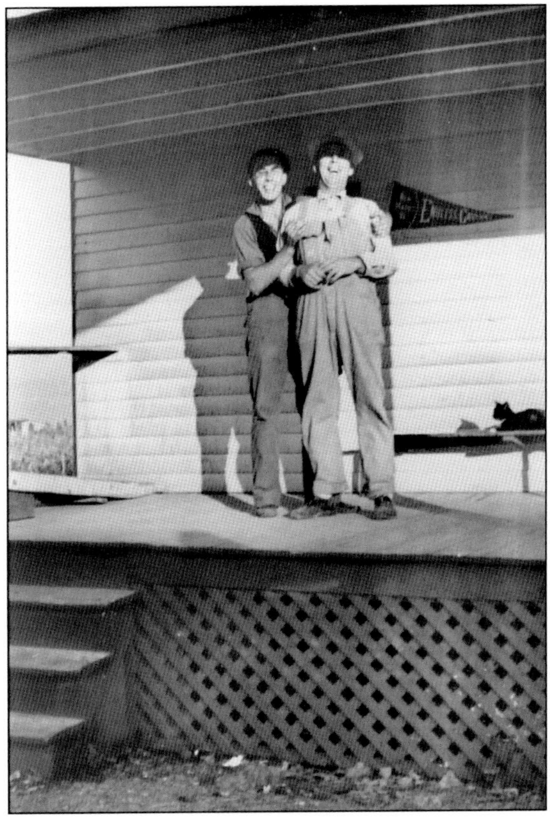

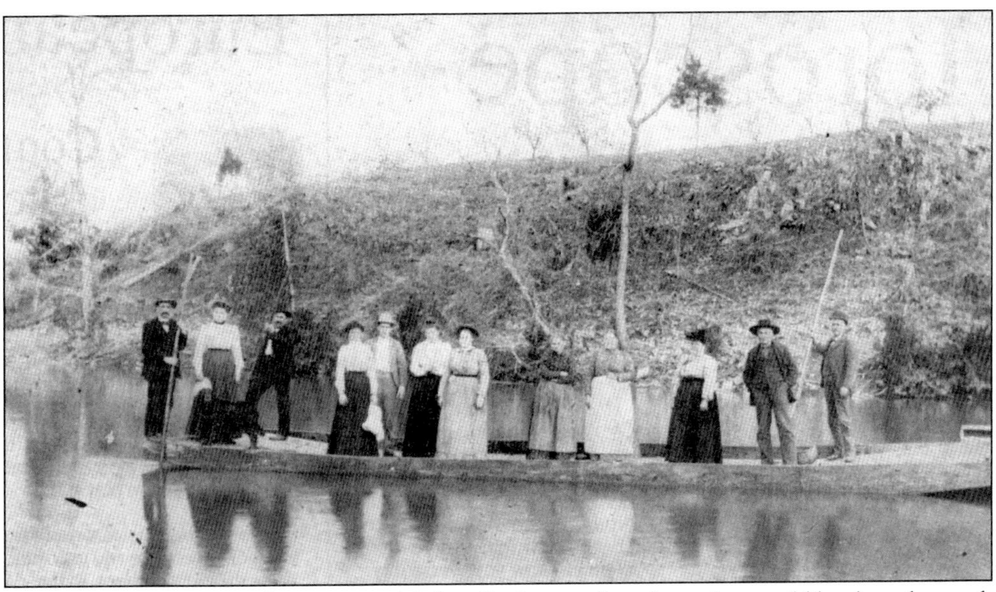

Jim Manor of Manors Mill ran a "gundalo" or flat-bottom long boat that could haul sand, gravel, produce, and people along the Shenandoah River. On occasion, pig iron from the local furnaces may have been hauled as well. As early as 1798, New Market had the Shenandoah Navigation Company, which chartered commerce downriver. (Nancy Branner Stewart.)

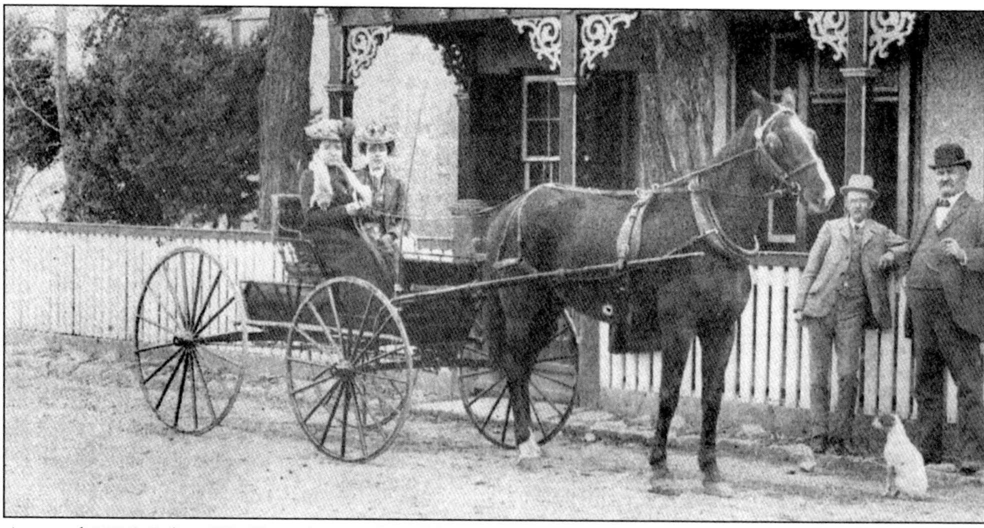

Around 1895, John W. Clinedinst, the older man second from right, is visiting the home of his friend Col. Phillip O'Bannon (far right) in Sperryville. The lady at left is tentatively identified as Louise O'Bannon sitting in the Piano-Box Buggy manufactured by the J. W. Clinedinst Carriage Company in New Market. (John D. Crim.)

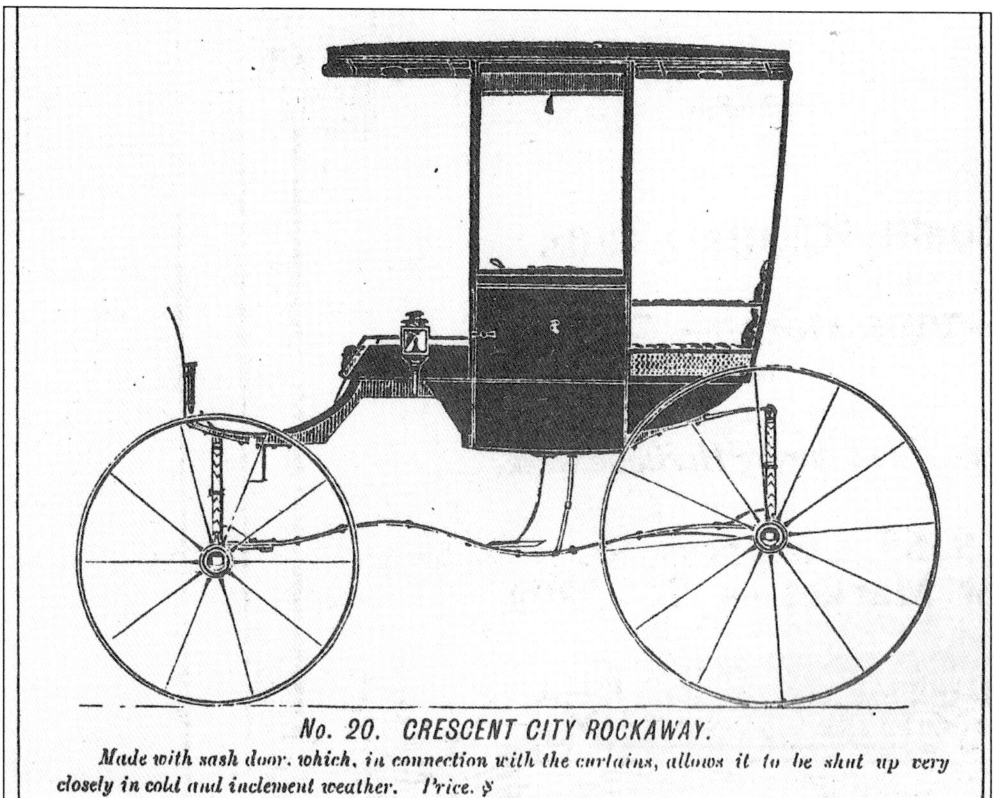

A page from the 1880 J. W. Clinedinst and Company Catalog shows a Crescent City (four passenger) Rockaway–style carriage that would have sold for $350–$500, depending on the accessories and gear ordered by the customer. (John D. Crim.)

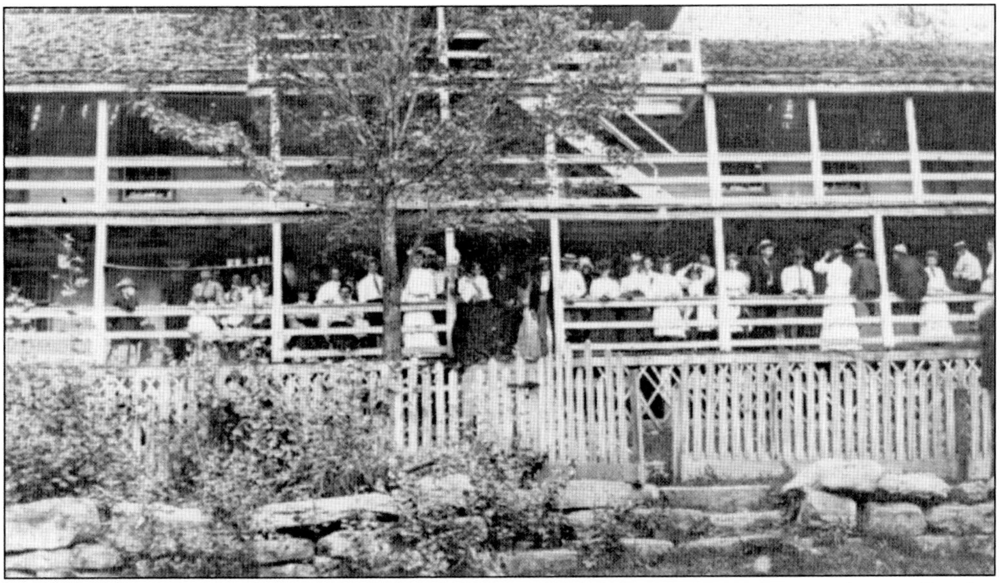

The Valley View Springs Hotel was built in the 1880s on the mountain just east of town. Similar facilities were constructed following a wave of national identification with mountain visits, clean air, and therapeutic results from bathing in healing mineral waters, and New Market was not about to be left out. While the majority of the hotels no longer exist, some, like Orkney Springs and Hot Springs, survive today. (*Shenandoah County Bi-centennial Book.*)

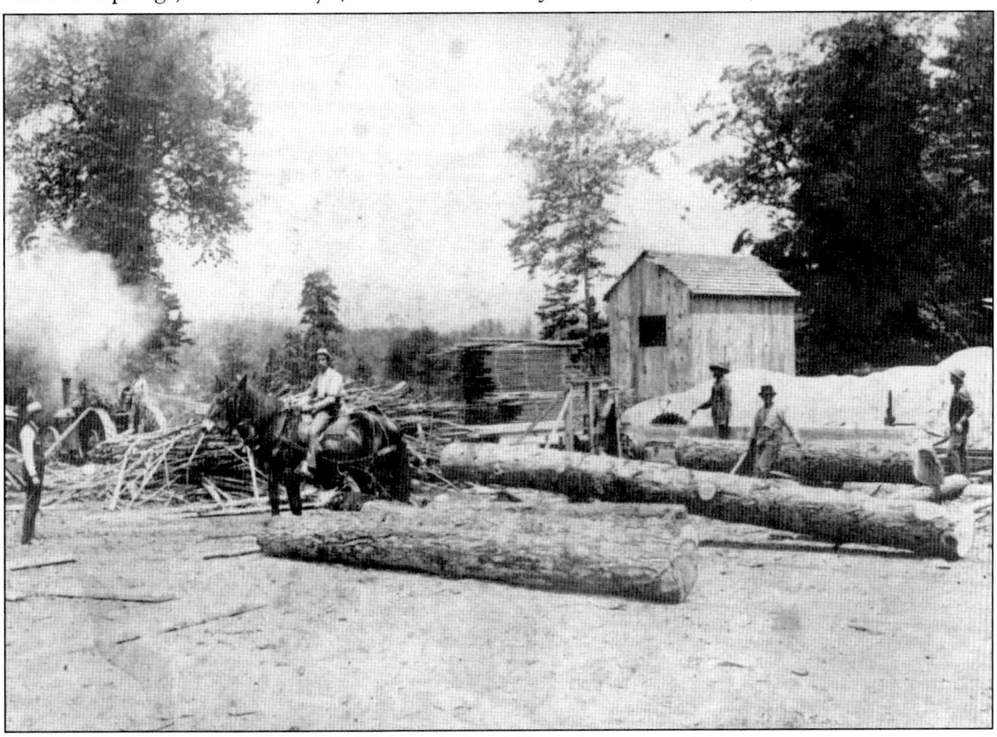

Hauling these massive white oak logs was a real chore before modern machinery. This sawmill was owned and operated by Atlas Lloyd up along the Massanutten Mountains. The steam engine at left powered the sawmill. (Nancy Branner Stewart.)

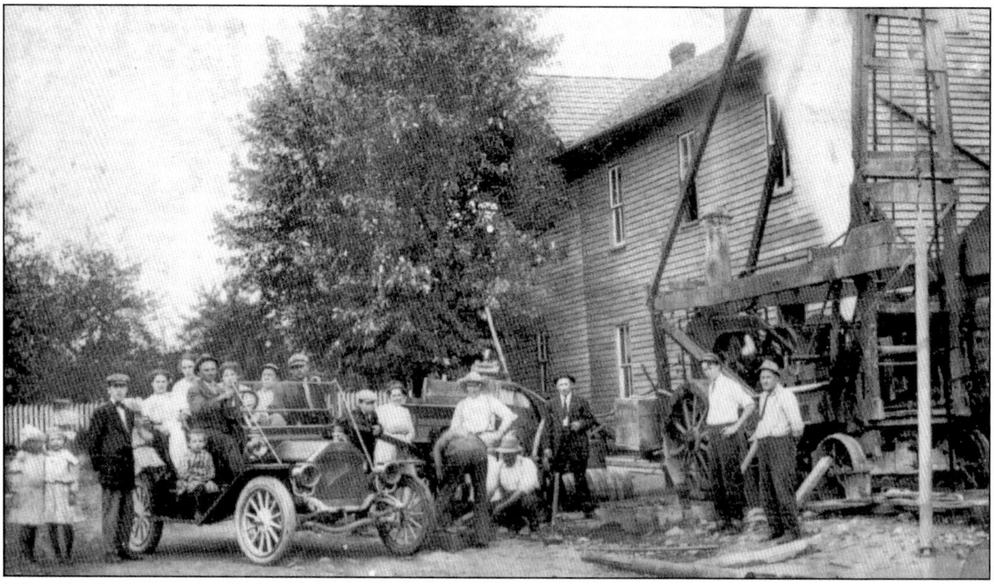

This B. B. O'Roark photograph captures a party in 1911 deepening the main well at Theis's corner at Lee Street and Cadet Road. The well pump–digging machine was powered by a steam-powered drill that would dig into the earth with long sleeves of steel to jacket the drill. The men would travel around the New Market area drilling for and improving water wells using the new technology. Wells were usually primed by dynamite, sending a huge explosion of water into the air. Seated in the brass-age Buick is W. J. Gochenour with a crowd of locals to see the commotion. (Nancy Branner Stewart.)

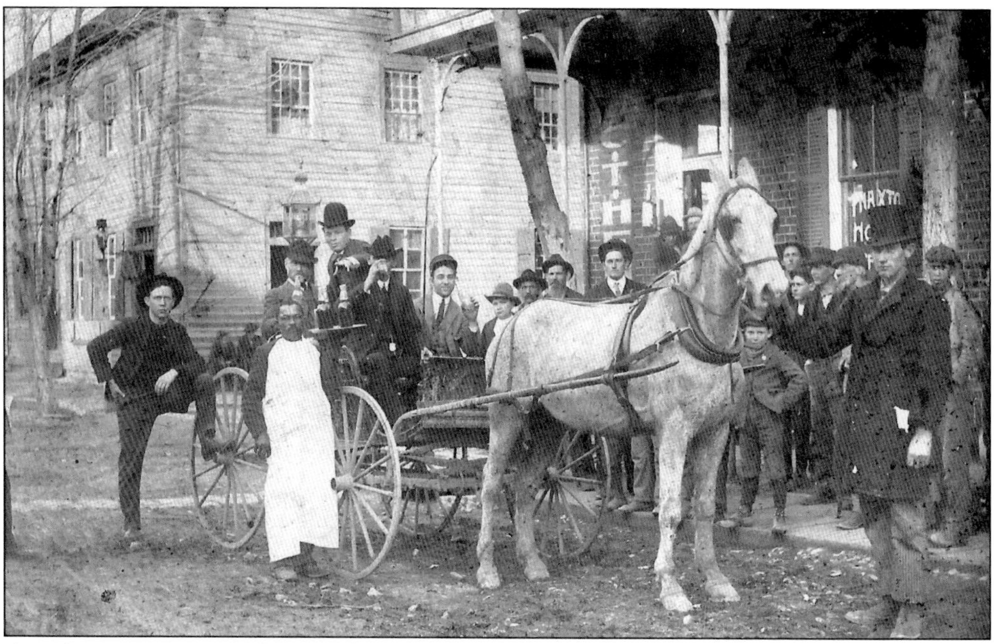

An afternoon group gathers at the Thaxton Hotel (today's Lee-Jackson), perhaps to try out the hotel's new drive-up service. Standing in the buggy is Emmanuel Sherry pointing at the camera. Milt Tusing is seated in the front right seat next to the whip. Holding the horse is William "Bill Bailey" Knupp. (New Market Area Library.)

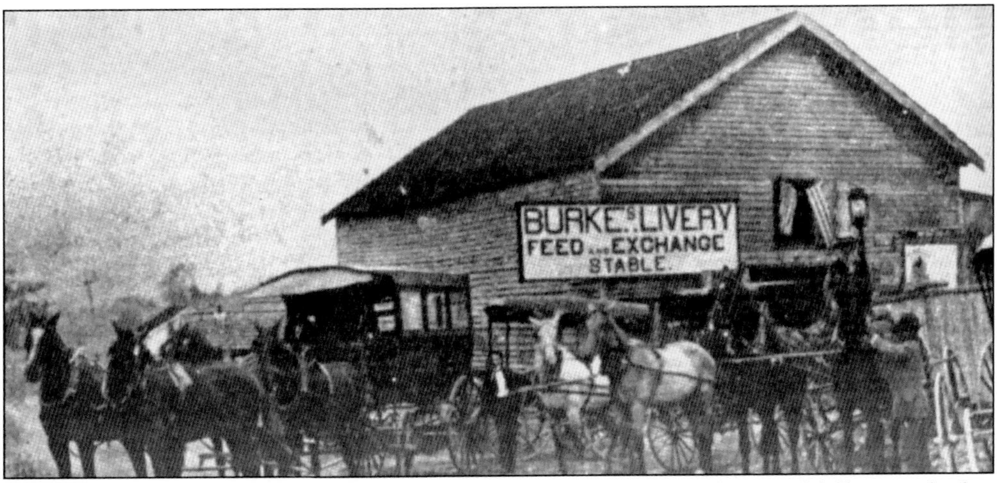

In 1887, the photographer (probably O'Roark) seized this moment with several different vehicles, which explains the operation of the Burke's Livery in multiple roles of business. It was operated by three Burke brothers, Joe, Charles, and John. Originally located near what is now Interstate 81 and the turnpike intersection in New Market, the stable rested weary horses and gave fresh horses for travel for United States mail carriers traveling to Luray Caverns and other routes into West Virginia. (Nancy Branner Stewart.)

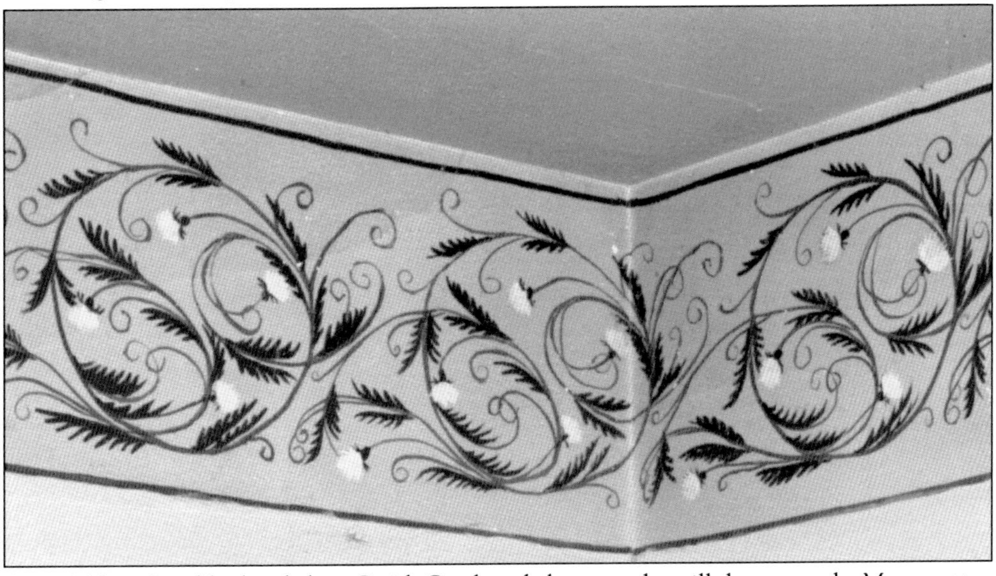

Artist Milton Strickler lived along Smith Creek and also owned a mill there near the Massanutten in the early 1900s. This beautiful grapevine fresco work was done in Page County, Virginia, by him in the 1920s for a prominent family home there. Strickler painted and decorated many homes, but unfortunately most of his works do not survive because people painted over them. His work was complex but not three dimensional. He made metal stencils for his one-dimensional forms to execute his simple patterns. His work was vastly different from William F. Rupp's (also from New Market) fresco work as a three-dimensional artist. Strickler was known to enjoy chewing tobacco while he painted and had a miniature spittoon tied around his neck. Fresco painting was a Shenandoah Valley tradition of artistic expression usually done for the prominent and mastered by few. What few works of Strickler's that survive are regarded as important 20th-century Virginia folk art. (Gary Bauserman.)

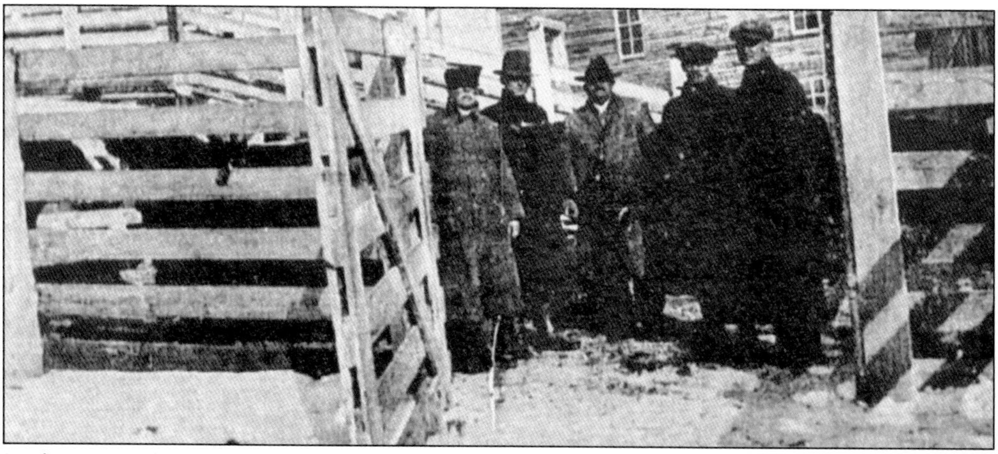

In the 1930s, the stock holding pen at the New Market Railroad Depot is holding buyers as well as livestock. The loading ramp to and from the cattle rail cars is directly behind the men. The depot was located one and a half miles out of town because New Market citizens did not want the railroad scaring their livestock within its limits. (Nancy Branner Stewart.)

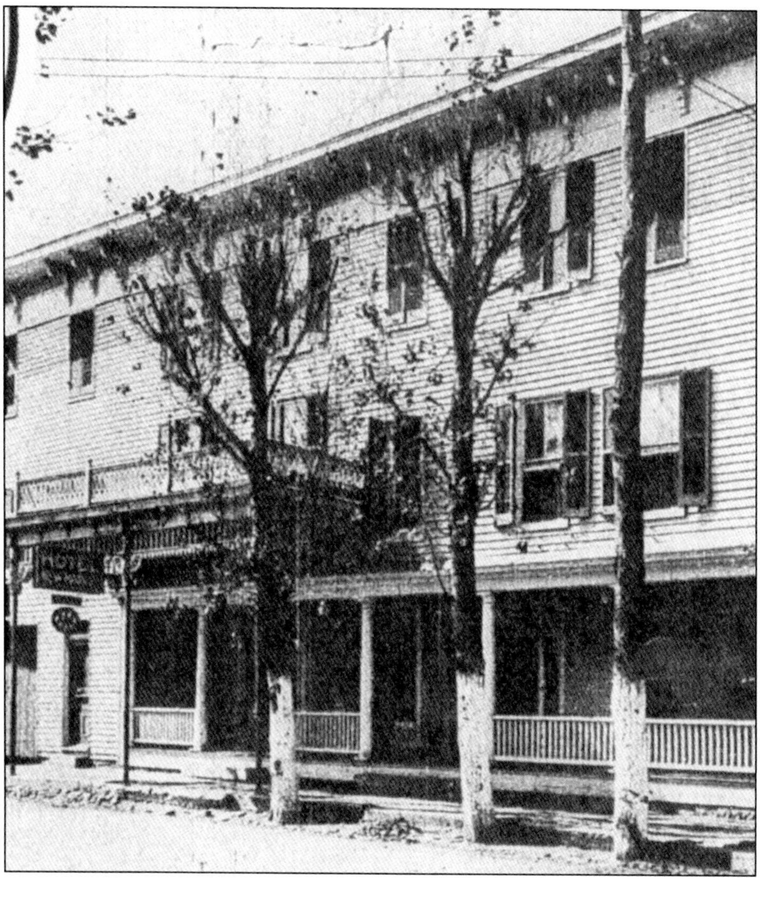

In the 1920s, the Hotel Grabill waits for new visitors. Automobiles were the principle means of transportation and tourism has been embraced, judging from the AAA (founded in 1902) sign prominently displayed. In later years, the building was torn down, and a public parking lot constructed adjacent to today's Jalisco Restaurant at 9403 Congress Street. (Nancy Branner Stewart.)

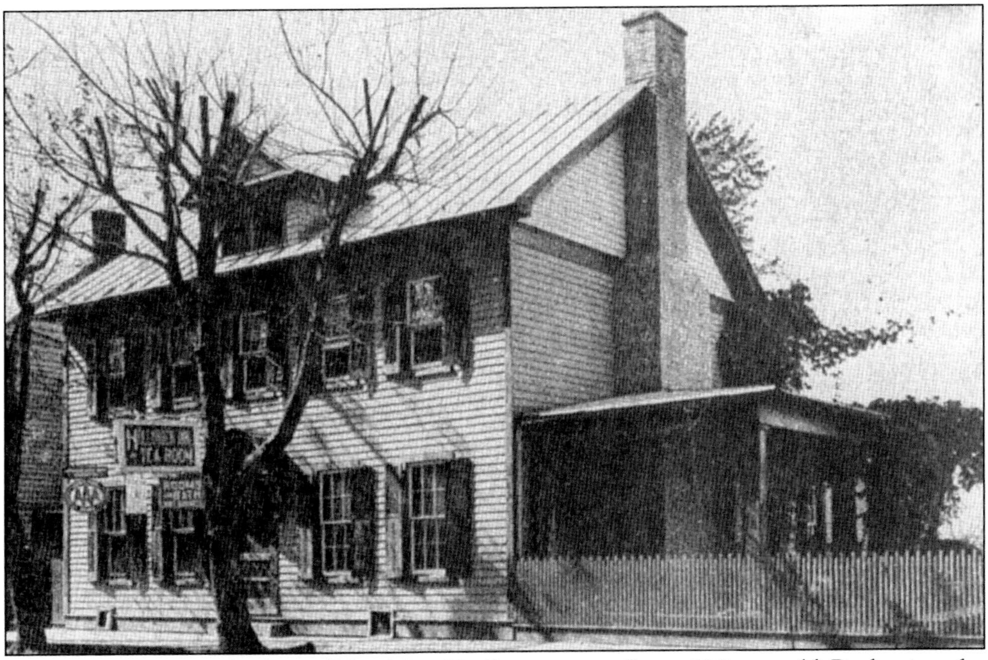

In this 1927 photograph, the Hollyhock Inn Tea Room was well over 120 years old. By the time the Roaring Twenties rolled around, this operated as an inn. The ladies that ran the Hollyhock Inn were sisters Ludy and Sue Burwell. The inn was a quiet, good, and wholesome overnight stay. The well-known Harry Byrd, former governor of Virginia, stayed there often while visiting New Market. Today Faye's Flowers at 9361 Congress Street continues the building's commercial legacy. (Nancy Branner Stewart.)

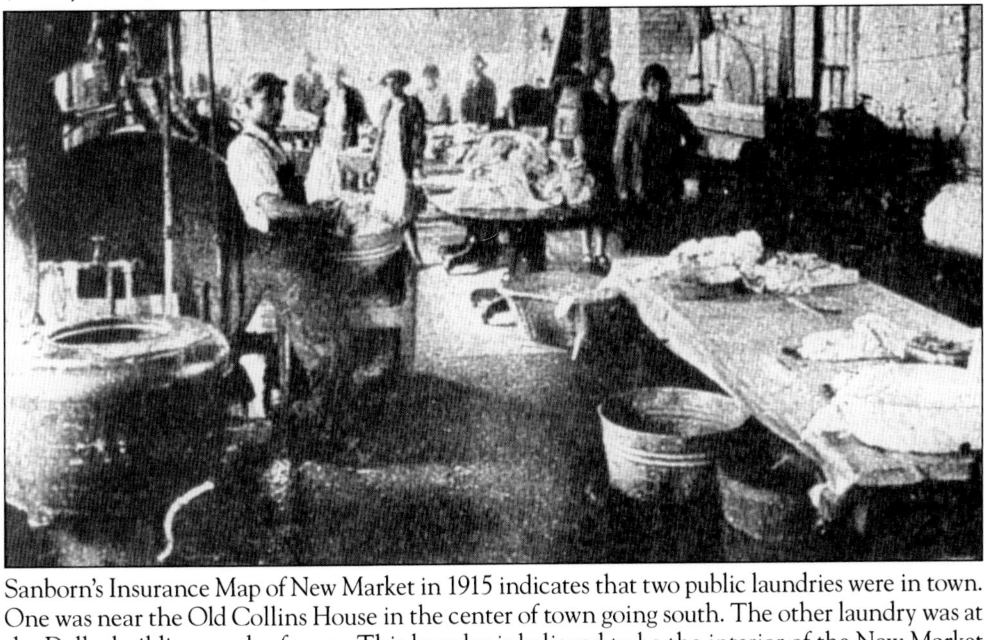

Sanborn's Insurance Map of New Market in 1915 indicates that two public laundries were in town. One was near the Old Collins House in the center of town going south. The other laundry was at the Dalke building south of town. This laundry is believed to be the interior of the New Market Laundry near the carriage house by the Collins House. It is an exceptionally rare and intimate 1927 view capturing a necessary day-to-day chore. (Nancy Branner Stewart.)

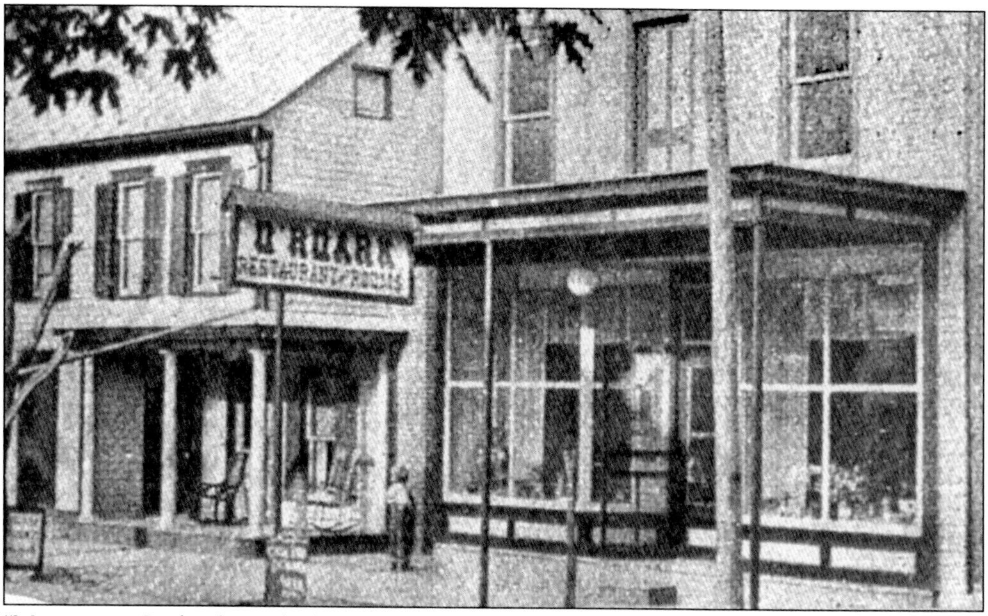

"Mmmm . . . Said to have the best ice cream in town," is New Market historian Nancy Stewart's reaction remembering O'Roark's Restaurant in town. The establishment was rather famous and was in business for many years feeding hungry travelers and locals wanting an outing. Every week during the fall season, they would have an oyster feast that everyone loved. These salted oysters were imported straight from the fishermen farming Virginia's Chesapeake Bay. Today these tasty native treats are endangered due to disease and pollution. Another similar Korean variety of oyster has been introduced and is prospering in the bay. (Edward "Casey" Billhimer, Dan Vaughn.)

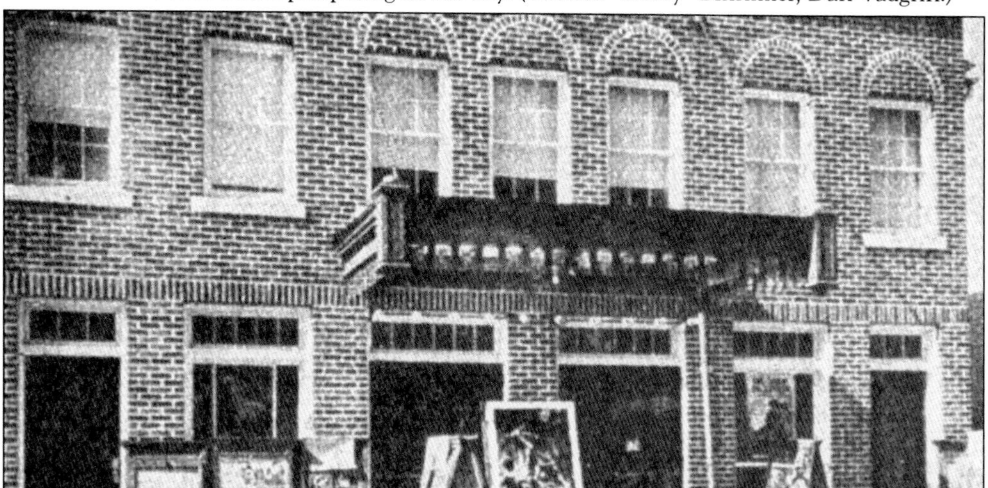

In the 1920s, the New Theatre played any number of westerns, comedies, serials, musicals, and others, some of which were current and some past their prime. The playbill in front appears to be advertising a good old Hoot Gibson cowboy western. (Nancy Branner Stewart.)

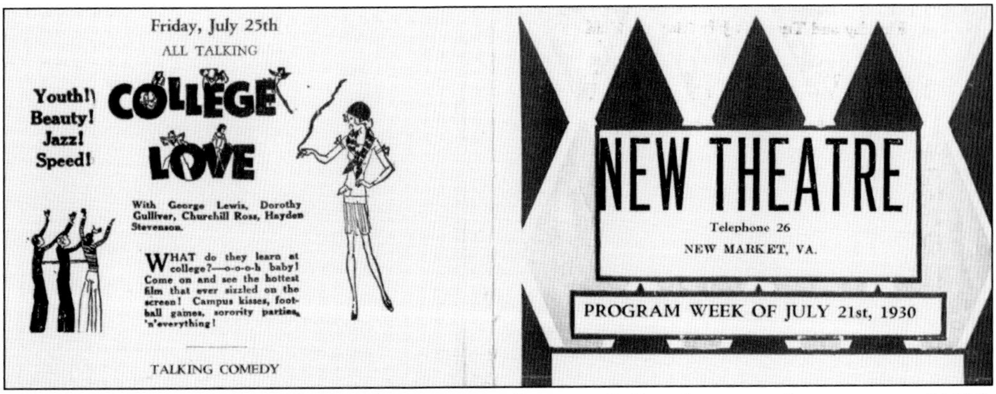

The New Theater shows off one of its newest offerings, *College Love*, in the summer of 1930. Promoting the "All Talk" aspect of the movie meant the end of the silent film era. Other features on the bill were Charles (Buddy) Rogers and Jean Arthur in *Halfway to Heaven* and also Ted Lewis with Ann Pennington and Alice Day in *Is Everybody Happy?* The fliers were printed in advance and handed out in local stores and streets. (John D. Crim.)

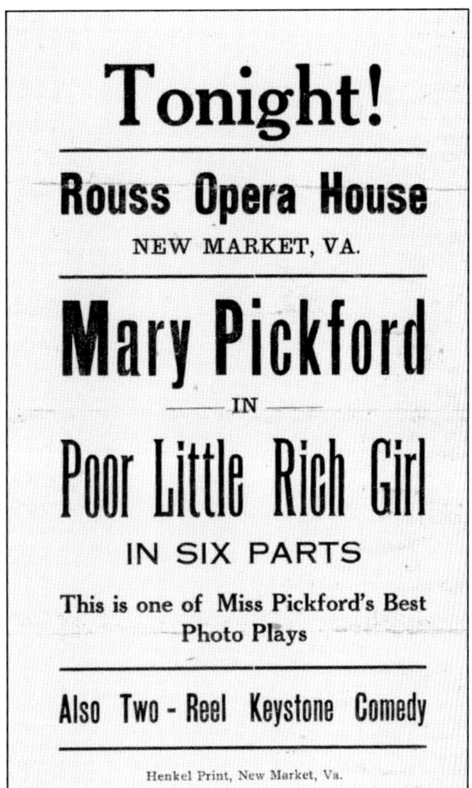

This flier for the Mary Pickford film probably came out around 1917–1920 and was probably shown as a six-part serial. Her role as Gwendolyn forever established Pickford as "America's Sweetheart" of the silent screen. The three-story Rouss Opera House regularly showed older film features as they were recirculated. Built by Charles Broadway Rouss in 1905, the building survives today at 9357 Congress Street. (John D. Crim.)

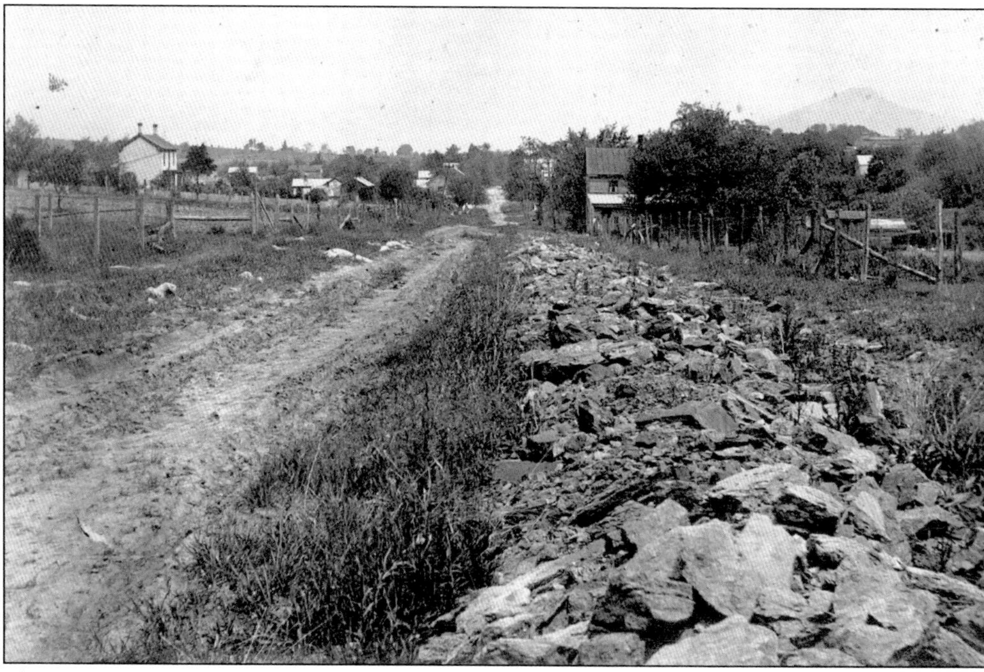

This is Lime Street (today's Cadet Road) looking north, possibly in the 1890s or early 1900s. The house at left exists today as 9541 Cadet Road, and the house at right survives as 41 Confederate Street. To the right, large rocks, exposed during years of roadbed erosion, are spoiled off to the side. They will be reused in building fences and house foundations along the streets. (Nancy Branner Stewart.)

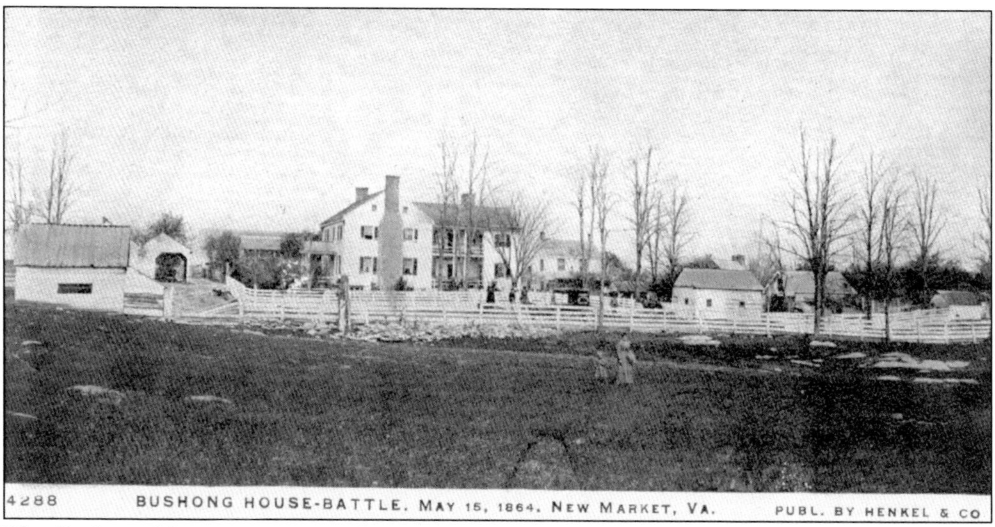

The Bushong House, appearing the same in about 1905 as it does today, contributed many different aspects to New Market culture. It left an indelible mark as the centerpiece of the Battle of New Market and the sacrifice of young lives by the VMI cadets and so many others. The house serves as a representative of an atypical, vernacular architecture in the Shenandoah Valley and an iconic tourist destination for those seeking to understand the Civil War. Today the house and the battlefield are beautifully maintained by the Virginia Military Institute. (Nancy Branner Stewart.)

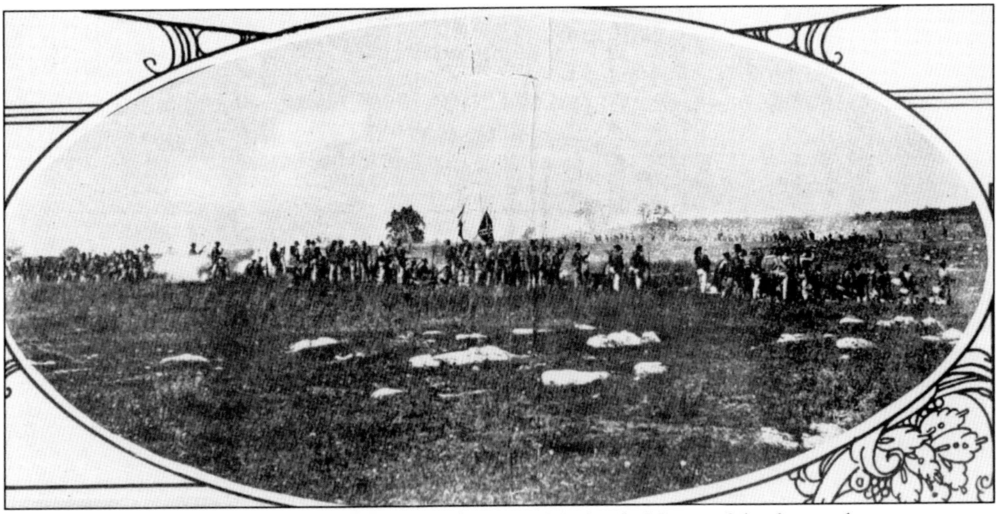

Originally reenactments were called sham battles. New Market held one of the first such reenactments ever in the United States. In September 1923, the U.S. Marine Corps and other military branches, including the U.S. Army, provided public entertainment and training for their armies in drills and fights with real strategies based on earlier tactics. (Nancy Branner Stewart.)

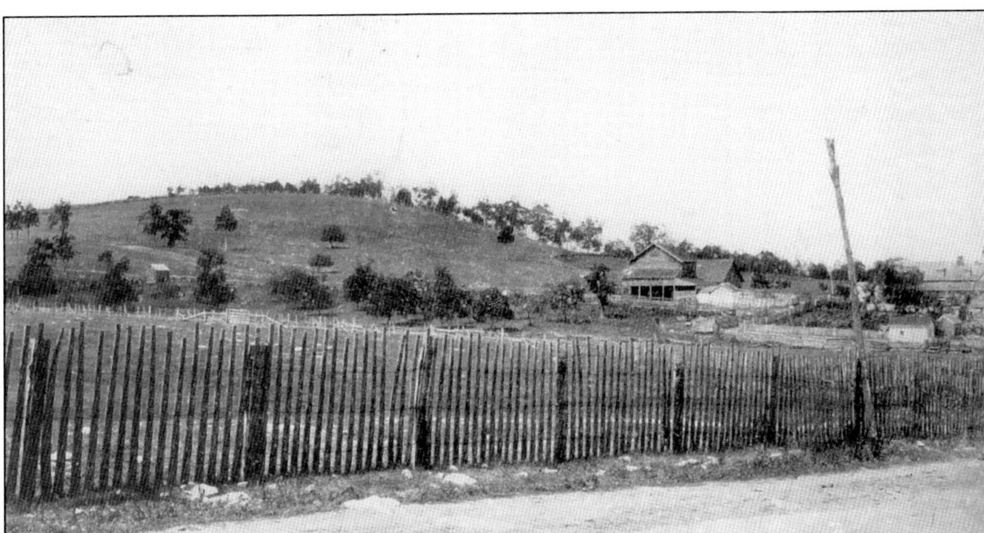

Madden's Hill was the location from which Confederate general John Breckinridge ordered an artillery duel during the first day of fighting in New Market. The firing went on into the early morning hours with no advantage to either side. On May 15, 1864, the VMI Cadets Corps first advanced down the hill. Their captain, Frank Preston of Company B, said a prayer for the day's battle. These brave lads had 18 Union rifled cannons aimed at them on the steep hill, and they were asked to charge in ankle-deep mud. They were successful and never wavered in their march despite many comrades dying all around them. (Jean Kite, Dan Vaughn.)

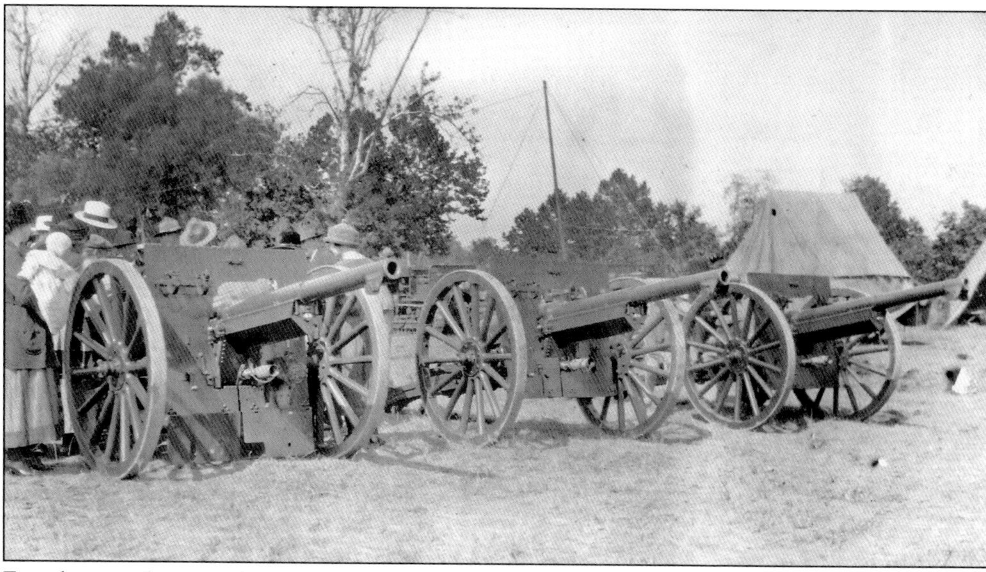

For almost 85 years, the New Market Battlefield reenactments have helped to educate the public and perpetuate the memories of those that fought and fell there. The howitzer cannons of the post–World War I era stand at the ready in this September 1923 sham battle. The battles have been witnessed by thousands of spectators. Reenacting has become a very serious hobby and work for some. Men and women involved in living-history interpretations and reenactors contribute greatly to the understanding of everyday life and the military history of this country. (Jean Kite, Dan Vaughn.)

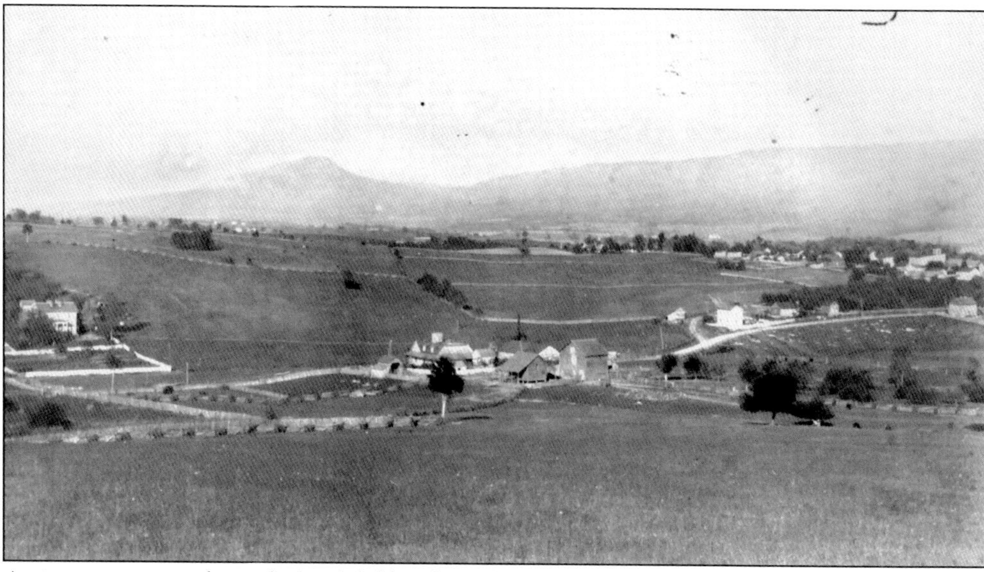

An impressive view shows the battlefield and its relationship and distance to the town of New Market taken from Madden's Hill just west of town at the site of the Confederate Artillery Battery. In the center of the photograph is the Madden farm and large spring, no longer existing, as it was buried by Interstate 81 in the mid-1960s. Further widening and expansion of this highway are being debated and clearly threaten historic sites and the natural grace so heralded of the Shenandoah Valley corridor. To the far left is the Shirley home, now the headquarters for the Shenandoah Valley Battlefields Foundation. (Jean Kite, Dan Vaughn.)

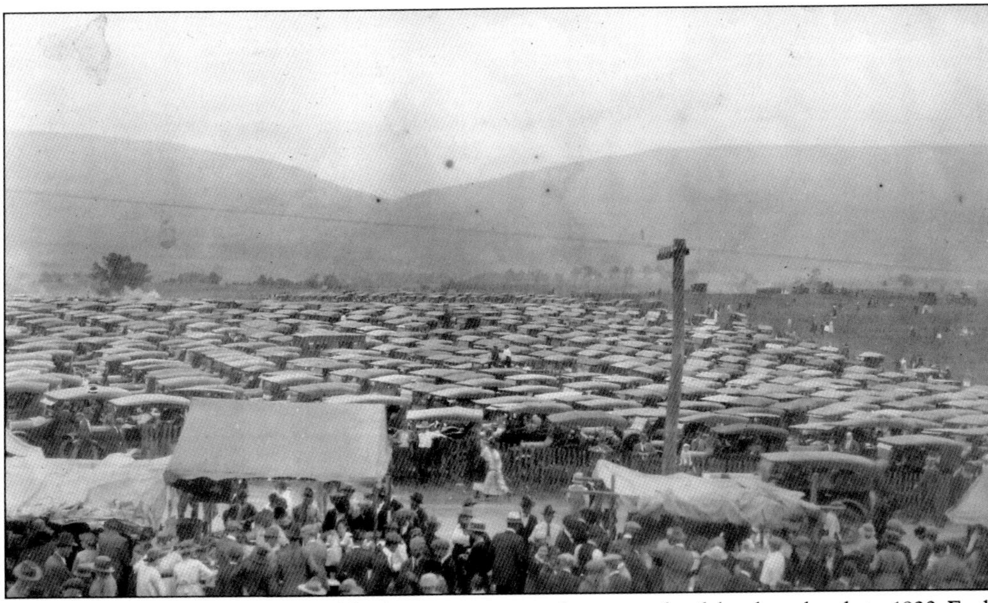

Tremendous crowds gather around food tents to witness the spectacle of the sham battle in 1923. Each year, crowds come to view the reenactors and pay respects to the men that fought here. The story of the Battle of New Market is retold annually on the original battle site. People come from all over the United States to see and participate in this historical recreation. (Jean Kite, Dan Vaughn.)

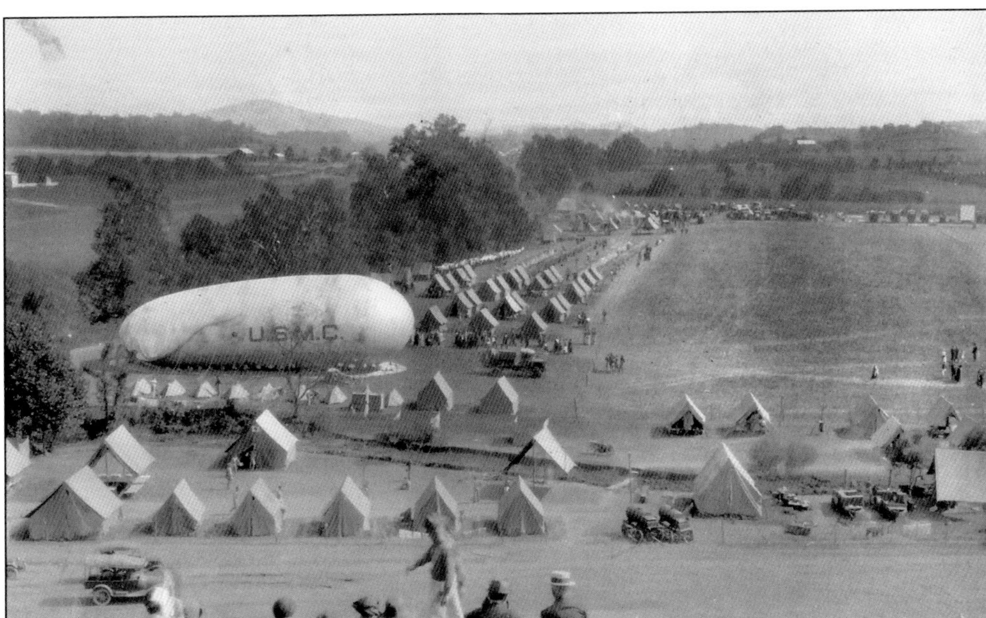

This dirigible aircraft was available for the U.S. Marine Corps at the battlefield for their first drills in camp. Below the aircraft are tents similar to the conditions Civil War soldiers endured the entire war. Note the tents are arranged in streets, which were a typical military aspect of camp life. The weekend reenactments created tremendous tourism markets for the economy of the local townspeople and those seeking Civil War history and the natural beauty of the Shenandoah. (Jean Kite, Dan Vaughn.)

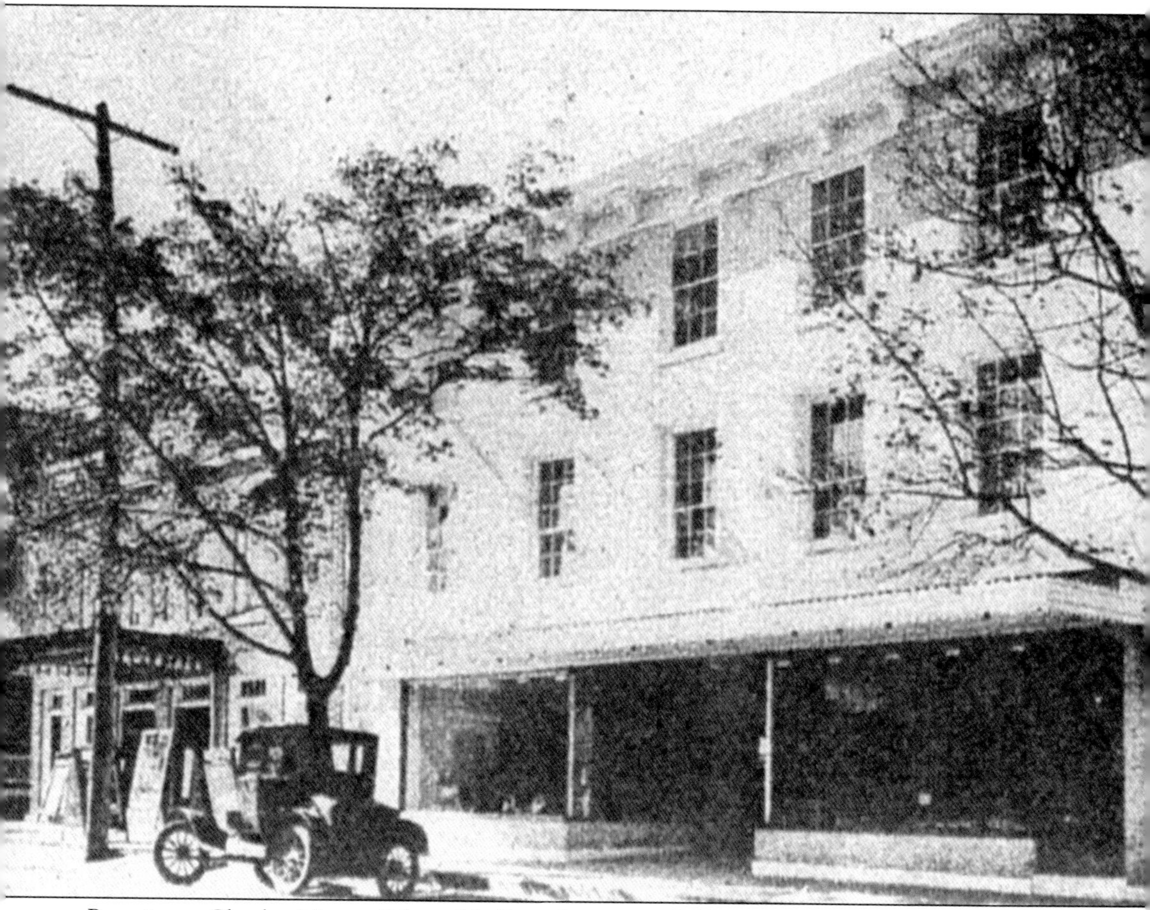

Proprietors Charles Moore, Edmond J. Rosenberger, and Abe Moore opened the New Market Department Store in 1927, offering a bit of just about everything a family might need. By 1937, Rosenberger had bought out his partners, and the store continued until closing in 1962. The renovated building still serves the community today as SunTrust Bank located at 9397 Congress Street. (Nancy Branner Stewart.)

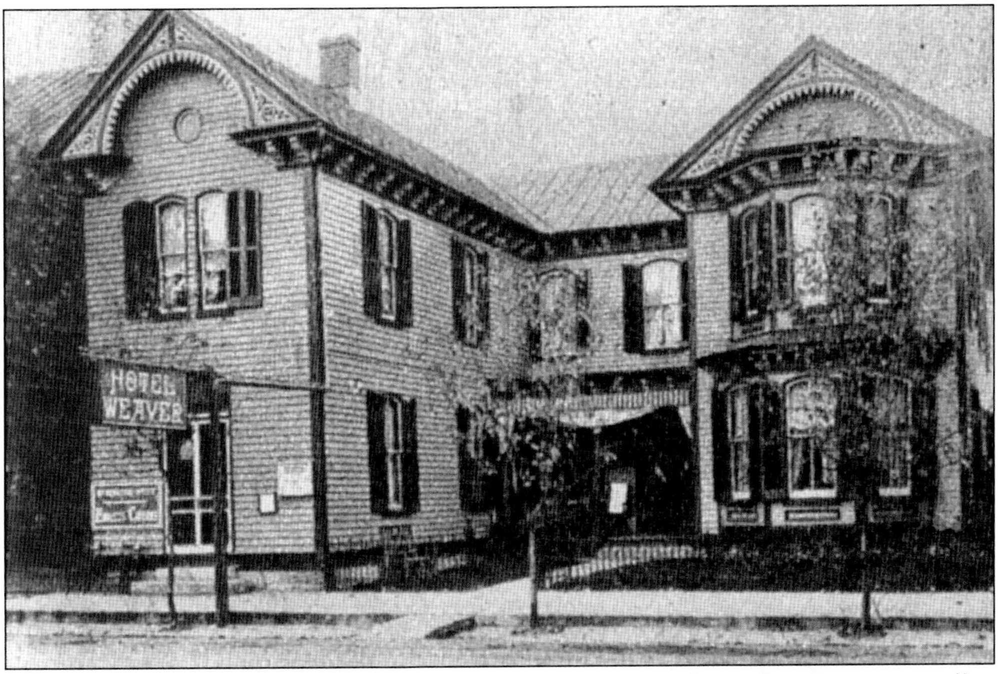

The Hotel Weaver functioned as a ticket and information office for Endless Caverns as well as serving travelers stopping in New Market on their way north and south. The building survives today next to the BB&T bank building as the Theis Chapel of Dellinger Funeral Homes, located at 9377 Congress Street. (Nancy Branner Stewart.)

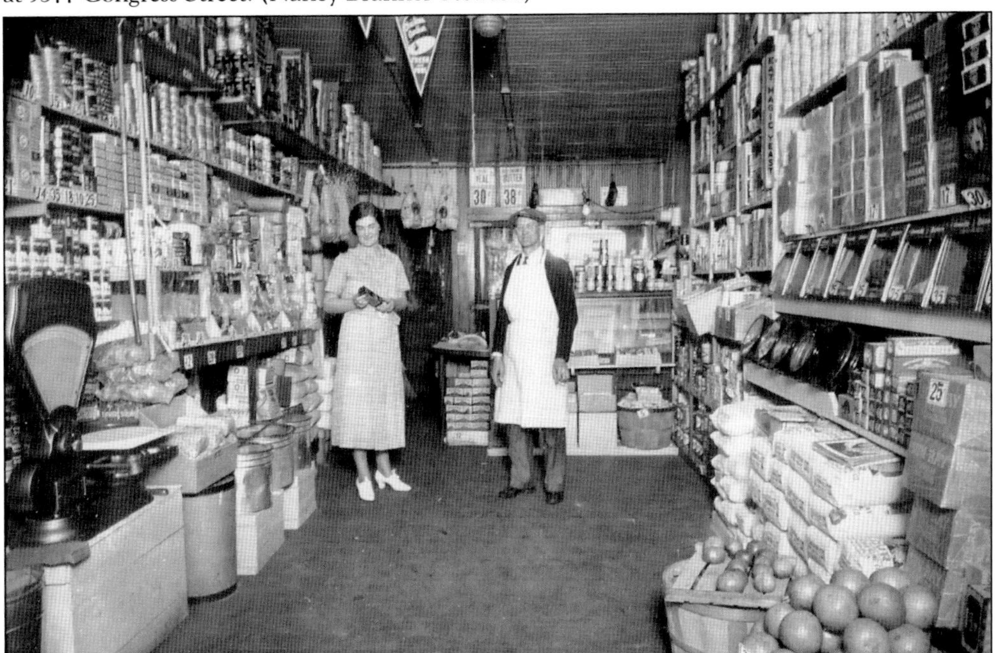
In the 1940s, Mrs. Norman Good makes a purchase in the Sanitary Meat and Grocery Market owned and operated by Preston Elwood "Crackerjack" Burkholder (right) for 32 years. Burkholder's store was open and serving the community until his passing in 1949. (Mrs. Maxine Burkholder.)

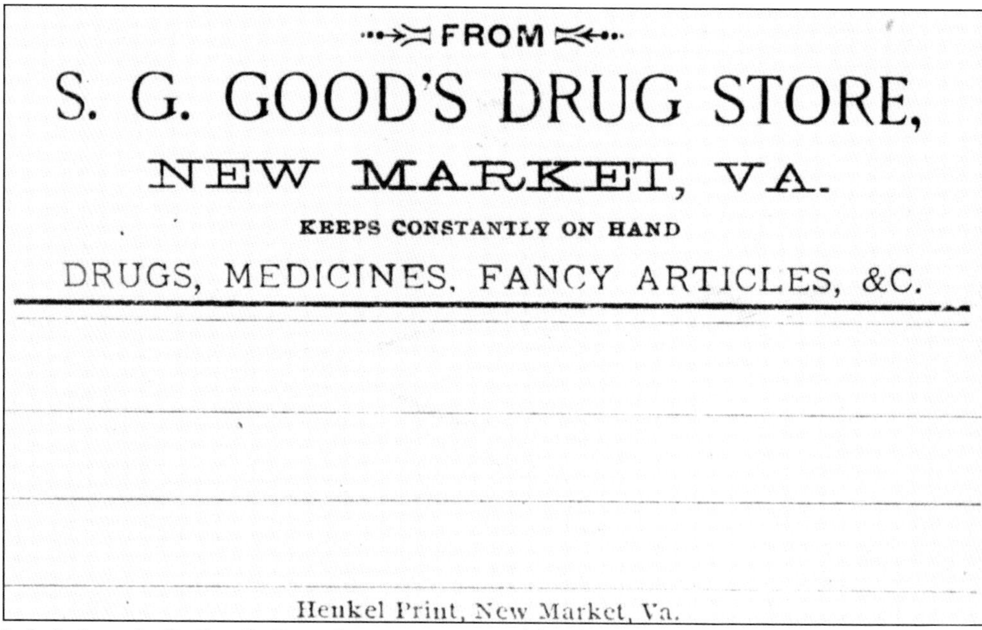
FROM

S. G. GOOD'S DRUG STORE,

NEW MARKET, VA.

KEEPS CONSTANTLY ON HAND

DRUGS, MEDICINES, FANCY ARTICLES, &C.

Henkel Print, New Market, Va.

Labels from S. G. Good's Drug Store were printed by the Henkel Press. Good's pharmacy was located on the northwest corner of Congress and Lee Streets at what is today 9437 Congress Street. (Mrs. Maxine Burkholder.)

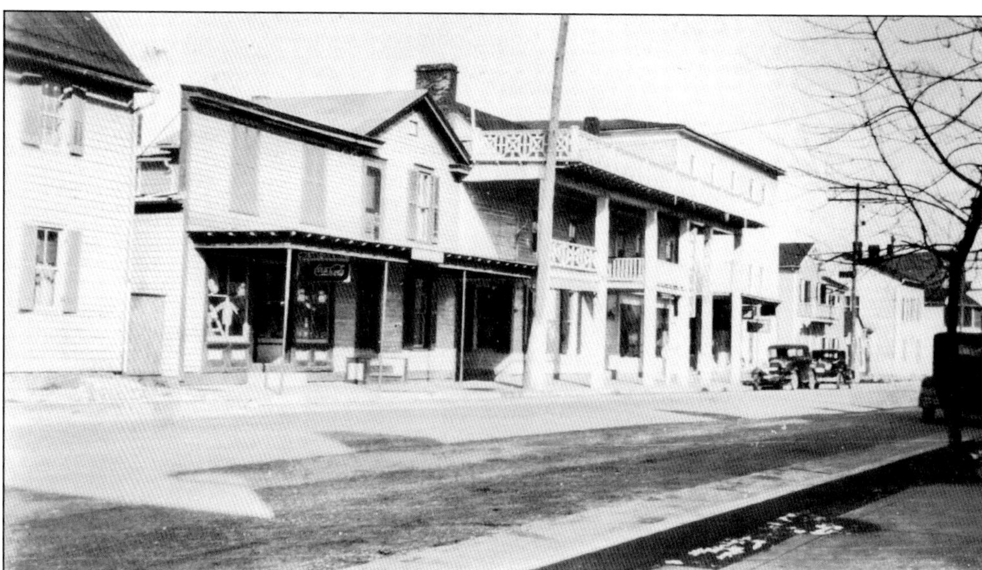

When this photograph was snapped, the building in the center was Mrs. Sine's store. The building at left was called Brocks Hotel, and the building at right was the Colonial Hotel. By 1950, the Colonial Hotel catered to the town for popular dances on the top floor, called the "Green Room." (Edward "Casey" Billhimer.)

On September 12, 1925, the town residents voted 116 to 105 in favor of installing New Market's Public Water Supply and Sewerage System, notwithstanding the opposition of those who circulated this flyer in the summer of 1925. The cost estimate was a staggering $85,000 by the American Industries Engineering Company at 140 Cedar Street, New York City. While the circular was printed by the same office that printed the *Shenandoah Valley* newspaper, the editor clearly favored the project in a September 17 article, saying, in part, "Now that this splendid step has been taken, the only course open to our citizens is to combine in good faith, though not in dangerous gullability [*sic*], and push this project over to the final success that it deserves and must get to place our town in a position to make the most of the opportunities that are literally cast at the feet of our people." (John D. Crim, Phillip Crown.)

CITIZEN

Do you know when you vote for that $85,000 water bond issue for New Market on Saturday, September 12, 1925, it means a first mortgage on your home and that you must pay it in thirty-five years? Further, do you know that this means that a sinking fund of nearly $2,500 must be raised a year, and the first year's interest $4,250, if floated at 5 per cent., and the handling of such a big sum would probably amount to $1,000, and besides the monthly upkeep for the use of the water? The above amounts with the $2,000 taxes you pay now would total a sum of probably $10,000, the first year.

Do you know if water is brought to New Market, it will be nowhere but in the streets; and if you wish it in your homes, it will cost from three to five hundred dollars to get it there?

Do you know unless your home is heated the pipes will burst every winter?

Do you know when the $85,000 is spent there is a strong likelihood the town will have no water and be everlastingly in debt?

Do you know Grim's Spring never can furnish enough water for New Market, and that spring has been dry more than once?

Do you know people who have lived here all their lives and have worked all around Grim's Spring say it goes perfectly dry, and do you know they know more about this part of the country than New York experts, who know nothing about weather conditions in these parts?

Do you know plenty of good water could be furnished from an artesian well sunk on top of Shirley's Hill at almost a fraction of the cost now proposed?

And do you know the $85,000 will not begin to get the water here from Grim's Spring, even if it were there, and no expert can insure a constant supply any more than he can that it will rain all the time, for the water on the mountain is rain water, and always has been?

Do you know that for one hundred years New Market has had almost the finest water of any town, anywhere, and less sickness from bad water?

Do you know that the very few fires we have had have not altogether been accidental, but our good wells and cisterns, which we have already at a big expense, have served us well?

Do you know New Market has never had a water shortage?

Do you know many of our towns with better showing than Grim's Spring have a water scarcity?

And do you know Harrisonburg, Staunton, and Winchester with all their money and modern water systems are having a water famine right now, a thing New Market ever had?

Do you know this is not the last chance New Market has of getting water? Later on, we could act on the sad experience other towns are having, and no doubt, profit by it.

Do you know you had better know what you are doing before you vote such a tax on us all, with no assurance of water?

Do you know, too, taxes are paying other people to come and examine our water when they might do well to look to their own water? And do you know you are paying an expert seven hundred dollars to tell you how to get rid of your money without a guarantee of value received for water in your town all of the time as we now have it. Think well before you act!

CITIZEN.

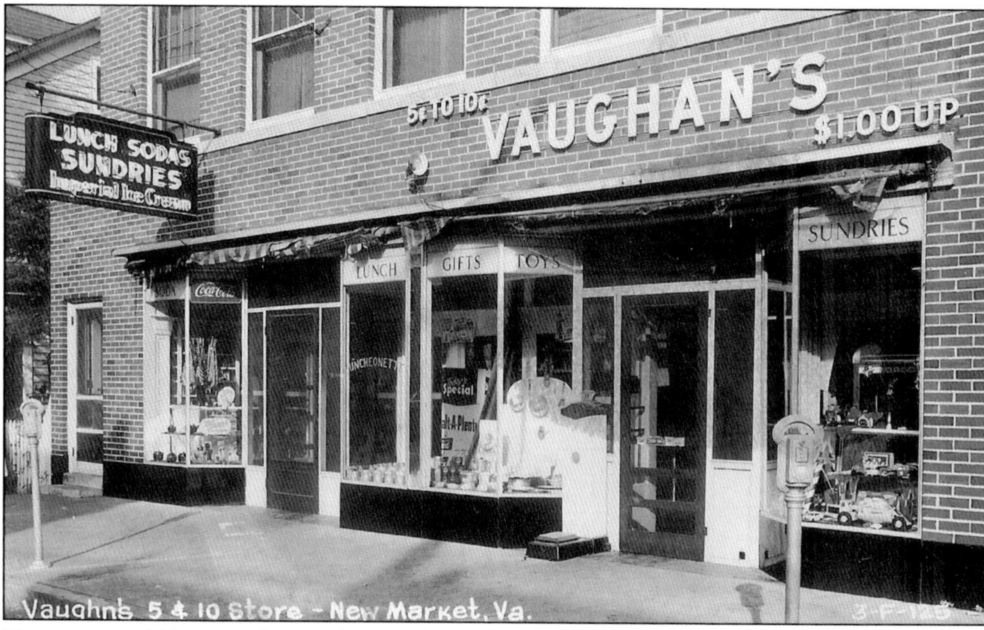

No town would be complete without a five-and-dime store, and Vaughan's was New Market's, pictured in the late 1940s. Shoppers could get just about anything they may want, including lunch. They were even able to check out the latest in comic books, despite the sign reading, "Please Do Not Read Before Buying." (Dan Vaughn.)

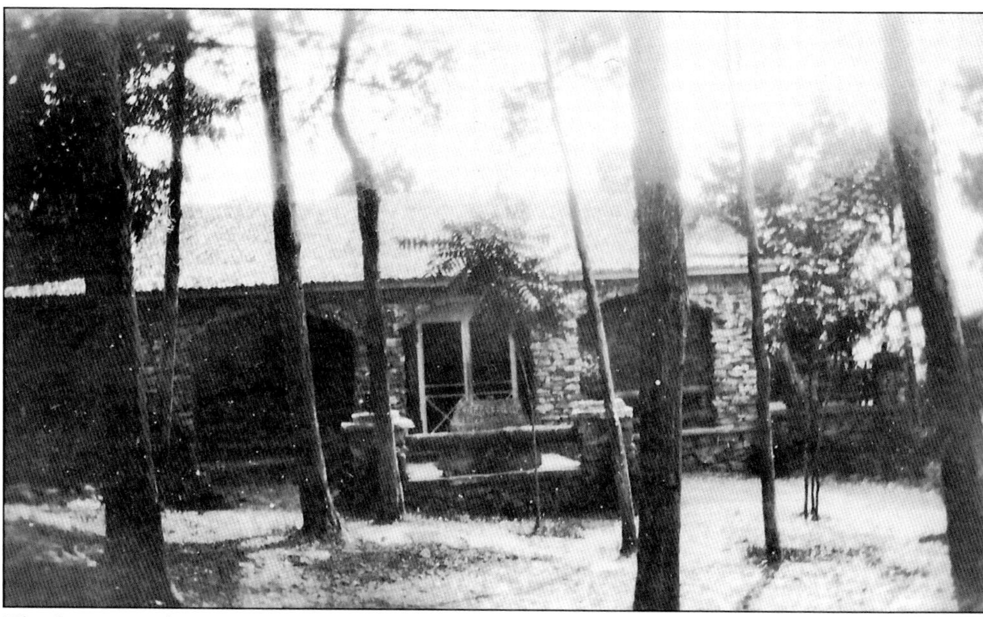

The house at the entrance for Endless Caverns was all constructed from native bluestone limestone laid in a whimsical naturalistic pattern. The caverns were discovered October 1, 1879, when two young boys were rabbit hunting along the Reuben Zirkle farm. The boys jumped a rabbit into the labyrinth. The cave was not opened and developed for tourists until about 1920. (Cathy Blackburn Mauck.)

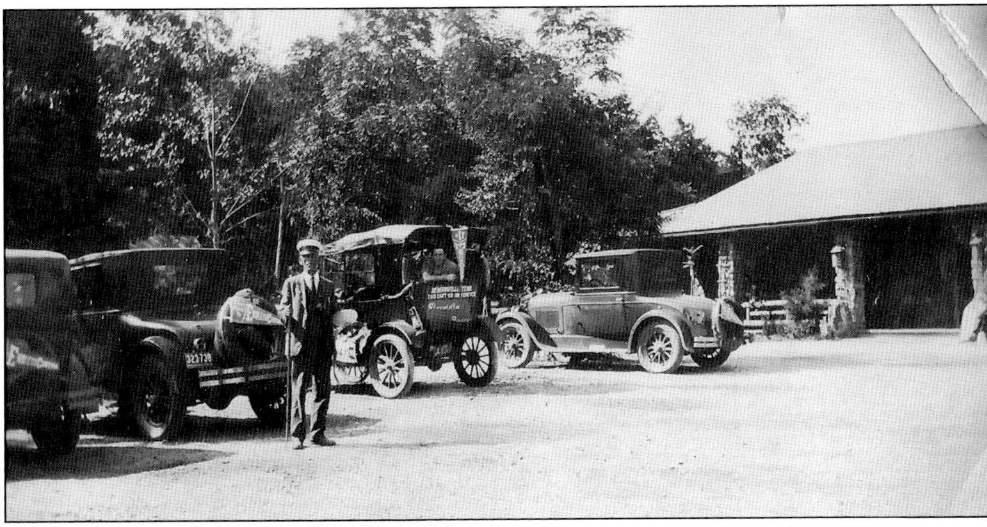

After the opening in 1920, Endless Caverns made an aggressive campaign to lure visitors en route to world-famous Luray Caverns, just over the mountain in Page County. About that same time, a beautiful cave was discovered in Mount Jackson, just north of New Market, called Shenandoah Caverns. Soon "cave wars" were prevalent, but all were working toward a booming economy in tourism in Virginia's valley in general. The cave wars were downright brutal in other areas during this period such as in Tennessee around Mammoth Cave. The caverns attractions in the valley learned later to work together. The man in the parking lot with his ever-present cane is Roland (Rollie) Newland, who was employed as a caverns guide, parking lot attendant, tour group excort, and also attached advertising banners to visiting cars. (Cathy Blackburn Mauck.)

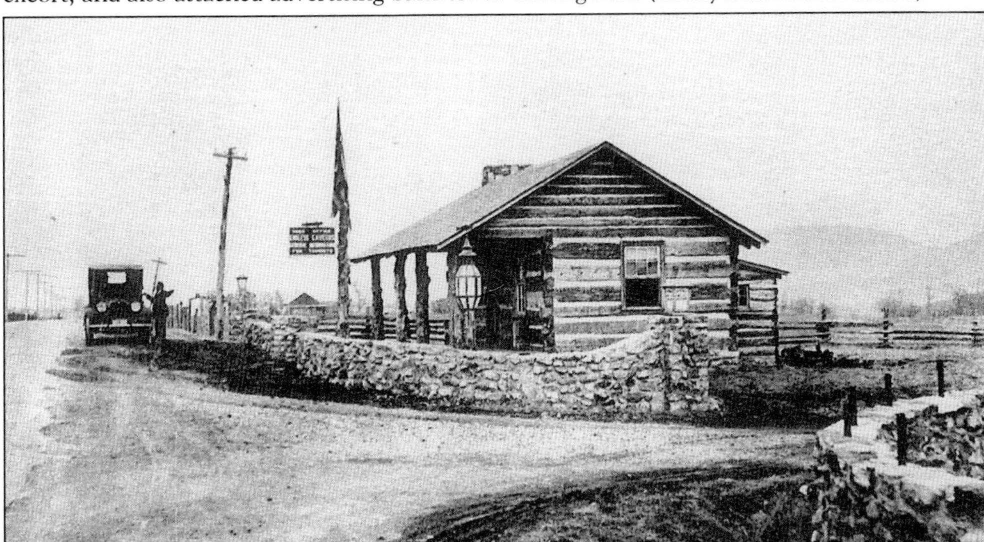

This cabin, dating from the early 1800s, was moved from the Mount Crawford area by Col. Edward T. Brown and restored to serve as the first main entrance to Endless Caverns, just south of New Market. The caverns are physically in Rockingham County, Virginia, but have always retained a mailbox in New Market, Shenandoah County, Virginia. The log cabin was a ticket area for the caverns or an area for old Valley Pike travelers to stretch their legs and get a cold drink. Many years ago, a new stone-wall entrance was erected with a brand-new road that went to the cave just south of the old entrance. (Dan Vaughn.)

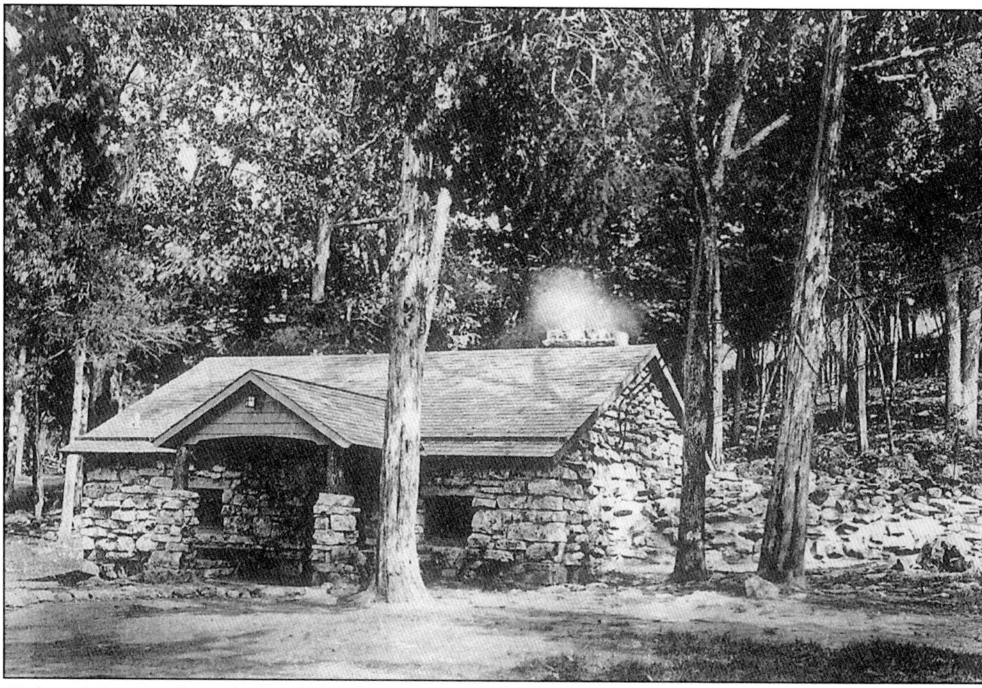

Colonel Brown bought and further developed Endless Caverns about 1919, adding a gift shop, campground, and later an art gallery all near this entrance building. For many years afterward, the Bourdeau family owned and operated the caverns. Today Endless Caverns has new ownership developing the property surrounding the caverns into an upscale RV camping area. (Dan Vaughn.)

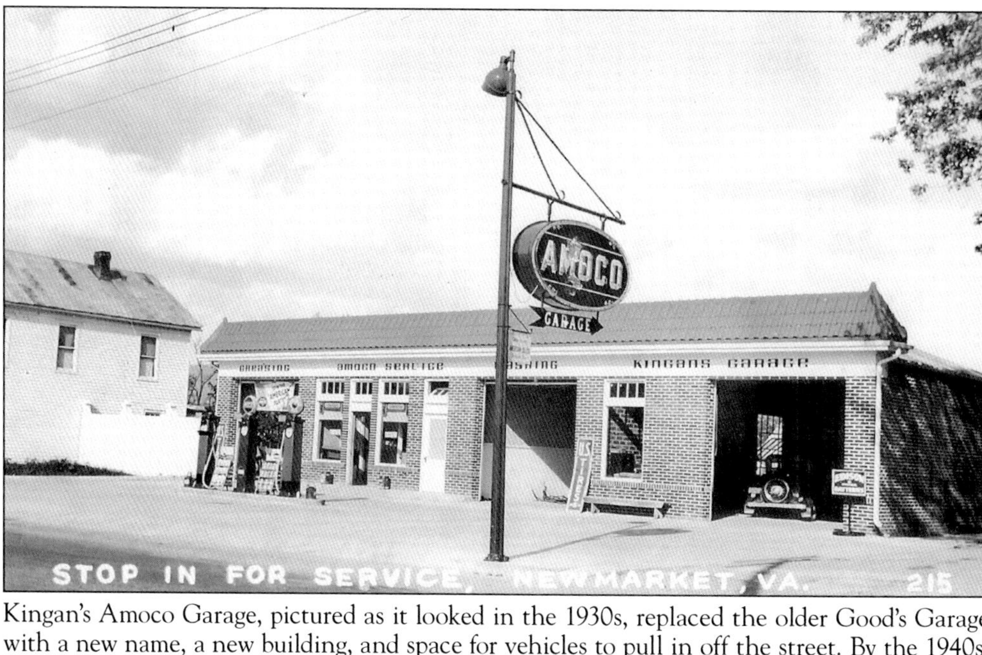

Kingan's Amoco Garage, pictured as it looked in the 1930s, replaced the older Good's Garage with a new name, a new building, and space for vehicles to pull in off the street. By the 1940s, the building had changed hands to become Harpine's Garage and still serves the public today as Greater Atlantic Bank at what is now 9484 Congress Street. (Dan Vaughn.)

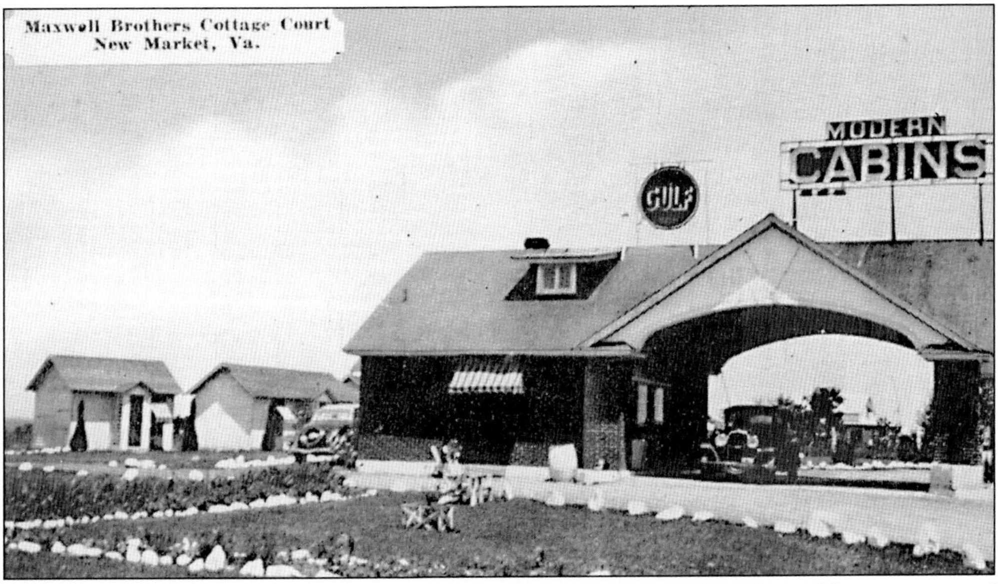

Along the Valley Pike, motels sprang up everywhere to accommodate the stable economics of tourism. The Maxwell Brothers Cottages were an exceptional, small motor cottage that was more modern as opposed to the homes open for traditional rent in downtown New Market. In the 1940s, the facility became M. D.'s Motel and Restaurant (M.D. stood for Mary DiTolvo). M. D.'s Chicken in the Rough restaurant franchise was popular with local residents until it closed in the late 1970s. (Edward "Casey" Billhimer.)

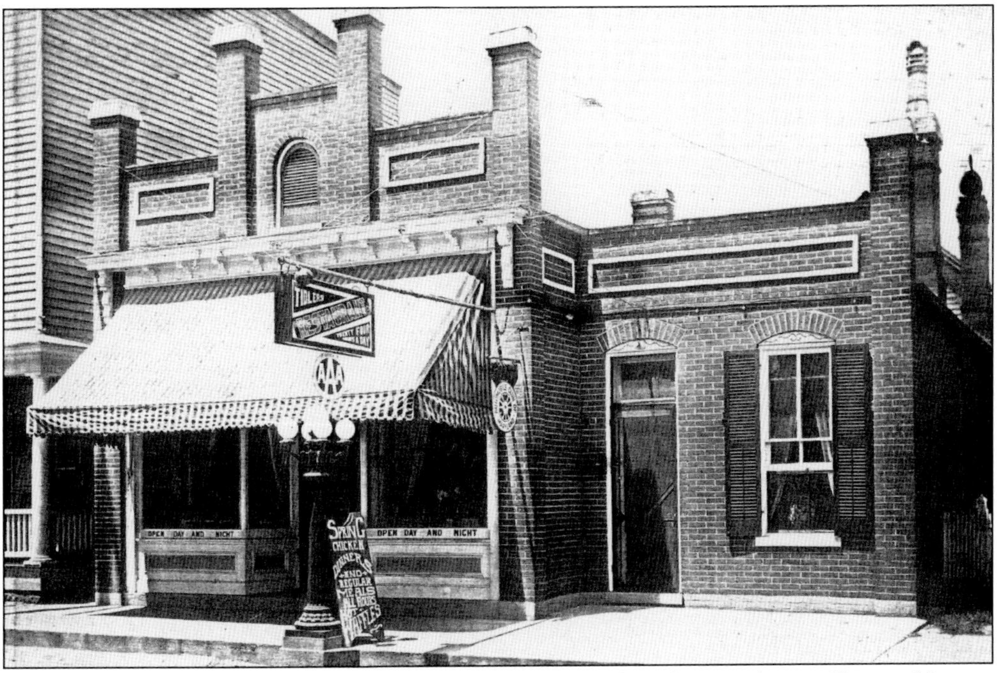

Tidler's Restaurant, shown in the 1920s, served spring chicken dinners, hot waffles, and home-cooked meals to the public 24 hours a day. Tidler's also embraced tourism, as evidenced by the AAA member sign and the endorsement from the Automobile Club of Maryland. The restaurant continues today as Jalisco's Mexican Dining at 9403 Congress Street. (New Market Area Library.)

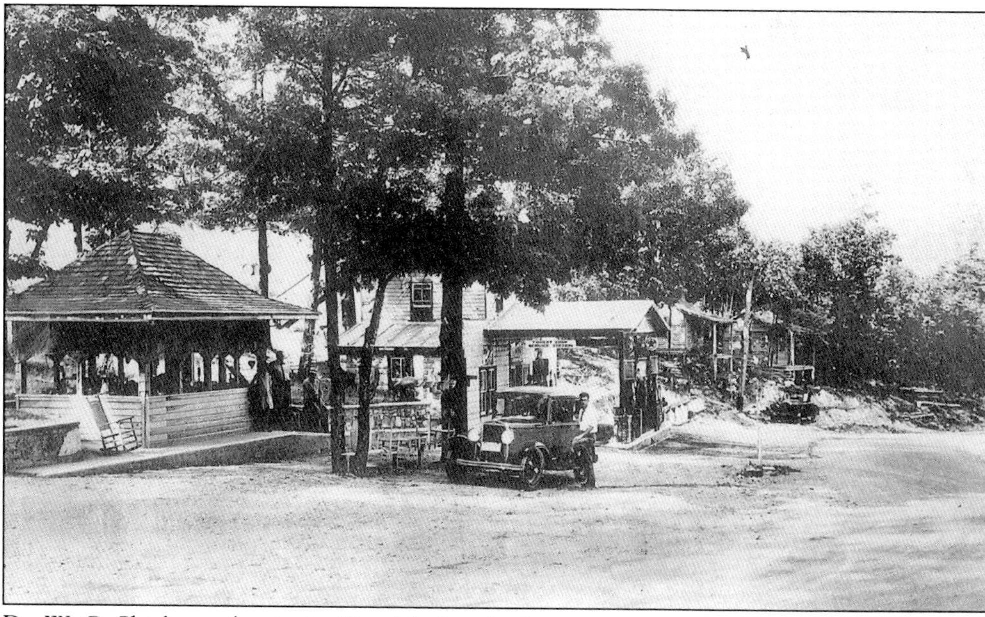

Dr. W. C. Shirley, a dentist in New Market, had an interest in tourism, and he started the New Market Gap Tourist Camp. Located at the top of the Massanutten Gap following the road over the mountain to Shenandoah National Park and Luray Caverns, the camp included needed food, fuel, shelter, and information for cars in the late 1920s and 1930s. According to the late travel expert Robert Harnesberger of Luray Caverns, "In those days it was normal to change a tire two to three times in traveling the twelve miles from Luray to New Market." (Edward "Casey" Billhimer, Dan Vaughn.)

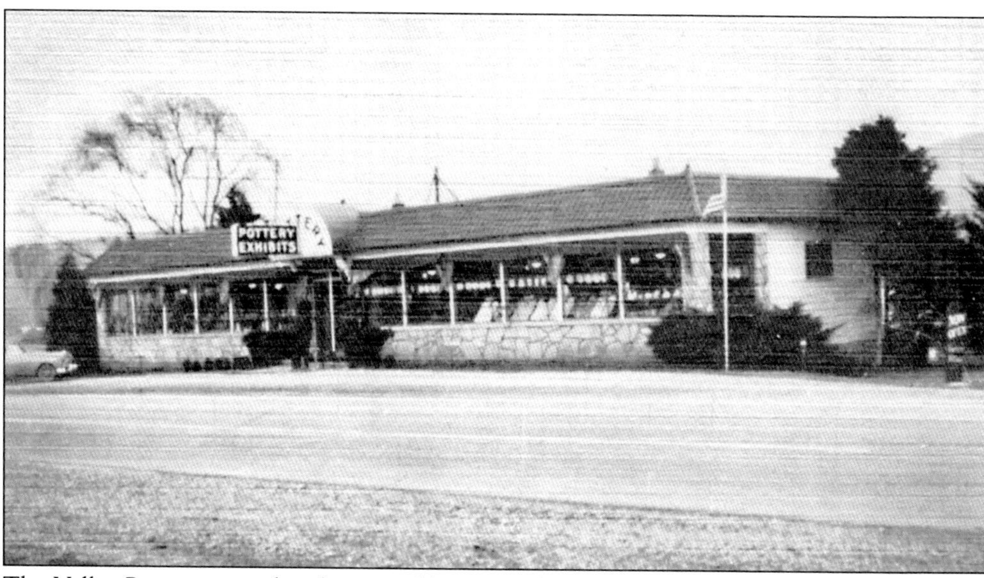

The Valley Pottery, owned and operated by Mr. and Mrs. Al Eichelman, featured pottery from many countries and the world's largest ceramic vase, which is over seven feet tall. Visible through a screen door in the back were the Eichelmans' two pet ocelots, which are spotted and striped members of the leopard family from South America. Their ocelots were about three to four feet long and weighed up to 35 pounds. (Edward "Casey" Billhimer.)

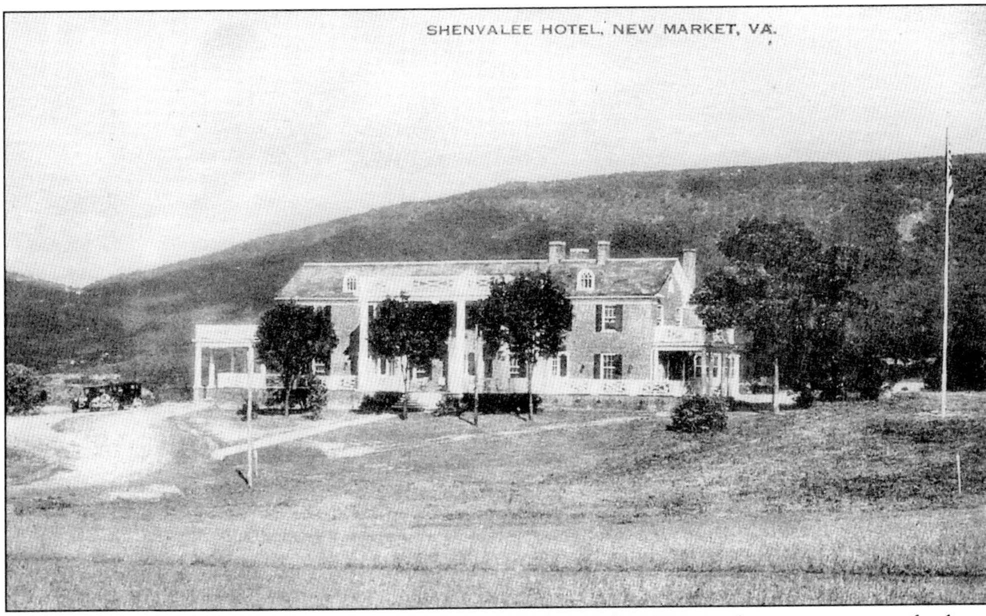

The Shenvalee Hotel and Golf Course began, in the mid-1920s, as the centerpiece of a large residential/recreational development that was to extend all the way to the mountain beyond. After the lodge, the clubhouse, and the nine-hole course were completed, the Depression halted further development. The addition of 18 holes and the resumption of residential construction since then have made the Shenvalee a premier attraction for the town. (Dan Vaughn.)

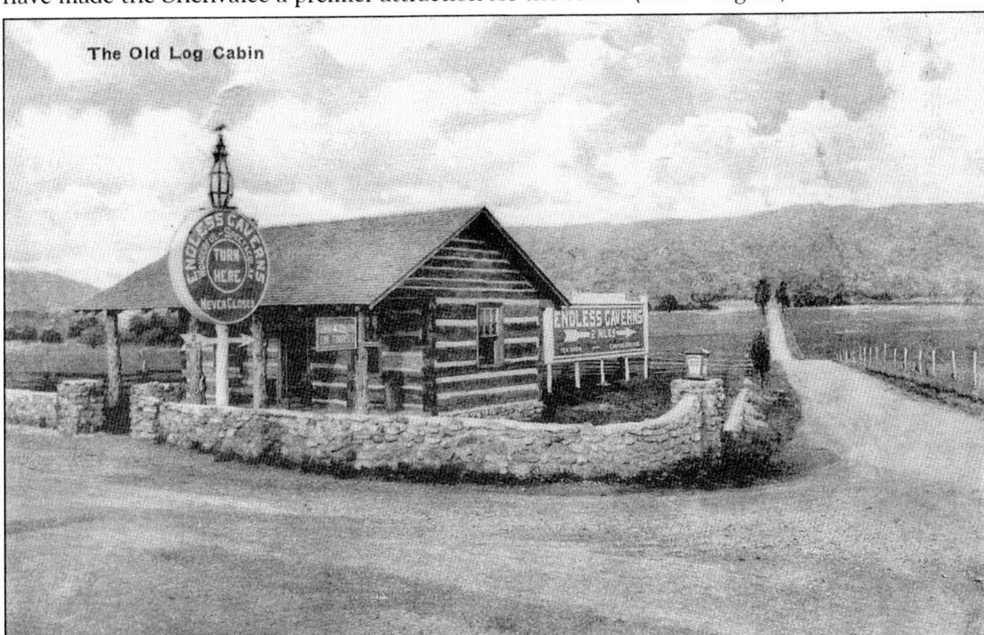

The 1920s saw Endless Caverns making use of this existing road and restored log cabin as its first entrance, providing information and directing travelers from Route 11. Hundreds of visitors by train were ferried by every conveyance available daily from the station to the attraction. The caverns were never closed, offered overnight camping, and featured a tea room that was air-conditioned utilizing the constant 55-degree temperature of the caverns' air. (Dan Vaughn.)

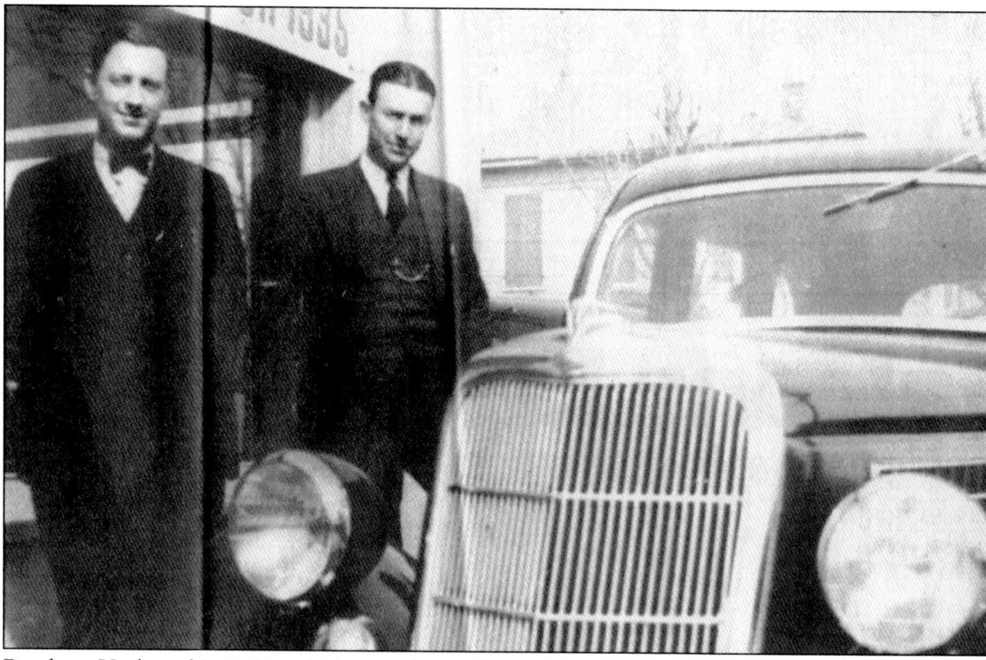

Brothers Herb and I. C. "Pete" Moyers show off new 1935 Fords at their newly opened dealership on the corner of John Sevier and Old Cross Roads. Their first car sold after World War II went to returning veteran Jack Tusing, a Japanese POW and survivor of the Bataan Death March. After World War II, the brothers moved the business to south Congress Street. (New Market Area Library.)

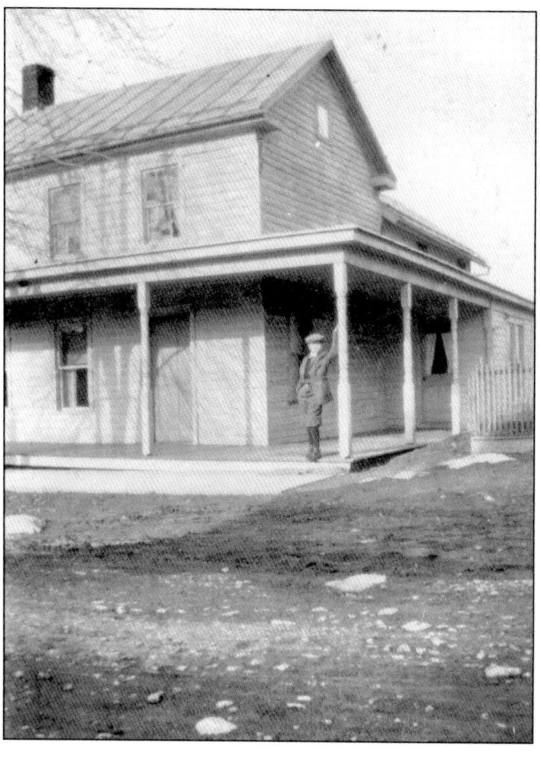

Pictured is the boyhood home of the late O. Braxton "Bracky" Theis, seen here in his youth on the porch. He was later undertaker of New Market during World War II. Bracky was friend to all who knew him because of his kind and generous nature. He was a real New Market character, with an encyclopedic memory of the history of New Market few will ever have. This house still exists as 9463 Cadet Road. (Nancy Branner Stewart.)

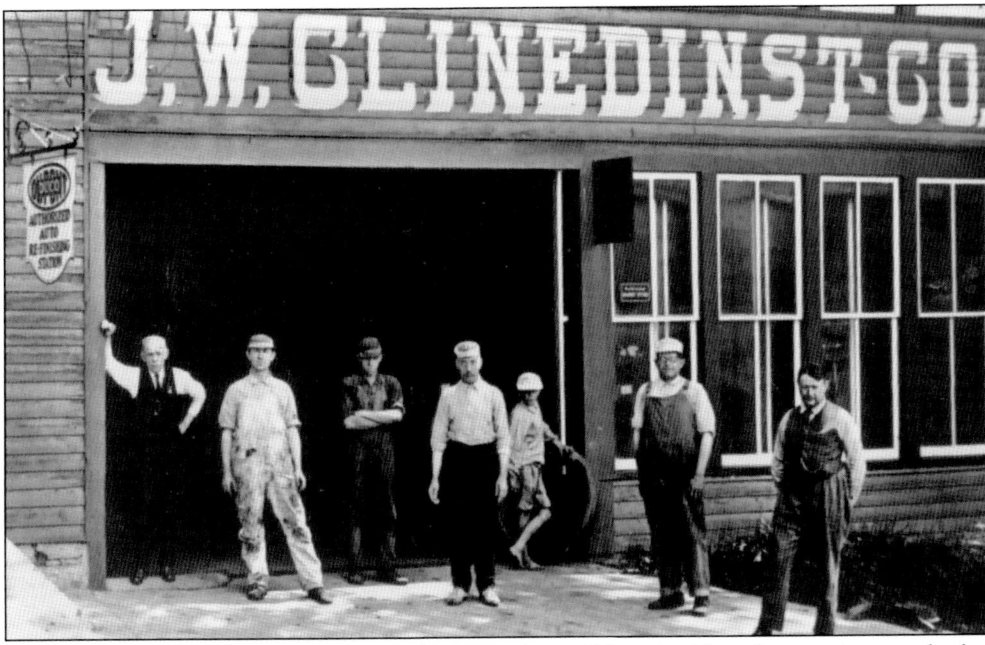

By 1925, the J. W. Clinedinst Company had remade itself from building fine carriages and other horse-drawn vehicles to building their own Clinedinst car and then to automobile repair. The men are, from left to right, Harry Drebbin, A. C. "Sleepy" Higgs, Raymond Drummond, John Grove, young John C. Crim (at the door), and owners John D. Crim and Jacob Crim. The crew brought all their talents and craftsmanship to automobile restoration, which continued in business until 1952. The small sign in the window by the door announces the company's support "For Governor Harry Byrd." (John D. Crim.)

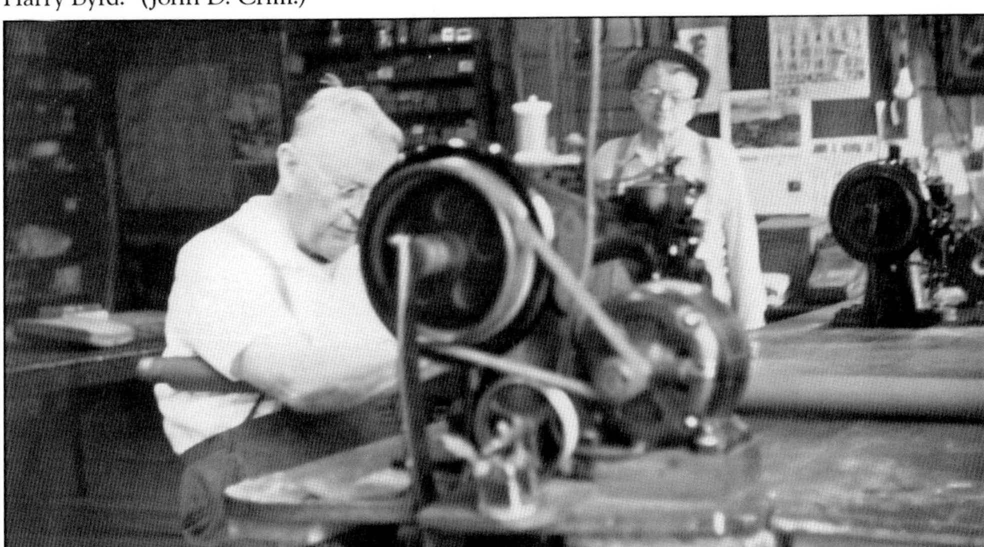

In the back (trimming) room of the old Clinedinst carriage factory, Jacob Crim demonstrates his skill at trimming and upholstery. He's working with a roll of goods at their big Singer World War I surplus tent-making machine that could easily sew an inch of tent canvas. His older brother John waits to reposition the convertible top or car seat material they are repairing. The photograph appears to date from 1949. (John D. Crim.)

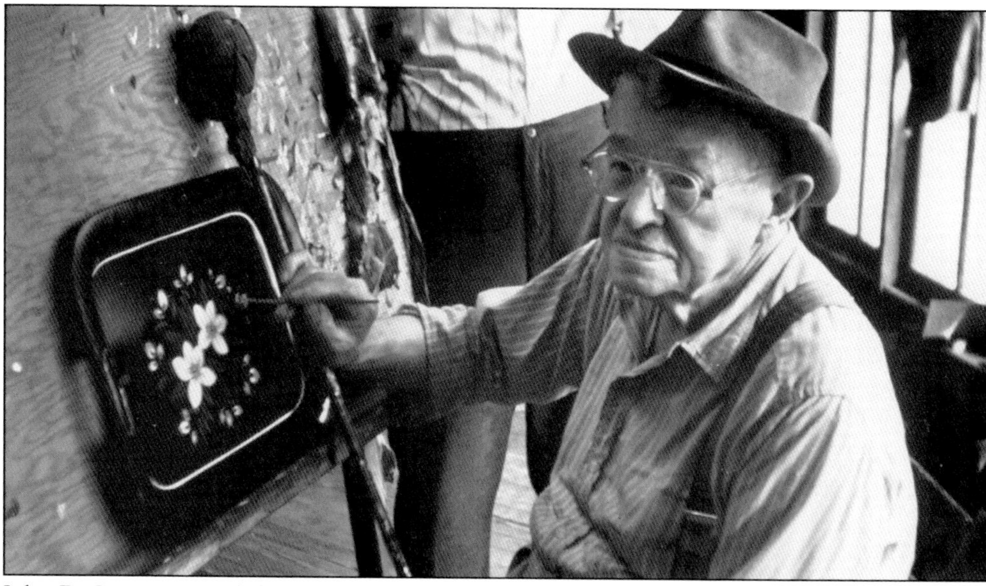

John D. Crim pauses while painting one of his tole trays. He apprenticed to John W. Clinedinst's Carriage Factory about 1886 and, for the next seven years, was required to pinstripe the same carriage wheel over and over until Clinedinst could finally find no fault. During the 1930s, Crim brought those skills to the painting and decorating of hundreds of tole trays until shortly before his death in 1959. (John D. Crim.)

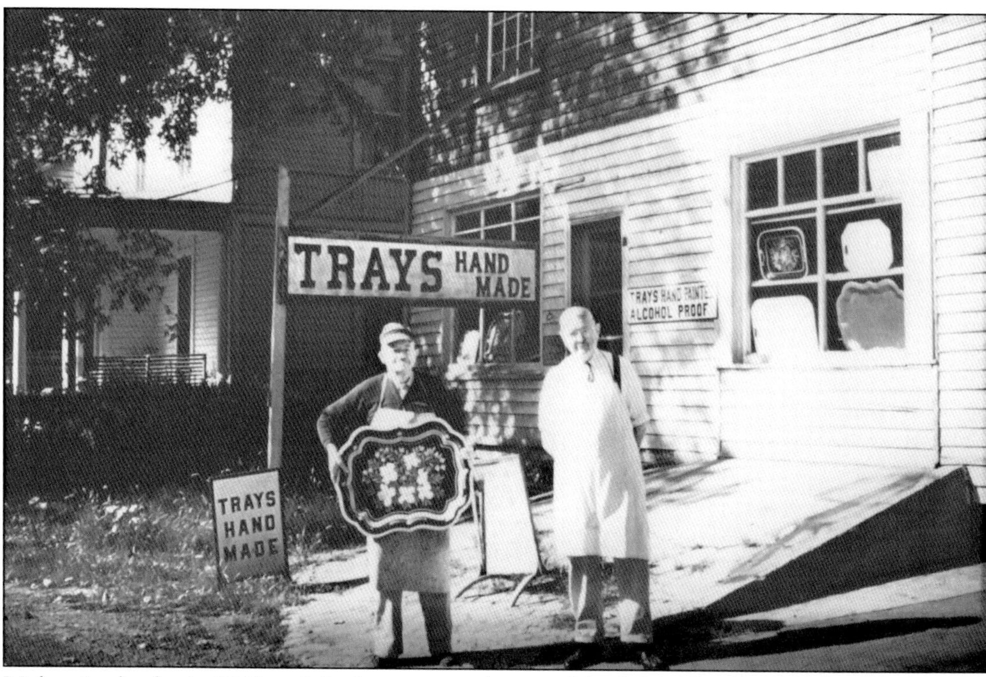

It's late in the day in 1949, and the last two employees of the J. W. Clinedinst Carriage Company, brothers John D. and Jacob E. C. Crim, stand outside the factory. They have watched the passing of the factory's carriages and buggies. Like the Dodge Brothers and Oldsmobile before them, they built the Clinedinst automobile but then turned to automobile repairs for a living. Could they know it's late in the day for them as well? (John D. Crim.)

Seven

Life on Congress Street

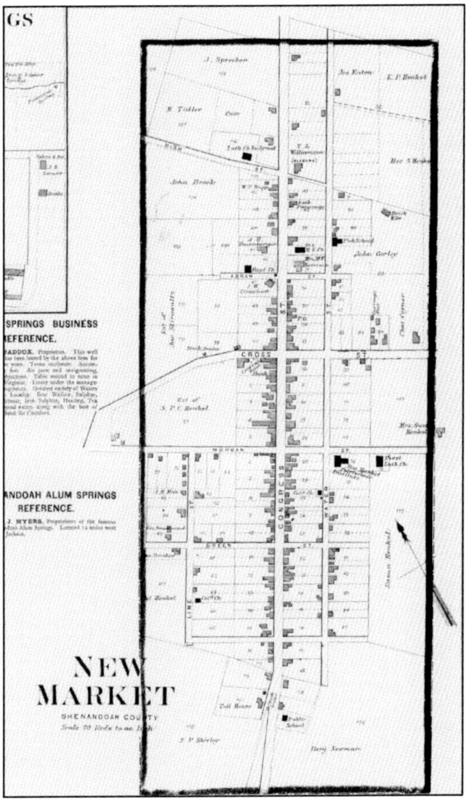

The *1885 Atlas of Shenandoah and Page Counties* by D. J. Lake and Company shows the layout of the town in excellent detail. Since then, several street names have been changed. Water Street is now John Sevier Road, Lime Street is now Cadet Road, Morgan Street is now Lee Street, Abram Street is now Seminary Lane, and High Street is now Breckinridge. (John D. Crim.)

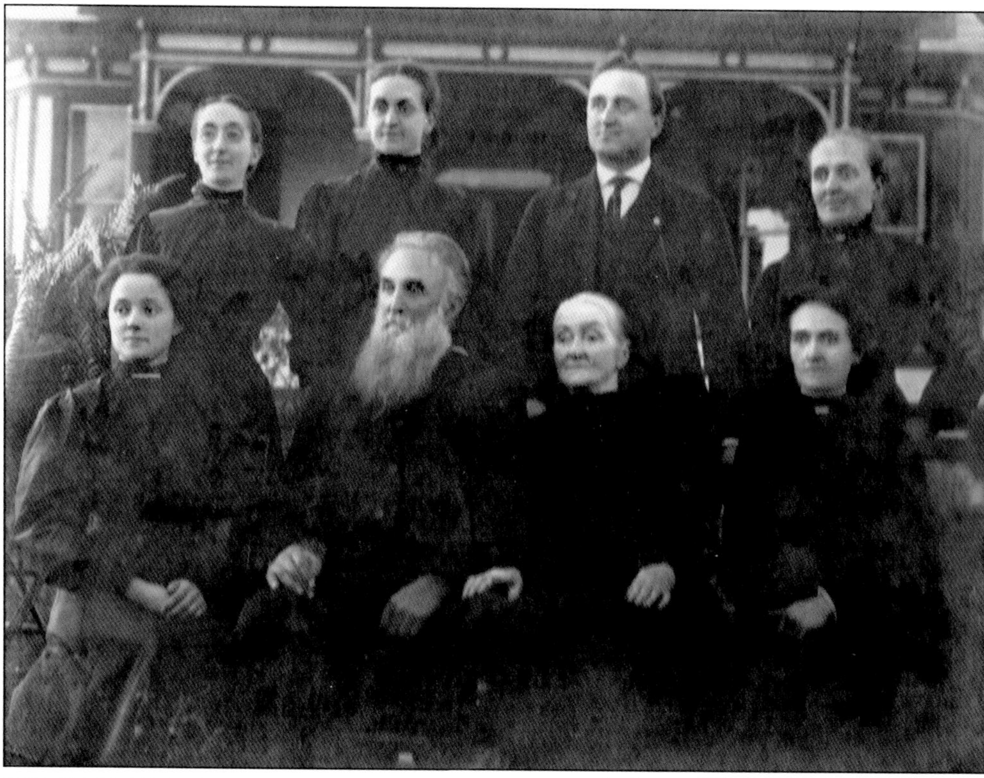

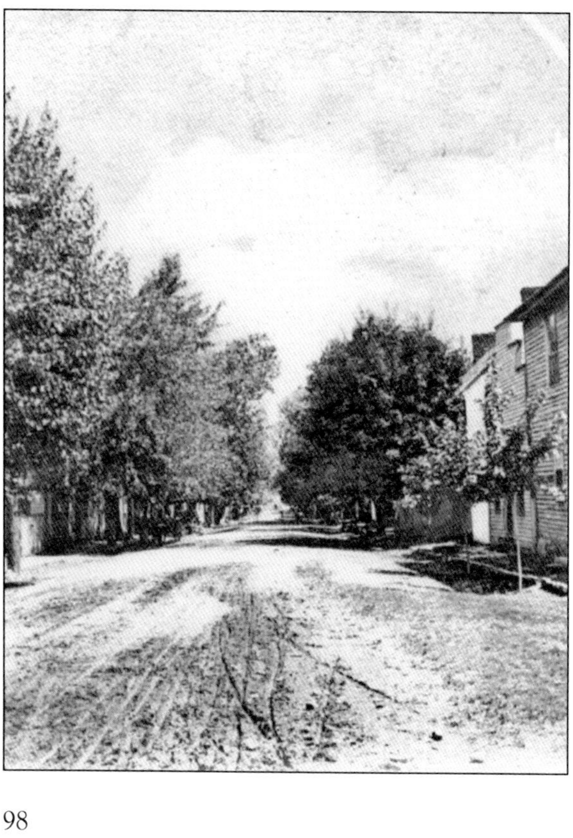

In front of the old Driver home is the Driver family, prominent New Market residents. Posing for the family portrait in about 1890, they remind us of how fragile time is and about the ties that bind in families. From left to right are (first row) Mystie Driver Kline, Rev. John Franklin Driver, Sarah Catherine Rife Driver, and Pearl Driver Coffman; (second row) Catherine Elizabeth "Lizzie" Driver, Emma Driver Wampler, Dr. William Franklin Driver, and Ida Driver Kline. (Cathy Blackburn Mauck.)

This is a timeless, lazy summer afternoon view looking north showing a rut-pitted Congress Street. New Market had progressive roads at this time, so one could imagine the rough and tumble roads elsewhere in the backcountry of the valley. The trees still adorn the street, greeting the weary traveler with a reminder of more graceful times. (Nancy Branner Stewart.)

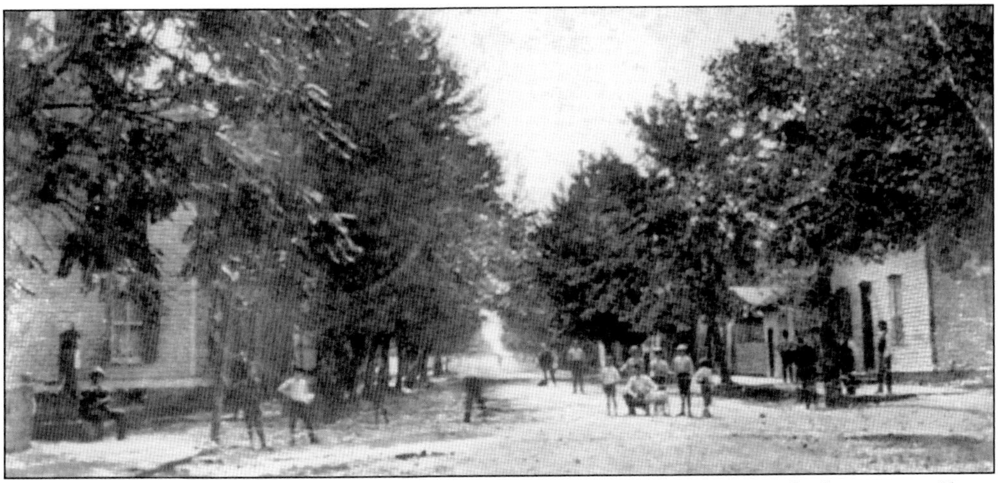

An early-1900s, high noon view near the corner of Lee and Congress Streets finds a group of boys and onlookers in the street in front of Elon Henkel's home (right). Traffic does not appear to be a concern. Perhaps they are admiring the dog, or maybe the dog's interest in a game of marbles has temporarily halted the action. The old town pump at left provided plenty of cheap refreshment. (Nancy Branner Stewart.)

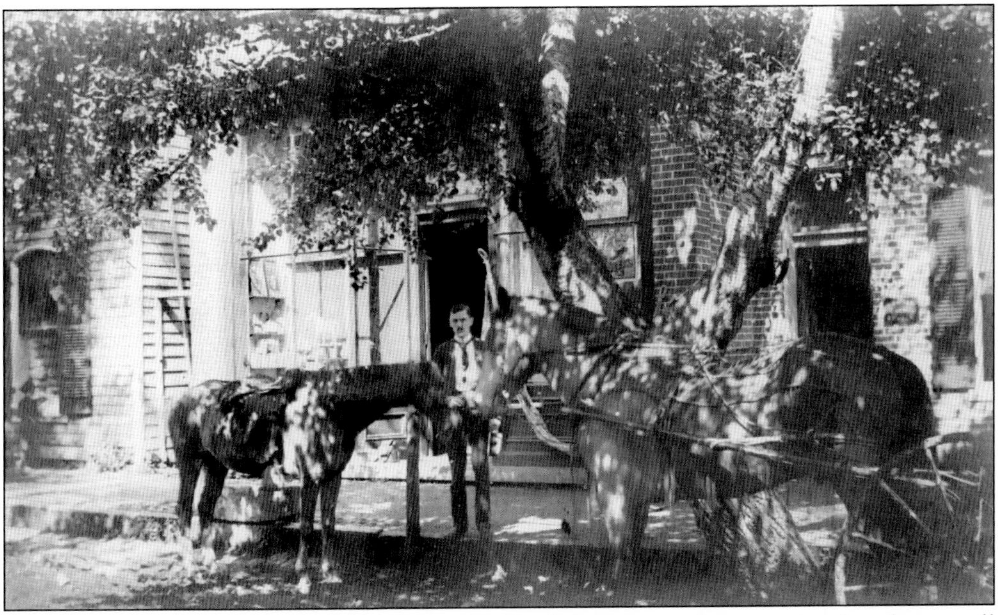

It's noon in the early 1900s, and Dr. Casper C. Henkel appears to be preparing for a house call on horseback, leaving his small office at right. The saddlebags, on the step in the entrance to the mercantile store behind him (now Jalisco Restaurant), may also be part of his equipment. At far left, a small boy investigates the activities in a room of the American Hotel. It's a typical summer day in the heart of town. (New Market Area Library.)

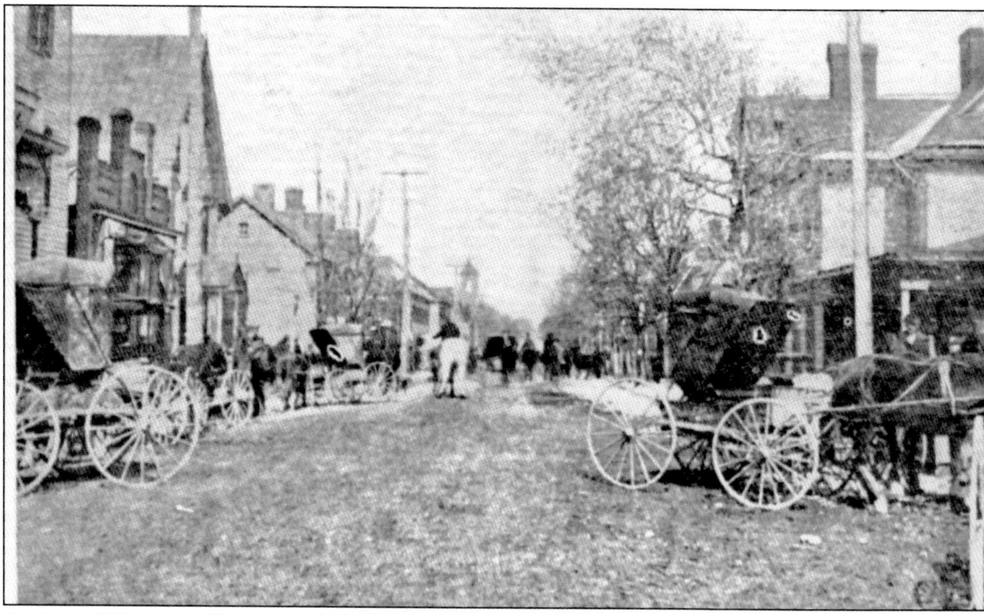

A view of Congress Street in 1908 illustrates how common horses were for transportation at that time in the valley. Perhaps one of these carriages could have been manufactured in town at the Clinedinst factory (the Cadillac of carriages for the period). Impoverished by the Civil War, the valley had been gutted by "The Burning" in 1864 of barns and homes and the slaughtering of livestock. If one were to take away the blacktop and vehicles today, a person would scarcely note a difference in appearance of the town from this early-20th-century postcard. (Nancy Branner Stewart.)

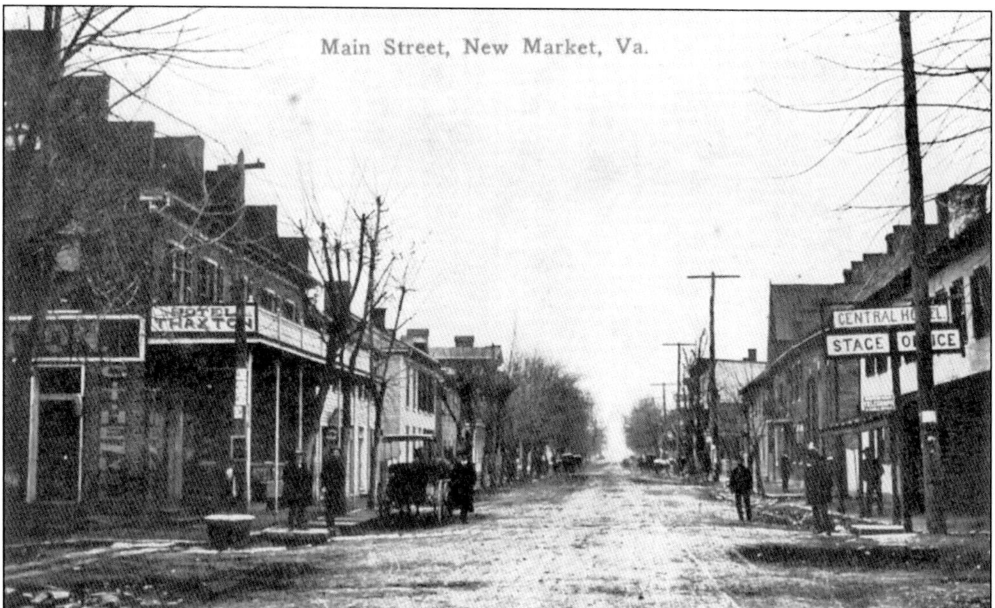

The view looks south on Congress Street from the Crossroads. Its winter in 1912 judging from the long coats, patches of snow, and general lack of activity. Several people appear to be looking at the camera or perhaps watching for the southbound stage, which was chronically late. (Dan Vaughn.)

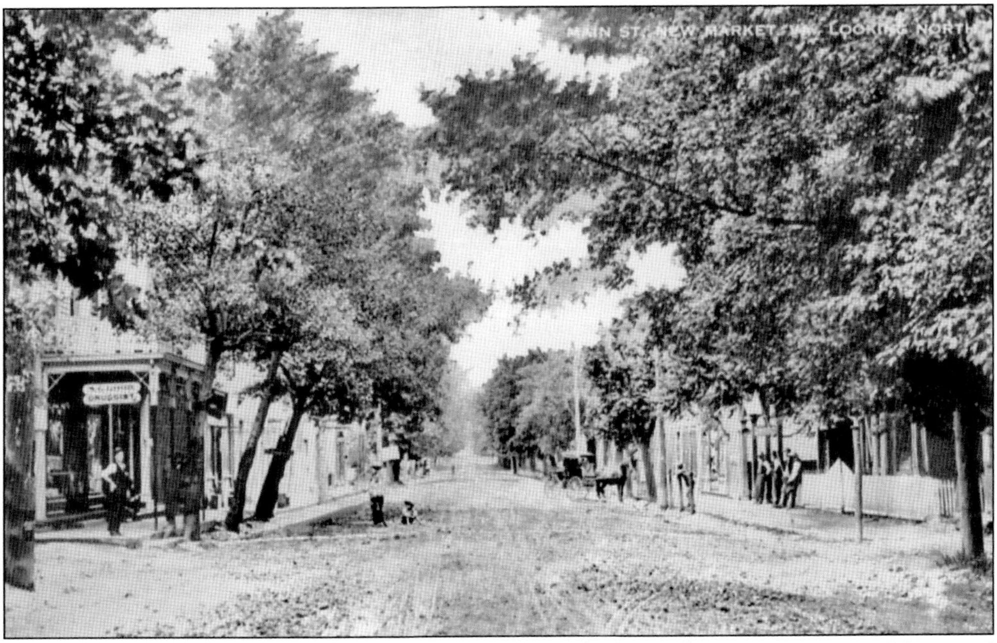

This view of a lazy summer afternoon faces north from the intersection of Lee and Congress Streets. S. G. Good's Drug Store is at left, and his building exists today as 9437 Congress Street. (Dan Vaughn.)

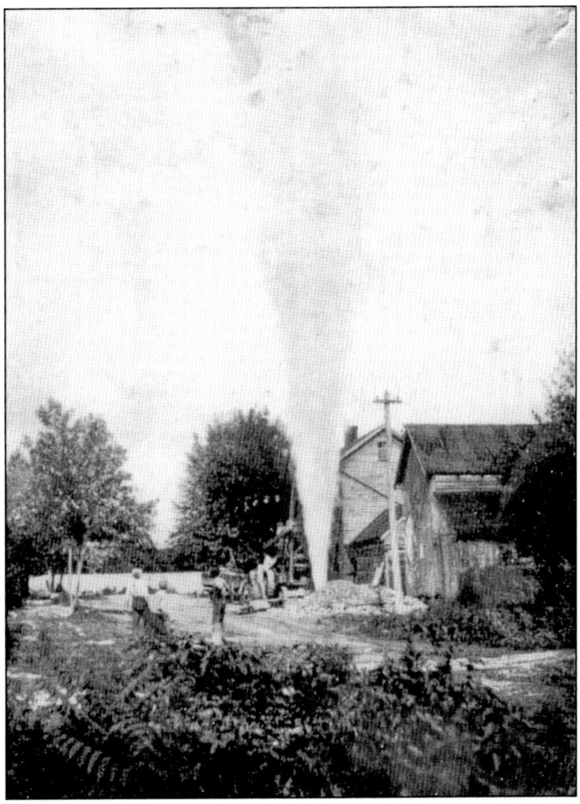

Here is an example of early well drilling in town near the old Theis home using explosives to prime the draw of the water in an upward flow. New Market has always been known for the wonderful resource of water from Colonial times even to this day. One New Market resident stated in a recent newspaper article about the town's water resources, "I do not think God is making more of it." The town is very close to major underwater streams or aquifers according to geologists. (Nancy Branner Stewart.)

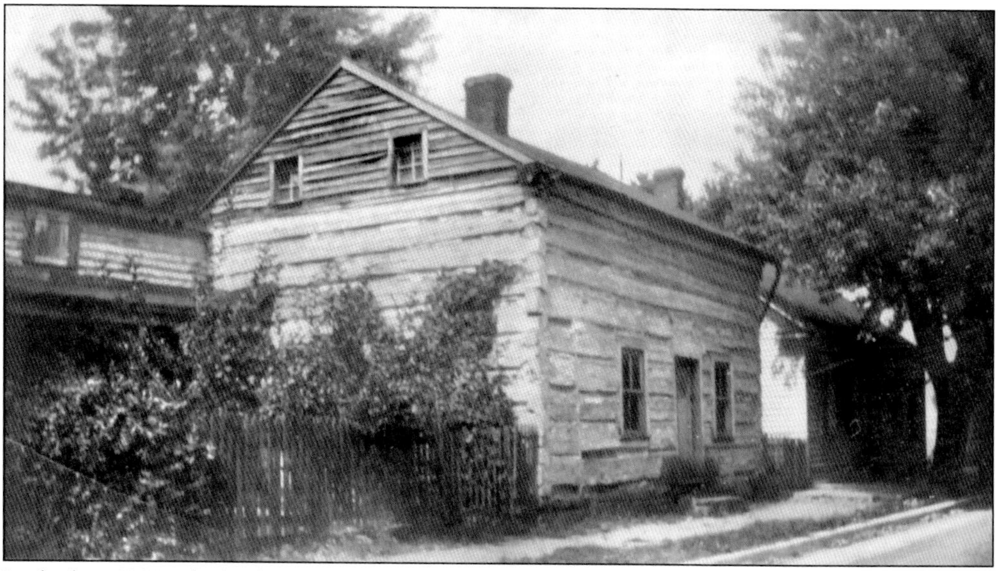

In the late 1800s, the log house was home for Gustavus Wickes, the town's street lamplighter. The evenings saw his stooped, familiar figure carrying a small ladder and can of coal oil (kerosene) from post to post, making the town a little brighter wherever he went. The building served other uses, such as a ticket office for Luray Caverns and the Valley Trading Post. The brick home at 9305 Congress Street replaced it around 1979. (John D. Crim.)

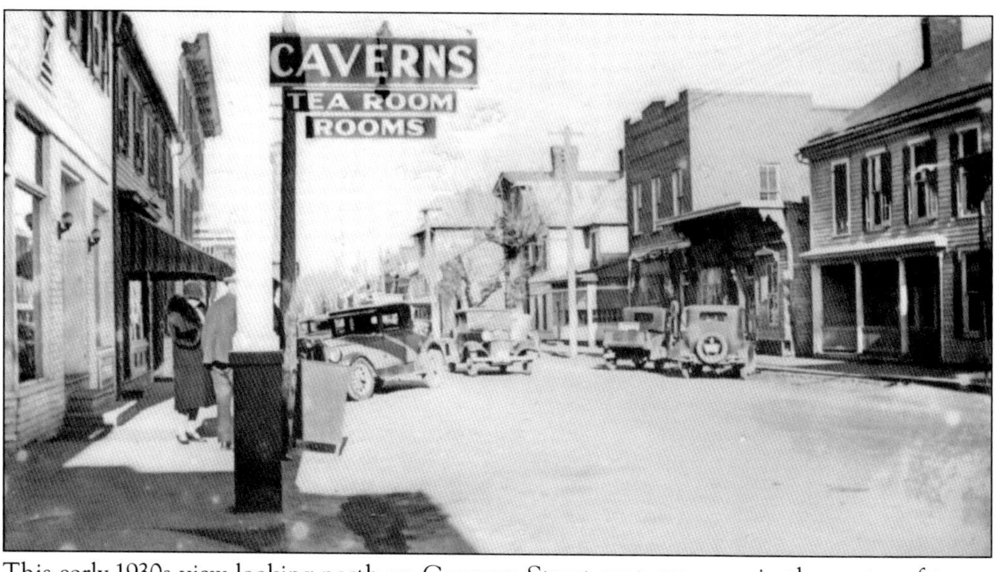

This early-1930s view looking north on Congress Street captures noon in the center of town. Rising in the center background is Dr. C. C. Henkel's fine two-story brick residence that remains today. In front and to the right of Dr. Henkel's is the stylish Victorian office building that currently houses the law offices of James Weissenborn at 9404 Congress Street. (Janet Theis Dellinger.)

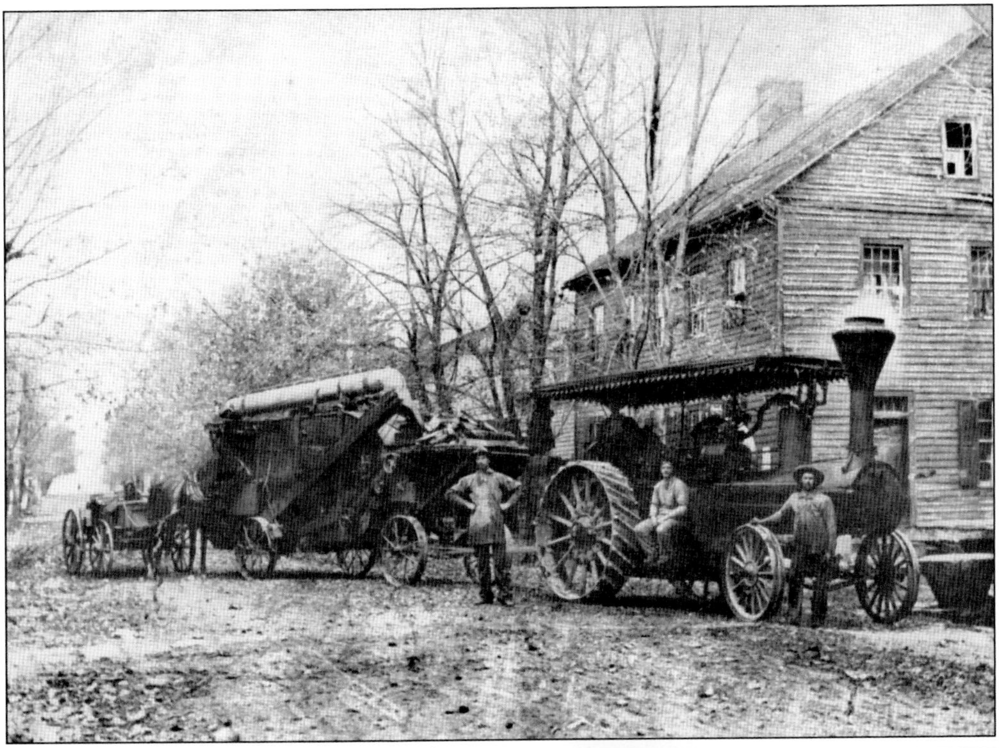

Minnick's (a local family) thrashing machine was pulled through the valley every harvest season during his operation to thrash wheat. The steam-driven tractor, thought to be a Frick brand, rumbled through town for this classic agricultural view right at the Crossroads, in front of the old Lee Jackson Hotel (today Public House Restaurant). Steam-powered thrashing was essential in the valley before 1945 as a large portion of the nation's wheat was grown here. The men would thrash the wheat next to the barn. Iron hooks fastened to the barn secured the movement of the rickety thrashing machine. They also wanted the machine as far away as possible to keep the sparks from setting the barn afire. (Nancy Branner Stewart.)

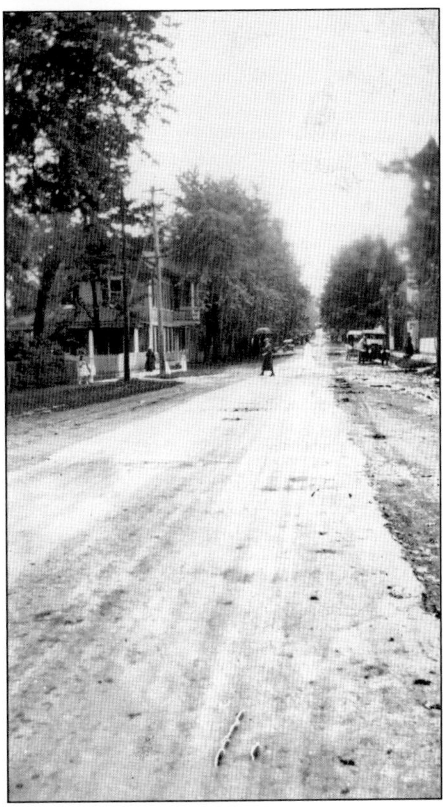

Two young women cross Congress Street at Seminary Lane around 1910–1915, perhaps to stop by Ms. Williamson's Seminary (at left, not pictured) from which the little girl is exiting the gate. Although the sky appears to be overcast, their parasols still protect their fair skin. (Nancy Branner Stewart.)

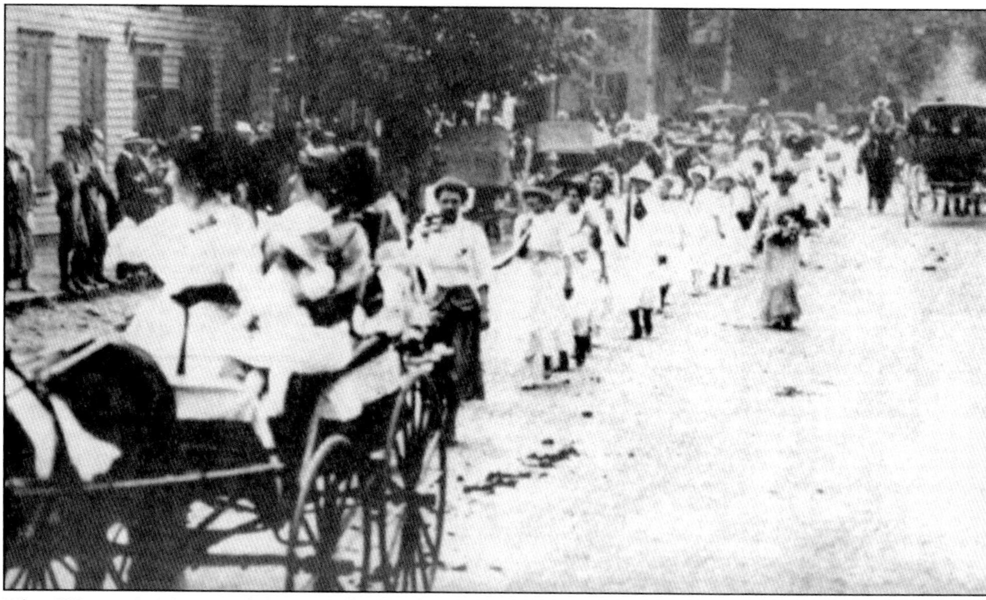

The Women's Memorial Society leads the May 12, 1898, parade commemorating the Battle of New Market. One of the more important ceremonies of the day's events commemorated the unveiling of the Confederate Veteran's Monument in St. Matthew's Lutheran Church Cemetery. Construction of the monument was made possible by contributions and the tireless efforts of the society since its founding in 1867. (Nancy Branner Stewart.)

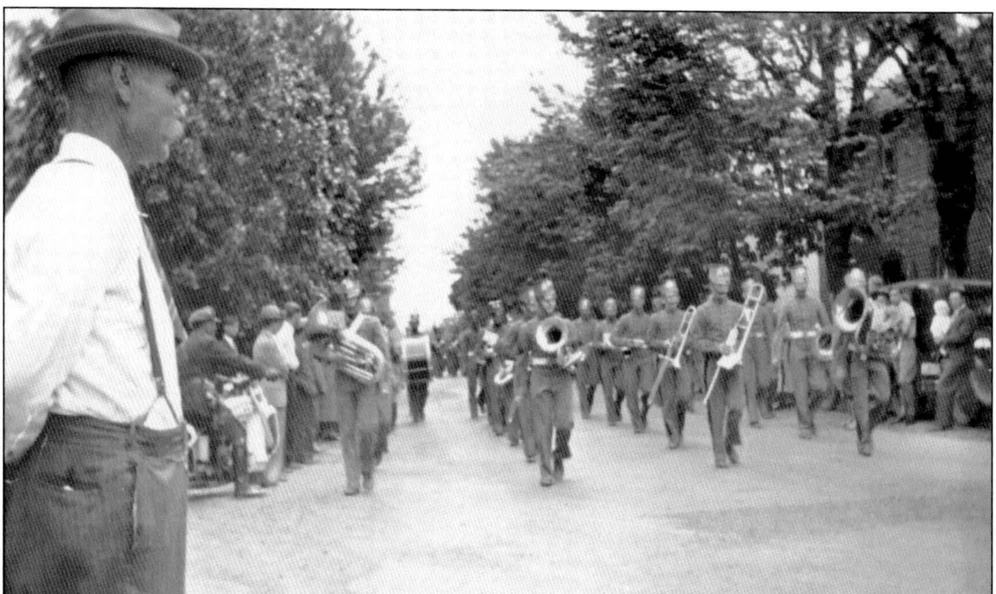

G. A. "Dutch" Tidler, at left, prepares to review the VMI Corps Band, with the rest of the corps marching behind, during a May 15 parade, probably in 1934 on the 70th anniversary of the battle. After beginning at the Shenvalee Lodge and marching for three-quarters of a mile, the band is approaching the corner of Congress and Breckinridge, near the Lutheran church, and most of them appear to still be in step. (Janet Theis Dellinger.)

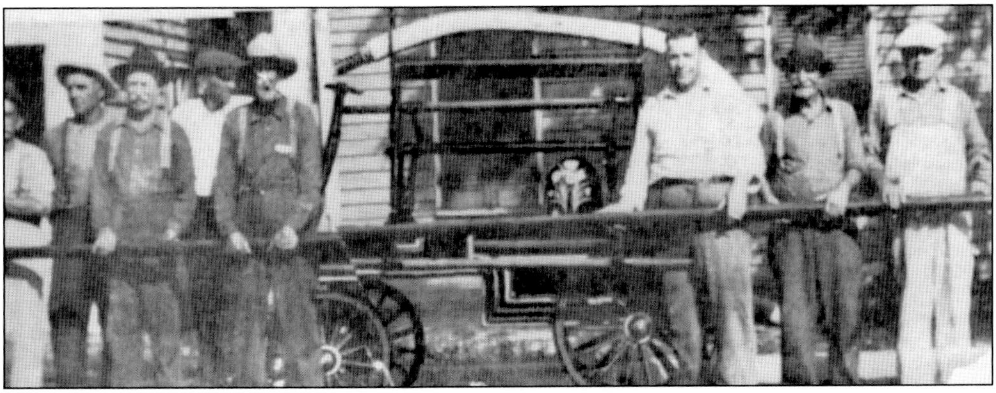

An unidentified group of men pose in the 1930s or 1940s with the town's first fire pump, which was horse-drawn and hand-operated. The fire pump was restored and hand-decorated by John D. Crim and can be seen at the New Market Fire Department at the south end of town. (Nancy Branner Stewart.)

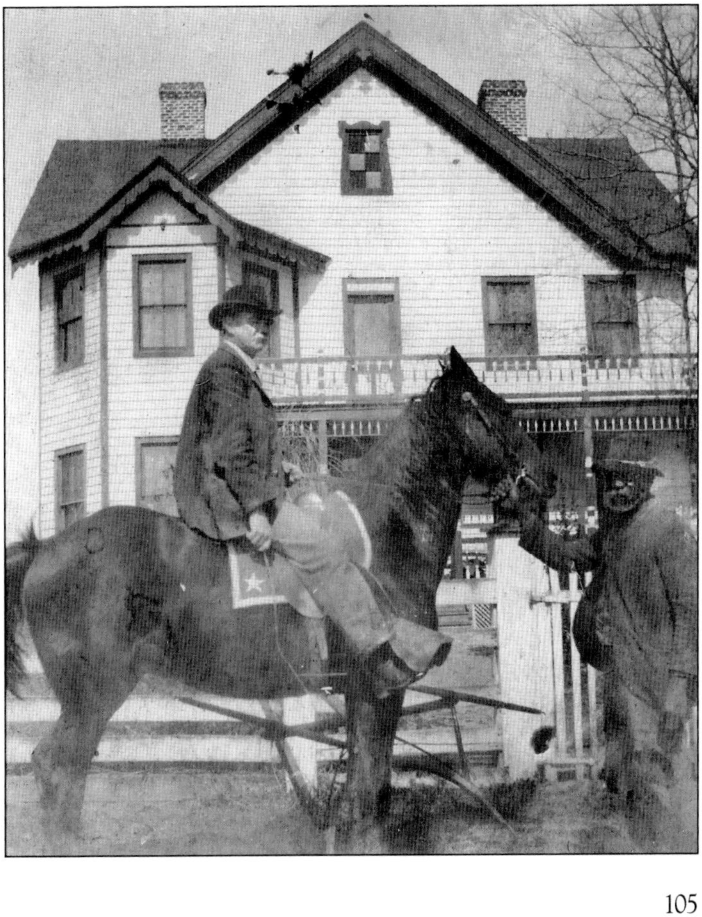

Two men pose for the camera at the old Driver residence. The identities of the two men in front are not known but it may possibly be Dr. William Driver and a local, unidentified African American man. It appears that the man on horseback is on a military saddle, and it may be a time of a Confederate reunion after the war. The Driver house has many interesting Victorian features. The painted windowpanes in the attic and the elaborate, ornate gingerbread on the porch were a statement of prosperity in an economically war-torn area. (Cathy Blackburn Mauck.)

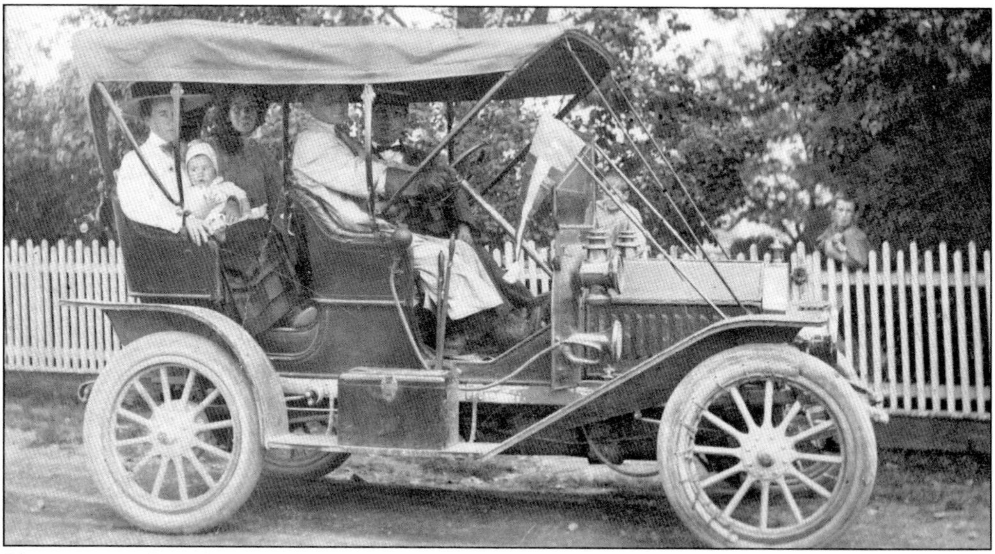

This group is thought to be the Gochenour "bunch," as they were affectionately called by locals, in front of Dr. Miller's house on North Congress Street. The brass-age automobile appears to be a Winton brand from about 1908. The car is decorated with a Confederate First National banner. It is possible that they were coming from one of the early veterans reunions held in different stations all around the country at that time. (Nancy Branner Stewart.)

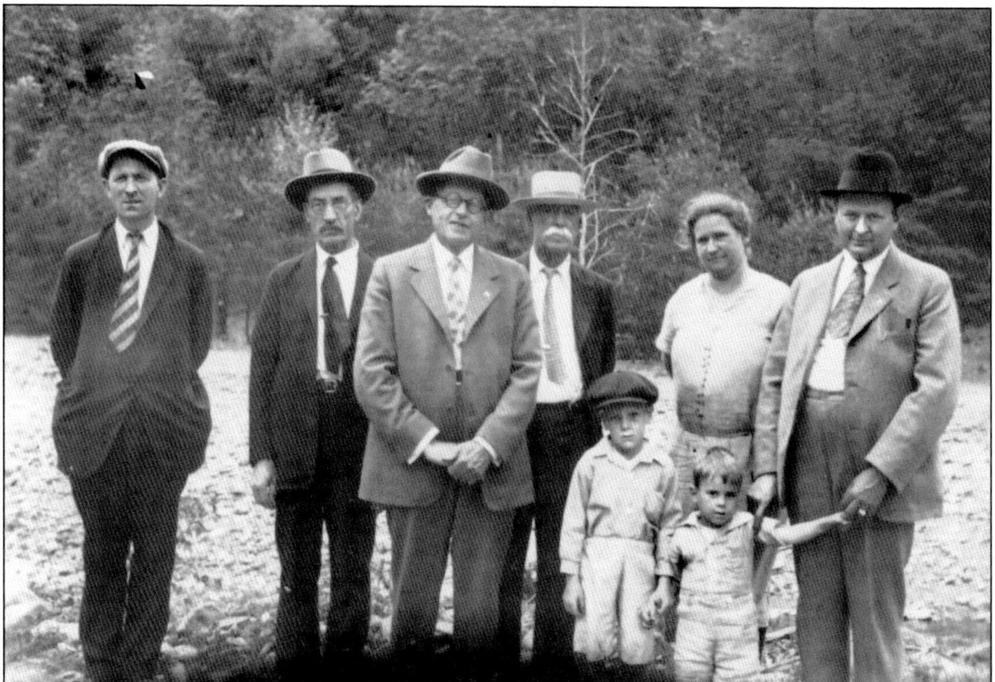

It's a great day in 1928 for a picnic down by the Shenandoah River, near the remains of Manor's Mill, which burned in 1927. From left to right are A. C. "Sleepy" Higgs, John Grove, John D. Crim, "Uncle Mike" Thomas, Behethland "Hethie" Crim, and her husband, Jacob C. Crim. The kids are Jacob F. Crim (about eight years old) and Mike Crim (about four years old) on the right. It looks like he is up to his old tricks, and Mike is pulling his father's finger. (John D. Crim.)

Born at 9349 Congress Street in 1910 and shown here at the age of five, Catherine Coleman (Crim) Miller shows an expression that vividly illustrated her approach to life until her passing in 2000. Her whole being was about self-sacrifice, community service, education, and hard work. Her piercing blue eyes, infectious smile, and helping hand behind the scenes steadied the lives of many young people she came in contact with. (John D. Crim.)

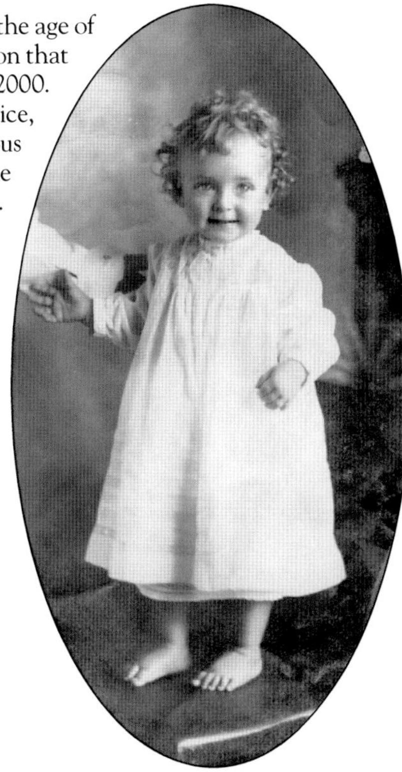

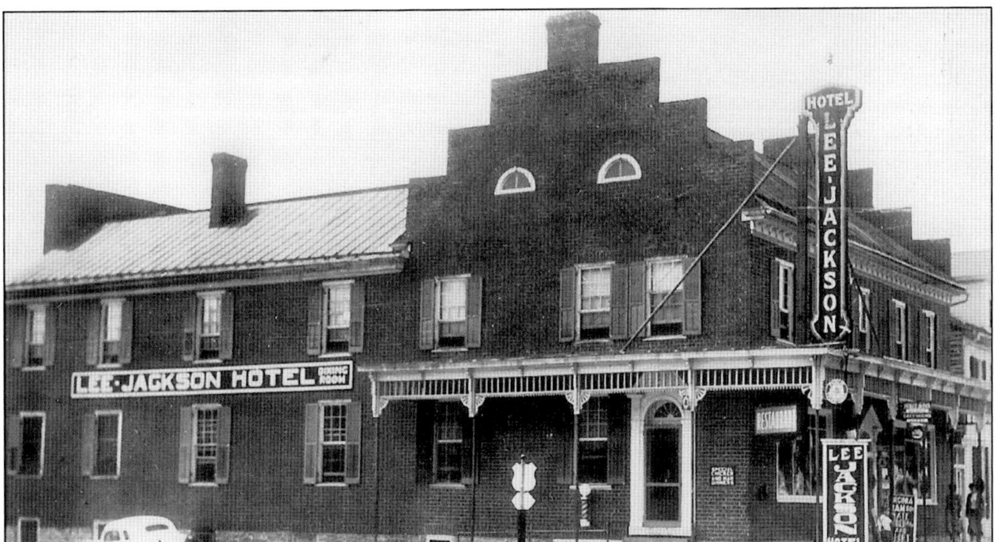

The Lee-Jackson Hotel and Restaurant at the Crossroads in the late 1930s is advertising its chicken and ham special for lunch. Virginia ham plates and short orders can be provided for Greyhound Bus passengers that stop in, while haircuts are available in the basement. The public telephone on the front corner of the building makes the Lee-Jackson a full-service stop for the weary traveler in New Market. (Dan Vaughn.)

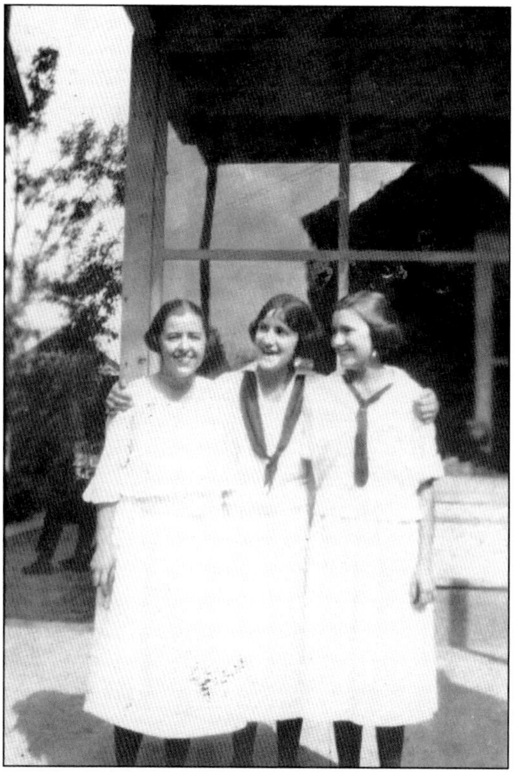

To celebrate their schoolwork being completed, these happy young ladies were photographed in 1923 right after graduation next to a storefront. Pauline Theis, Louise McNeal, and Irene Zirkle are identified. (Nancy Branner Stewart.)

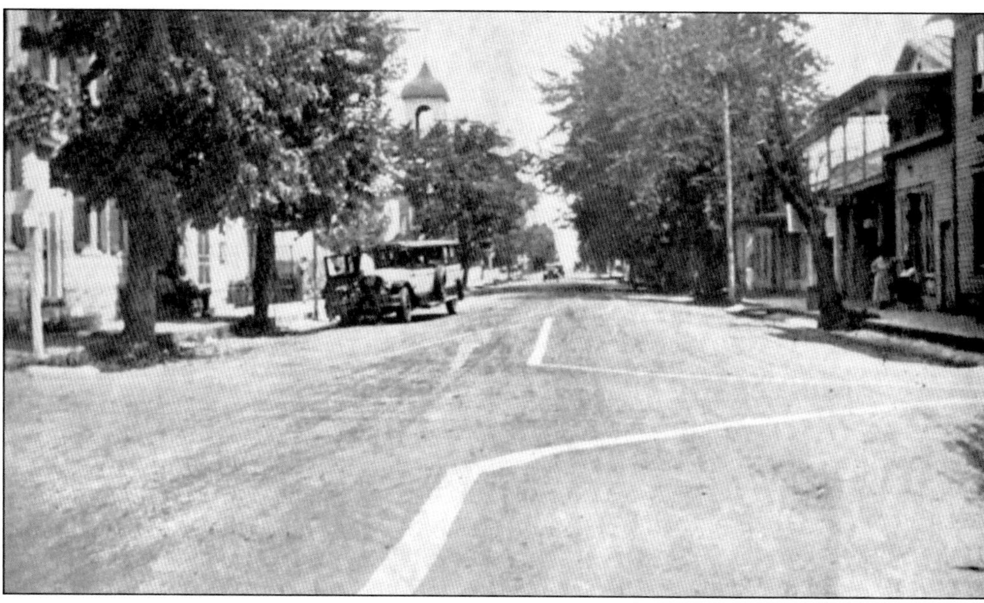

Congress Street was getting to be "downtown" with its own taxi shuttle, shown in the 1930s. The asphalt pavement was a new concept for this sleepy Virginia town in the 1930s. The awful condition of the road across the mountain in Page County was finally paved about 1933. Though much of the town gradually obtained these sophistications, it still retains the honest grace of an agriculture- and commerce-related town. Tourism has only enhanced the town's historic character that is quite uniquely New Market. (Nancy Branner Stewart.)

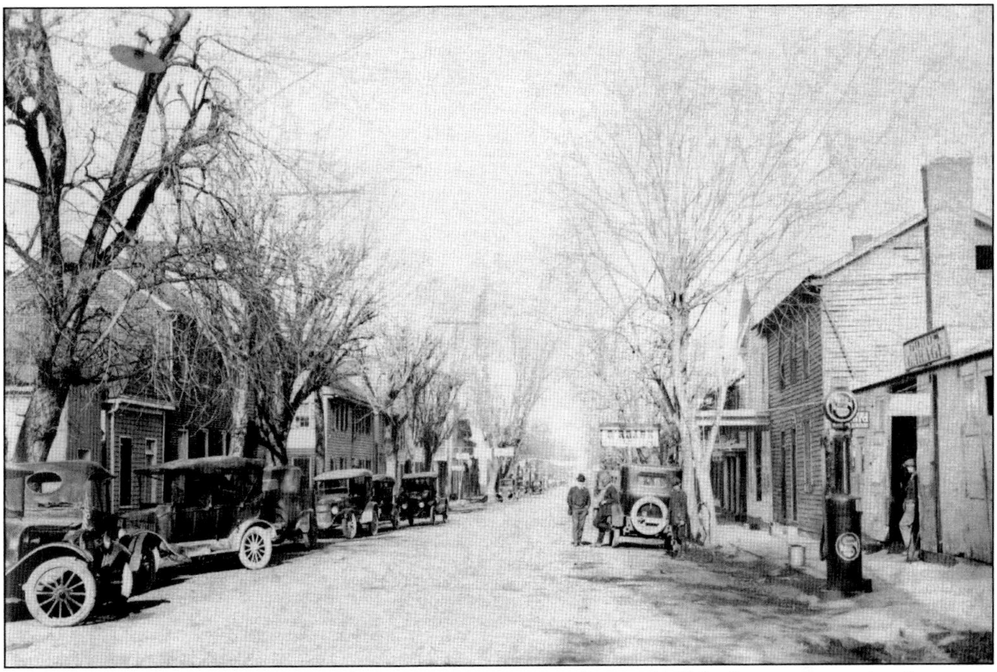

This spring view from Stuart and Congress Streets in the mid-1920s shows the early afternoon character of the town's business section. Good's Garage (right) is now a bank, while O'Roark's Restaurant has merely changed names. The two-story, brick Calvert/Collins house at left survives today, but the overhead streetlight, on the two wires in the picture's upper left corner, is gone, perhaps because it was too hard to change the bulb. (George Collins.)

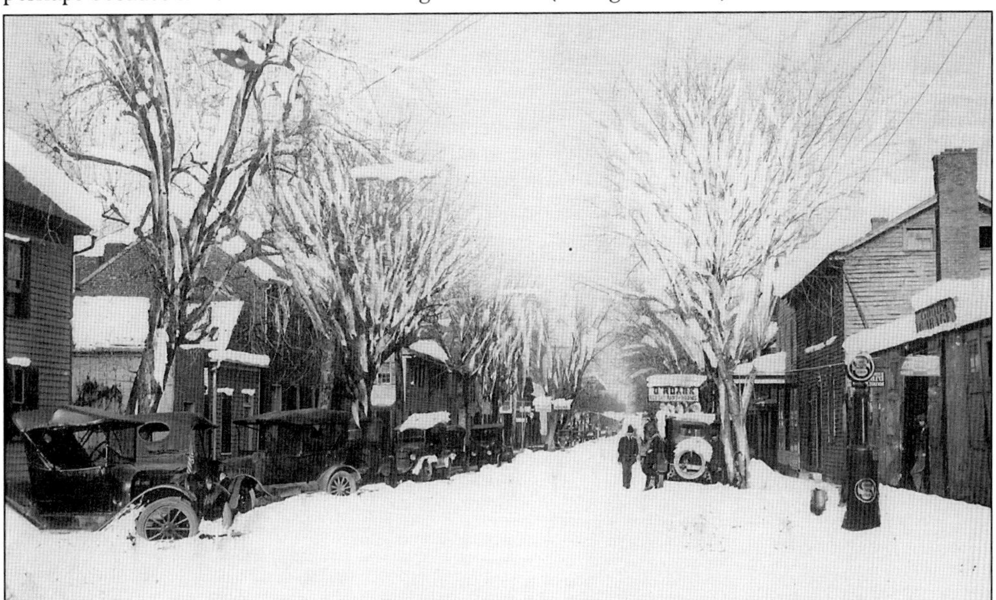

Now is this a winter view from the exact same location as the above photograph? Look very closely and see that all the details are identical except for the snow. The photographer has artfully altered the same negative and magically added the snow, making a spring scene into winter. (Edward "Casey" Billhimer.)

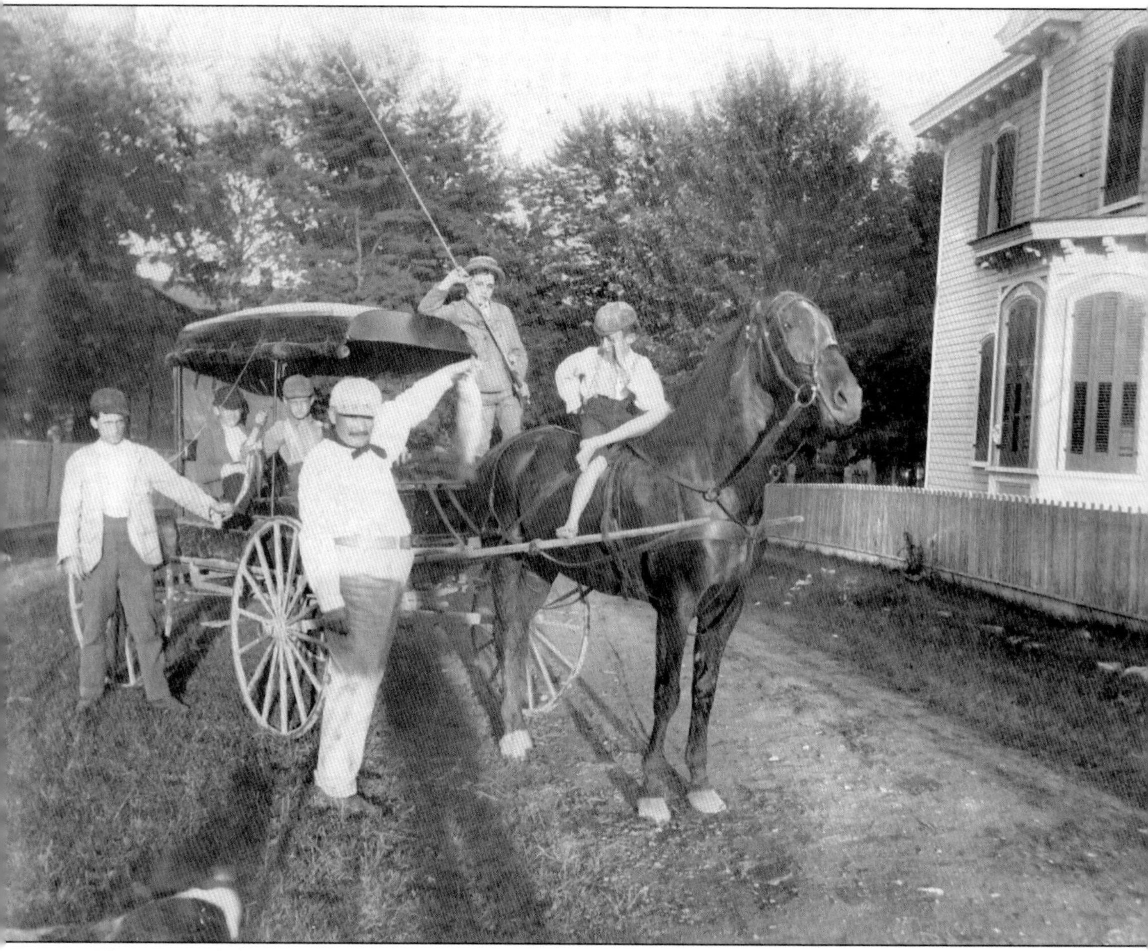

They went fishin' in the Shenandoah River and got a few. Jacob R. Clinedinst Jr. of York, Pennsylvania, holds the catch of the day around the spring of 1885 while his son, "little Jake," holds the rod. Seated in the very back of the two-seater is John D. Crim. His younger brother Jacob rides the horse. The group is in the alley (today's Seminary Lane) beside Jacob's brother John W. Clinedinst's house, which stands today at 9349 Congress Street. (John D. Crim.)

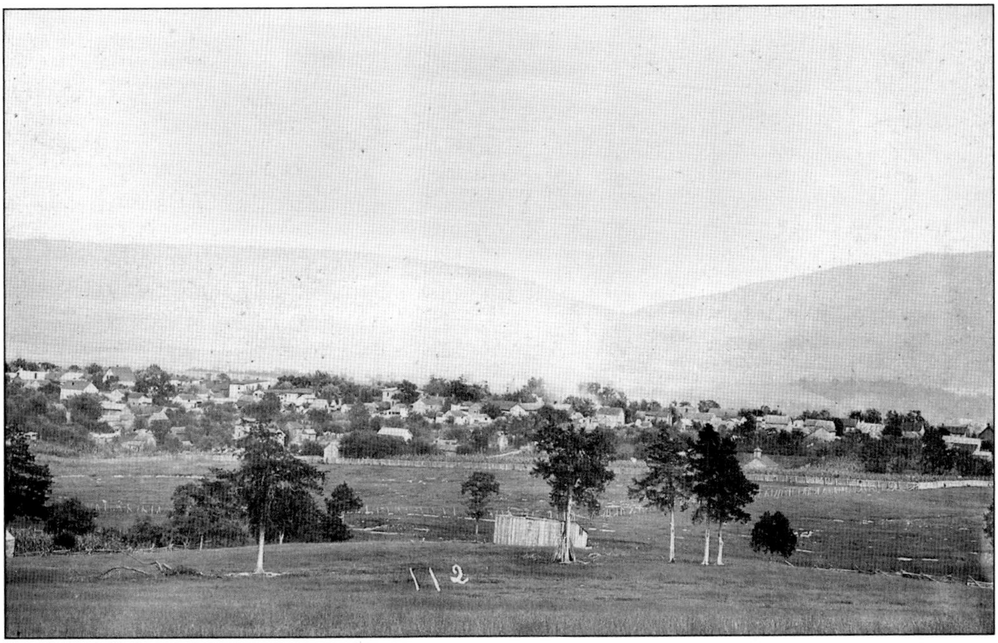

This rare view of New Market was taken probably from Williamson's Hill. The postcard view clearly shows the town's relation to the Massanutten Range. The gap was one of the reasons for early settlements there. Having contact with the other side of the mountain in Page County insured expansion of commerce from the tradesmen there. As it was then, it is today. These valley communities depend on each other in a very symbiotic way still today as they have in the past. (Edward "Casey" Billhimer, Dan Vaughn.)

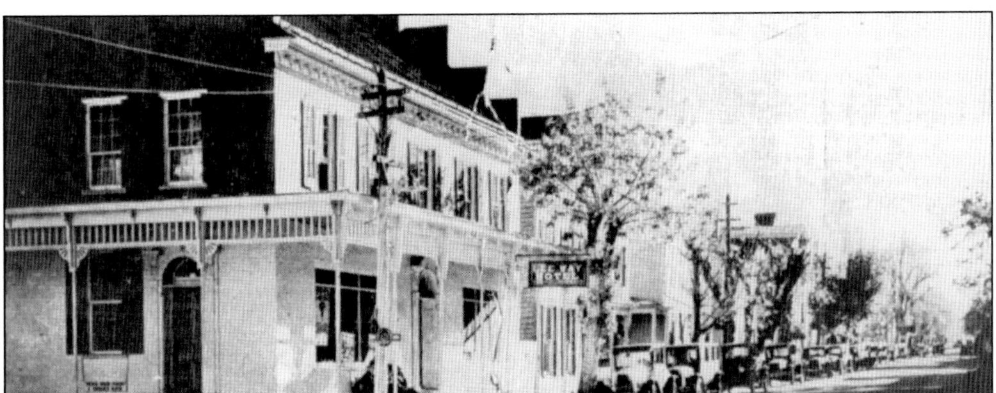

A late-afternoon view of the Lee-Way Hotel in 1921 looks south from the Crossroads at all the flivvers, or old automobiles, along the street. (Nancy Branner Stewart.)

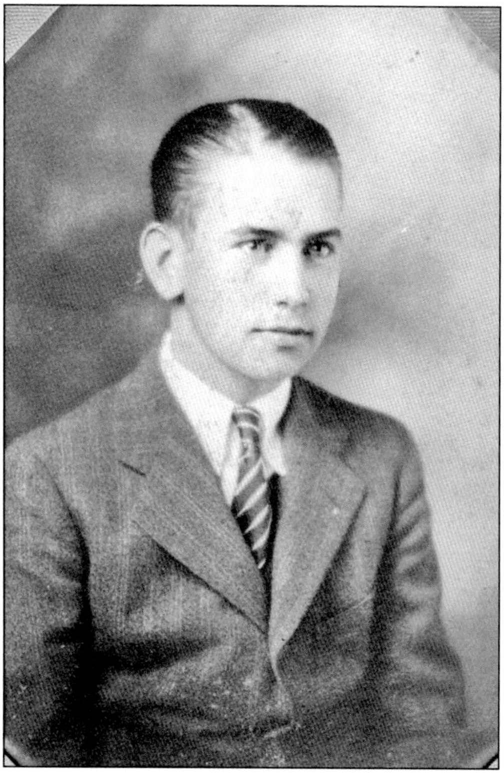

New Market citizen O. Braxton Theis is seen about at age 18. Bracky was known by both authors and by most locals as one of the grand old men of the town. He was truly a person that made a difference for his community. He was an excellent furniture maker and a collector of local relics, and he fancied local lore. He adored his antique Virginia-made "Kentucky" rifle collection because he understood that New Market was steeped in the history of the gun. Perhaps his occupation as the local undertaker at Theis Funeral Home gave him a greater understanding of what should be important to the living. His deep appreciation for his family and friends will be felt for some time. After his death in 2004, a great void was left in the fabric of New Market. (Nancy Branner Stewart.)

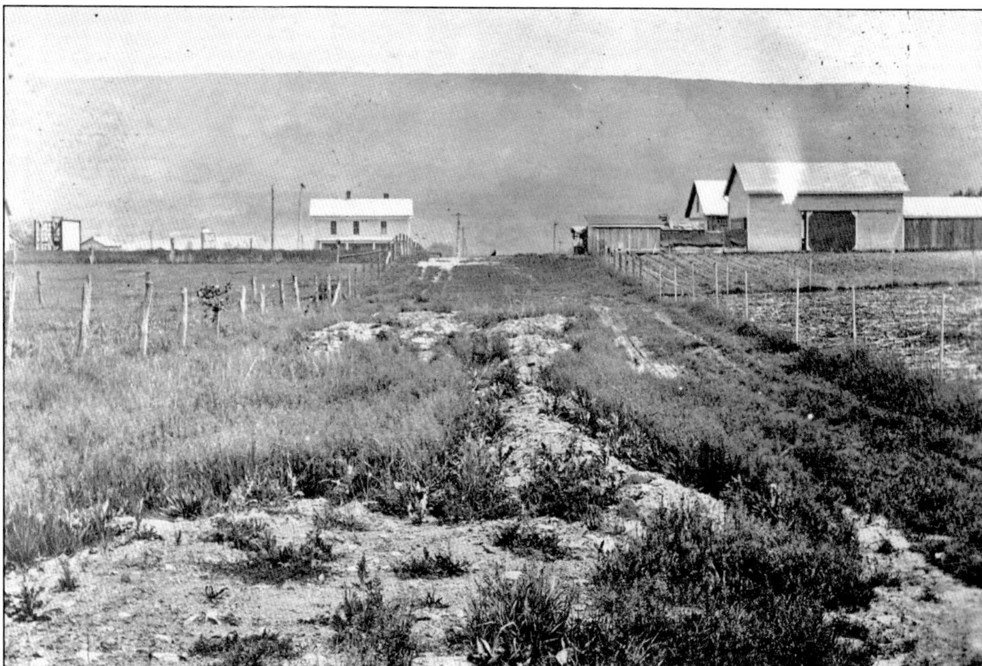

The picture appears to have been taken near the intersection of Stonewall Street and Cadet Road looking east along what will be Stonewall Street. The house may be the same one that is tucked behind Mountain View Guttering on Congress Street. (Nancy Branner Stewart.)

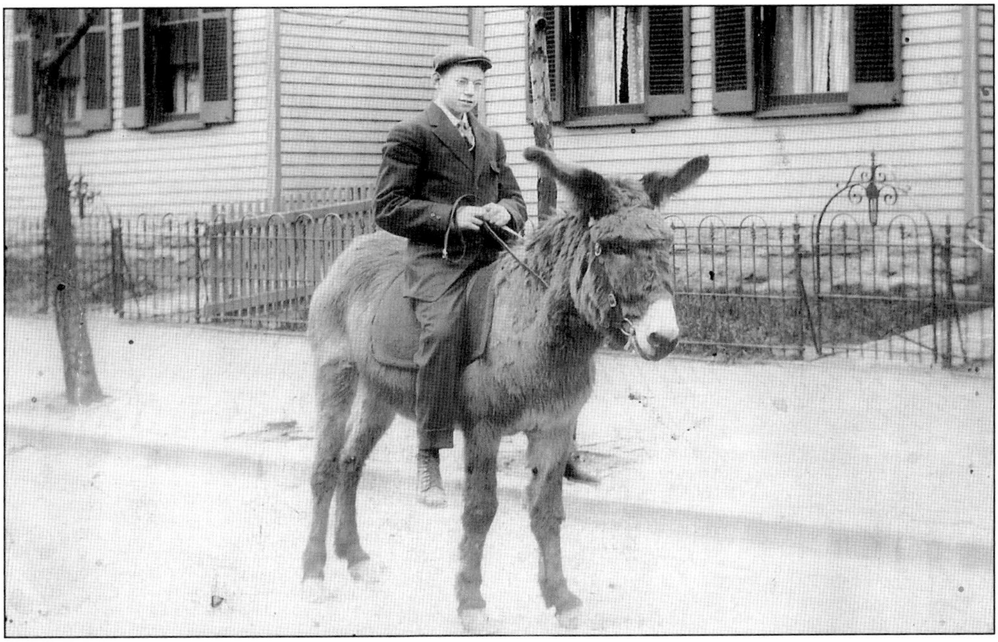

A young man thought to be Bracky Theis tries Ba'alam's transportation to get from here to there in 1908. Although not the most comfortable means of getting about, he had no gasoline concerns, nor did the young man have to pay tolls. Dating would have been a problem, however, since it does not appear to have a traditional rumble seat. (Edward "Casey" Billhimer.)

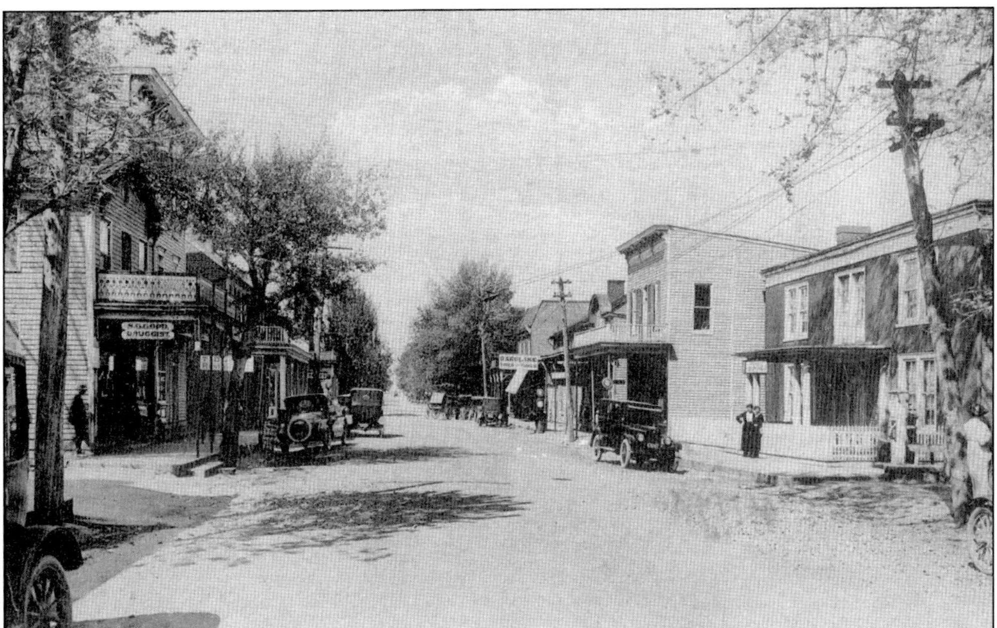

Spring is almost here in the early 1920s looking northeast from the intersection of Lee and Congress Streets. The old town pump is at right beside Henkel Nursing Home. Gasoline, tires, and tubes could be obtained at what is now a residence at 9420 Congress Street. The small sign at left advertises spring-cleaning, probably for automobiles. (Dr. Gene Comstock.)

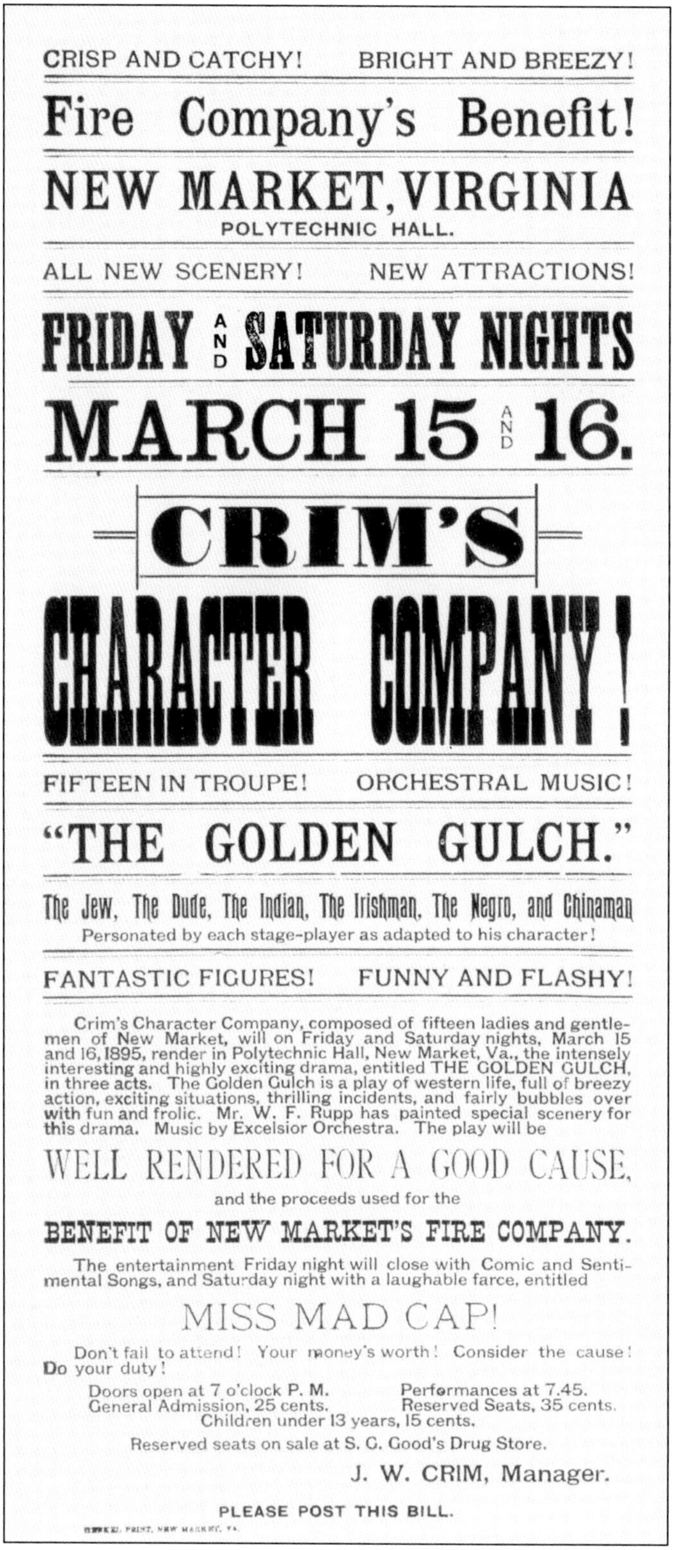
CRISP AND CATCHY! BRIGHT AND BREEZY!

Fire Company's Benefit!

NEW MARKET, VIRGINIA

POLYTECHNIC HALL.

ALL NEW SCENERY! NEW ATTRACTIONS!

FRIDAY AND SATURDAY NIGHTS

MARCH 15 AND 16.

CRIM'S CHARACTER COMPANY!

FIFTEEN IN TROUPE! ORCHESTRAL MUSIC!

"THE GOLDEN GULCH."

The Jew, The Dude, The Indian, The Irishman, The Negro, and Chinaman

Personated by each stage-player as adapted to his character!

FANTASTIC FIGURES! FUNNY AND FLASHY!

Crim's Character Company, composed of fifteen ladies and gentlemen of New Market, will on Friday and Saturday nights, March 15 and 16, 1895, render in Polytechnic Hall, New Market, Va., the intensely interesting and highly exciting drama, entitled THE GOLDEN GULCH, in three acts. The Golden Gulch is a play of western life, full of breezy action, exciting situations, thrilling incidents, and fairly bubbles over with fun and frolic. Mr. W. F. Rupp has painted special scenery for this drama. Music by Excelsior Orchestra. The play will be

WELL RENDERED FOR A GOOD CAUSE,

and the proceeds used for the

BENEFIT OF NEW MARKET'S FIRE COMPANY.

The entertainment Friday night will close with Comic and Sentimental Songs, and Saturday night with a laughable farce, entitled

MISS MAD CAP!

Don't fail to attend! Your money's worth! Consider the cause! Do your duty!

Doors open at 7 o'clock P. M. Performances at 7.45.
General Admission, 25 cents. Reserved Seats, 35 cents.
Children under 13 years, 15 cents.

Reserved seats on sale at S. G. Good's Drug Store.

J. W. CRIM, Manager.

PLEASE POST THIS BILL.

The Golden Gulch, a western comedy, had already been put on March 15 and 16, 1895, for the benefit of the New Market Fire Company and was apparently so well received that another final encore was scheduled for Friday, March 22. The cast was entirely local, and the play was managed by John W. "Button" Crim. It was to be his last production as he died in the fall, in his 52nd year. (John D. Crim.)

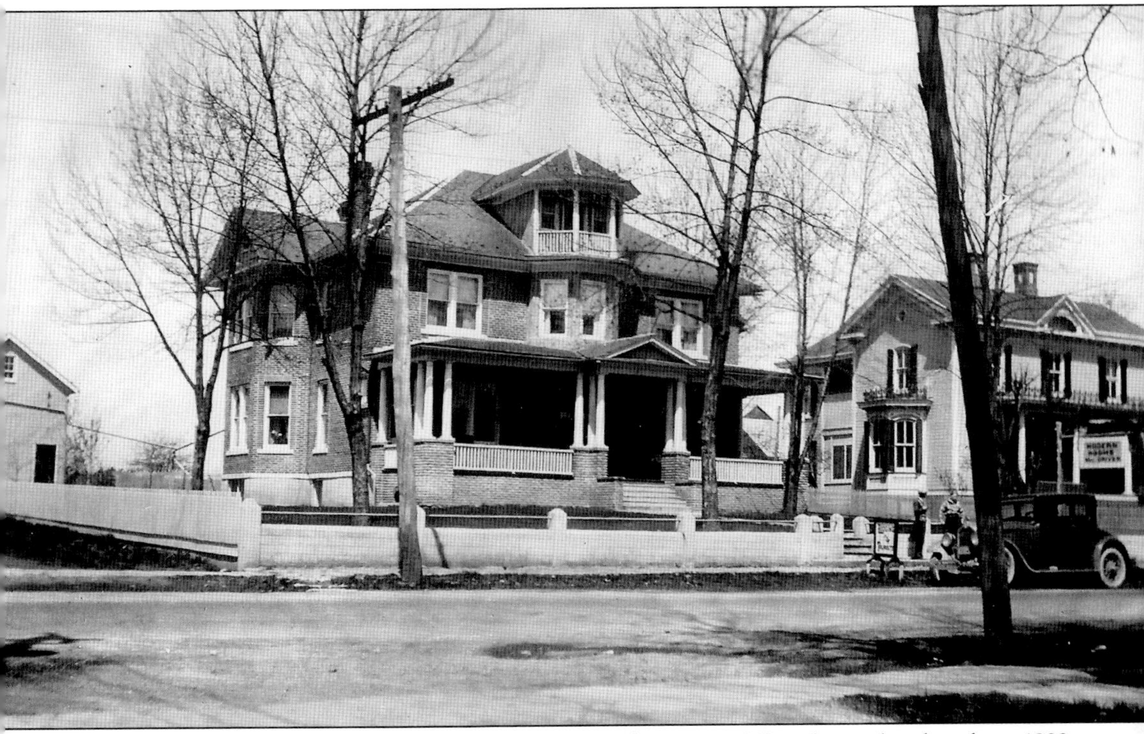

The imposing brick home at 9335 Congress Street was begun in 1917 and completed in about 1922 by Dr. William F. Driver. This late-1920s scene shows Mrs. Driver's signage advertising modern rooms and lodging for tourists. The house at right was occupied by the Good family at about that same time. (Cathy Blackburn Mauck.)

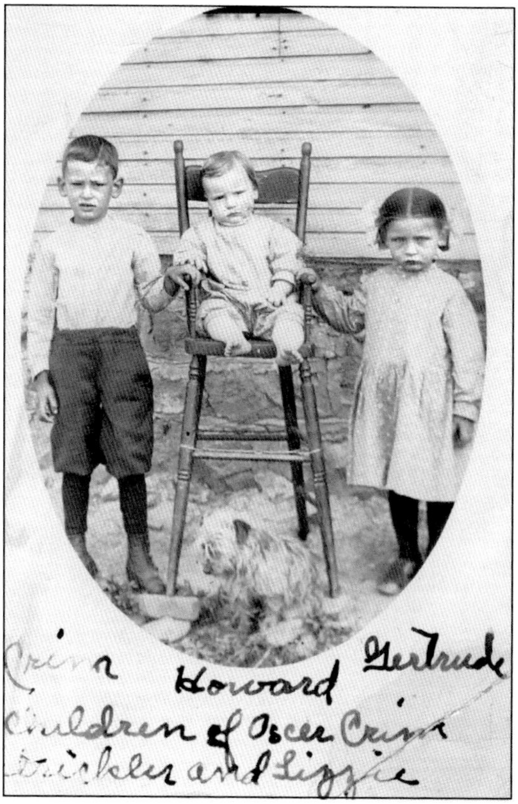

The children of Oscar Crim and Elizabeth "Lizzie" Strickler gather for an informal picture with their special friend around 1902. From left to right are Crim, Howard, and Gertrude, but there was no identification on the pet. (John D. Crim.)

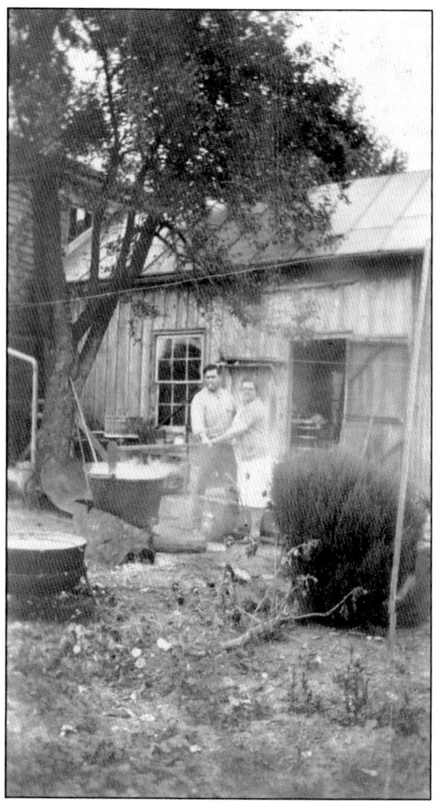

When it becomes fall in the valley, leaves become decorated with color and it is the right time for apple harvest and apple butter, a local German food tradition brought to Virginia from Pennsylvania. Seen here in the 1920s are Pauline and her father, Otis Theis (grandfather of Nancy Stewart of New Market) making the treat in their old copper kettle. It is a lengthy process of picking the right variety of apples, peeling and coring them, then *snitzing* them into cooking kettles with the proper amount of sugar and spices. As the apple mixture boils down for hours over a hot, white oak fire, a big 1800s penny is placed in the kettle for good luck and for preventing the apple butter from sticking to the sides. This tradition continues today, thank goodness, because it is so very tasty. (Nancy Branner Stewart.)

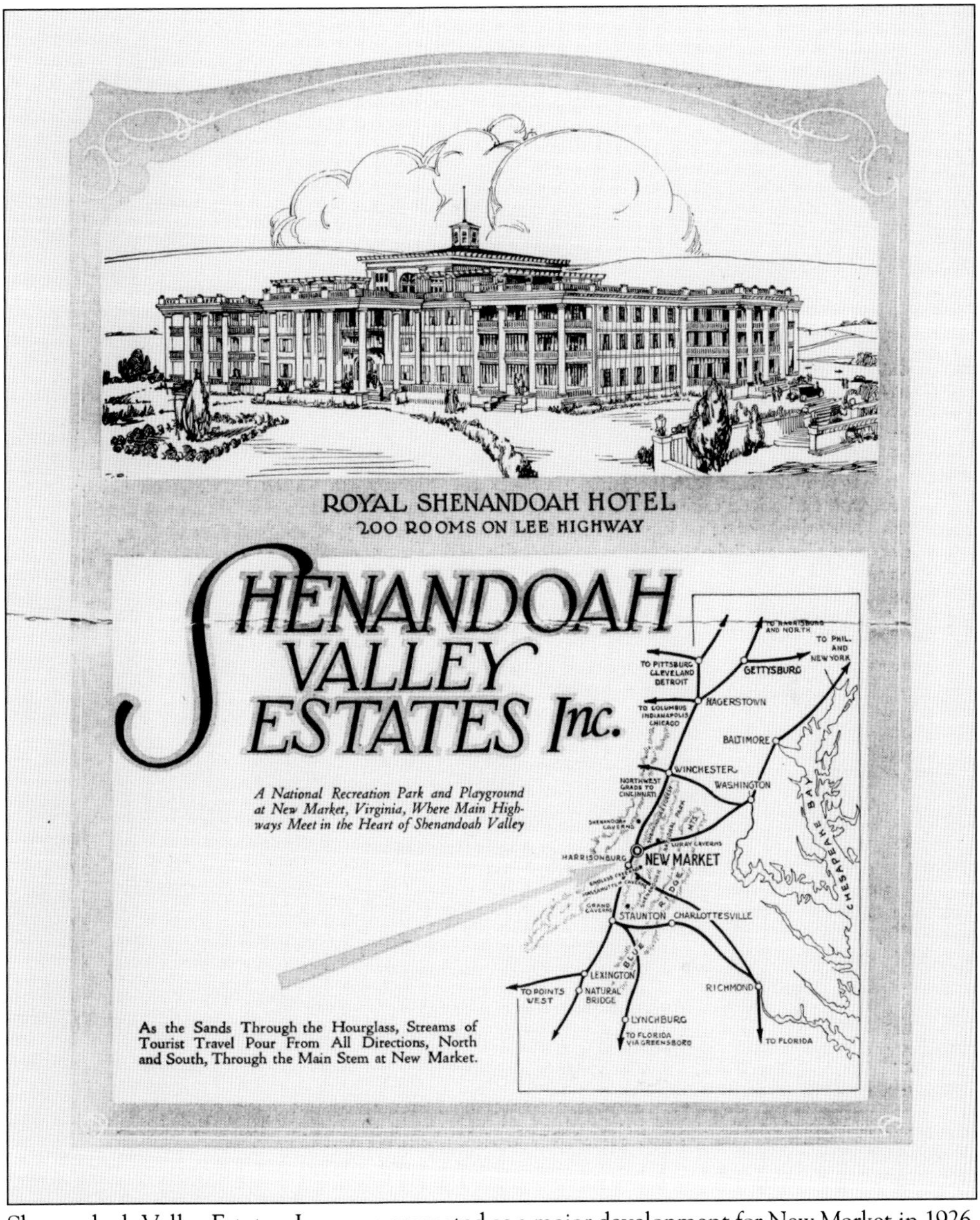

Shenandoah Valley Estates, Inc., was promoted as a major development for New Market in 1926. Plans included the 200-room hotel (shown), the Shenandoah Valley Golf Club with 18 holes and club house, a 20-acre Lake Shenandoah, tennis courts, polo grounds, an "aviation field," and bridle paths. Winding, boulevard-style streets would enclose a "beautiful restricted residential park" of about 2,000 homes stretching across Smith Creek and all along the Massanutten Mountain, east of Route 211. The Depression intervened, however, and only the Shenvalee Lodge and nine holes of the golf course were built and opened to the public. It wasn't until the 1960s that the 18 holes were completed, and since then, residential construction has taken place, although not on the scale of the original development. (John D. Crim.)

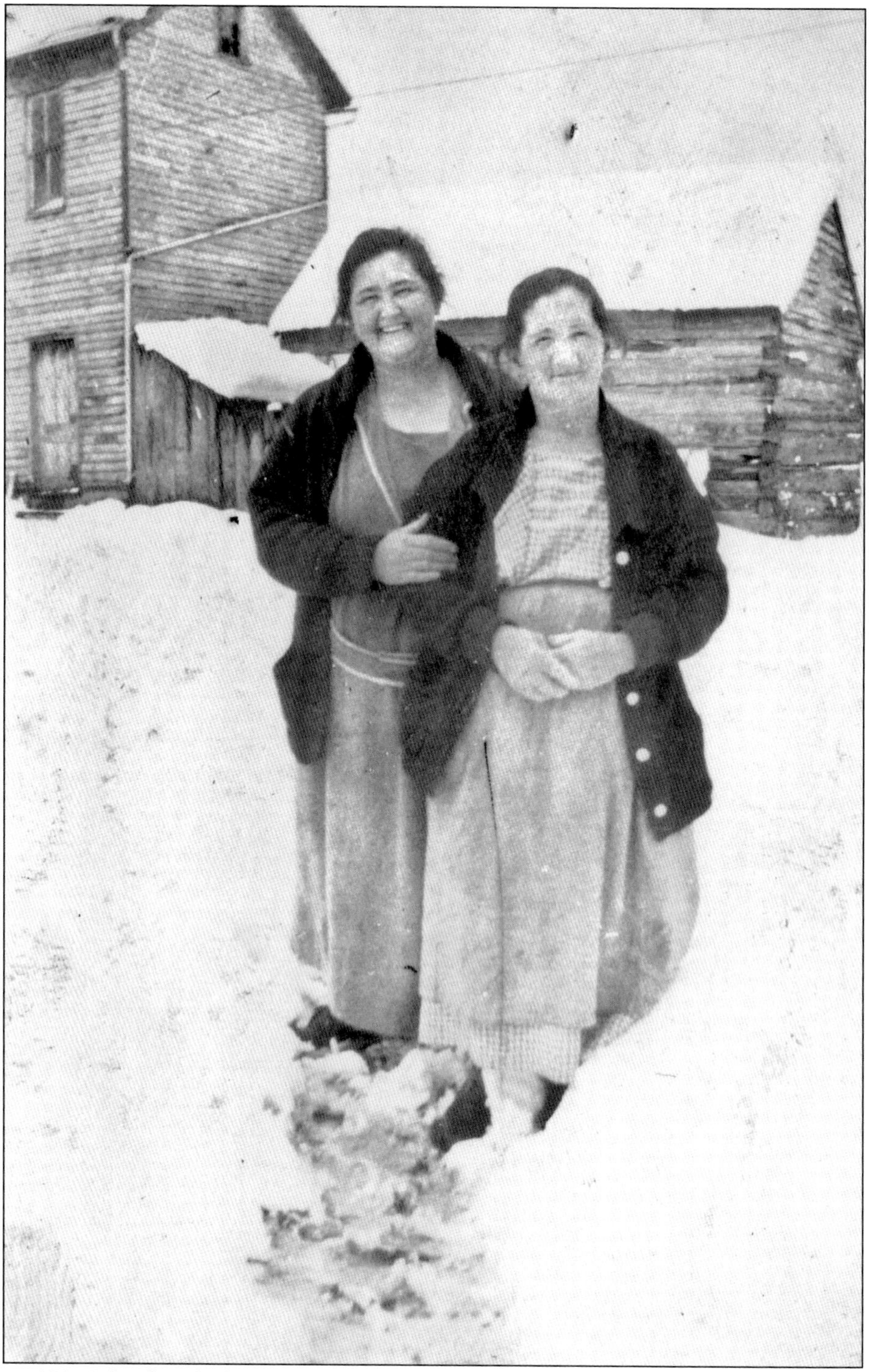

In the 1920s, Lily Theis (right) stands in the path made to her family's houses after a great blizzard blew through the valley. In those days, the winters tended to be much more severe and cold. In the background is the Theis home with the log meat house for storing salted pork and beef that provided sustenance for those cold months. (Nancy Branner Stewart.)

Eight

Beyond Congress Street

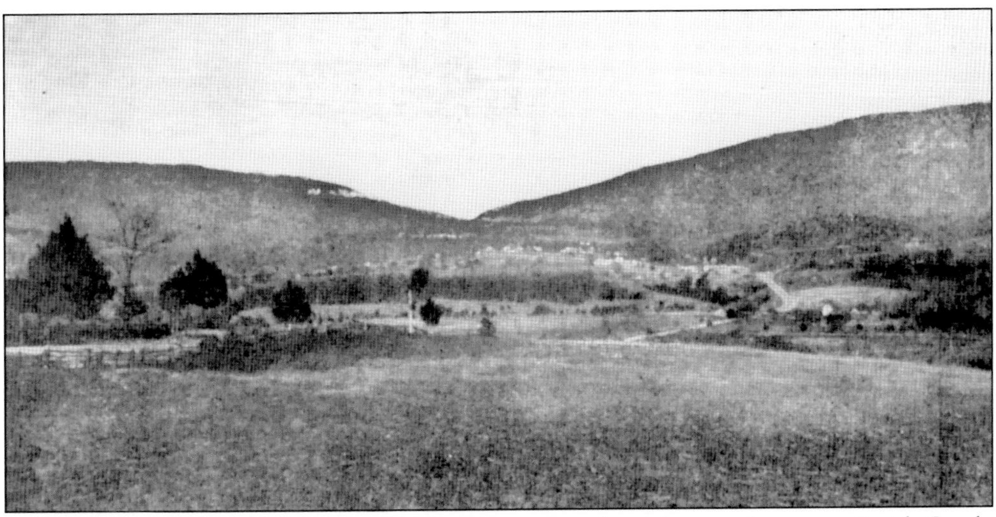

By 1900, New Market Gap displayed its bucolic scenery from the area known as Smith Creek, part of the Massanutten Range originally called "Massanutting" by the Native Americans, meaning "land of many potatoes" according to lore. Many hay and crop fields still thrive because of locals who farm the land. The land along Smith Creek is known for its incredibly rich soil and positive harvests. In the late 1700s and early 1800s, the creek retained its name from all the many blacksmiths found along its borders. Dirk Pennybacker's Pine Forge operated along the creek and gave birth to the most-advanced Colonial-period iron furnace in Virginia, named Redwell Furnace, in Luray in September 1787. (Edward "Casey" Billhimer.)

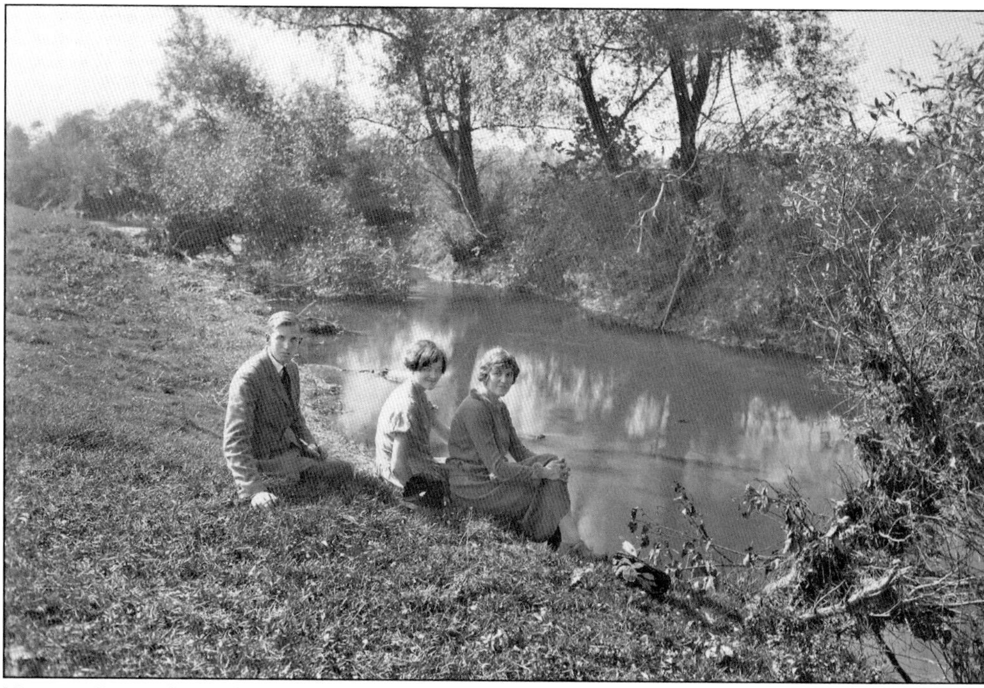
Virginia Driver (center) and friends enjoy a quiet afternoon outing along the Shenandoah River in the mid-1920s. The river appears high, perhaps after heavy rains, which may explain the debris lodged in the brush at right. (Cathy Blackburn Mauck.)

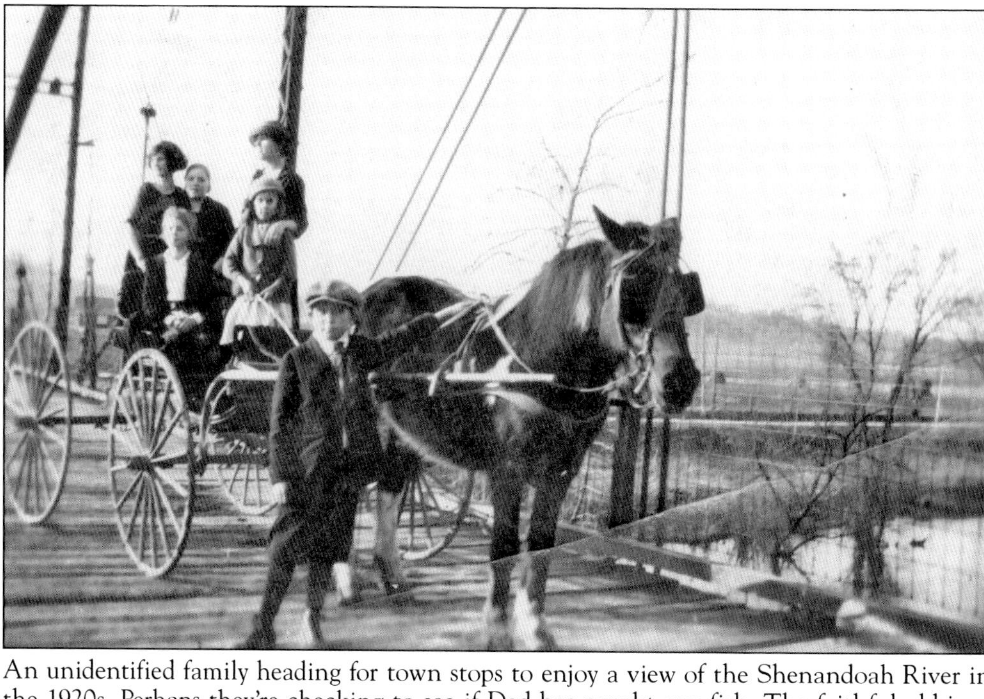
An unidentified family heading for town stops to enjoy a view of the Shenandoah River in the 1920s. Perhaps they're checking to see if Dad has caught any fish. The faithful old iron bridge quietly carried its weight (and everyone else's as well) until its more modern replacement. (Nancy Branner Stewart.)

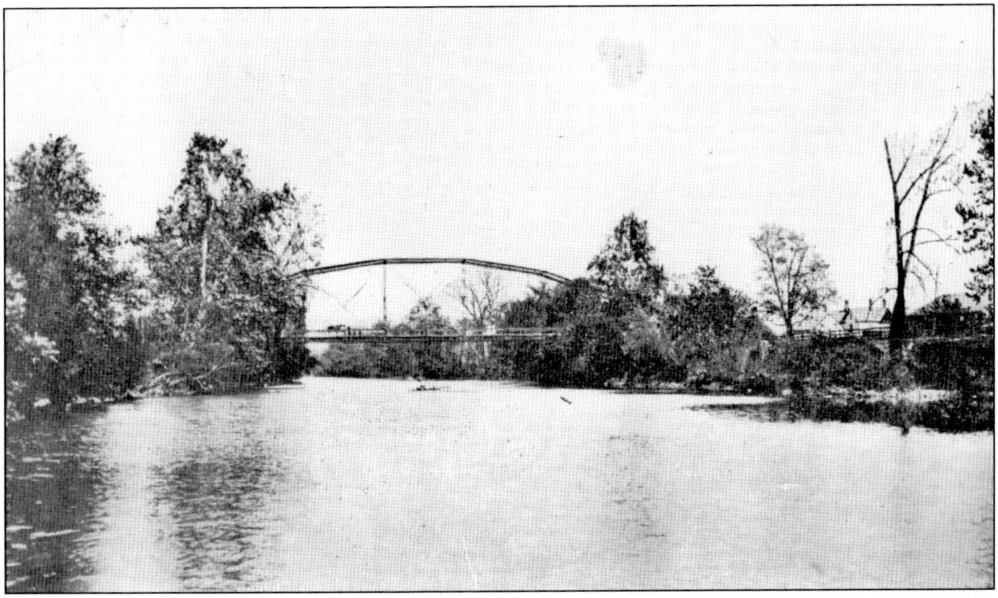

The great Shenandoah River, fabled in song and legend, is one of the few rivers in the world to run north. During the Civil War, Northern soldiers would get very confused by local residents when trying to ask in what direction the rebel soldiers had marched. Most times, the locals would say, "up the valley" or "down the valley." Their answer was not in direction but in how the river flows. This iron bridge was constructed in 1914 at Meem's Bottom crossing, where, in 1864, the retreating Union army narrowly escaped capture crossing the burning bridge to the safe shores of Mount Jackson after the Confederate victory at New Market. (Nancy Branner Stewart.)

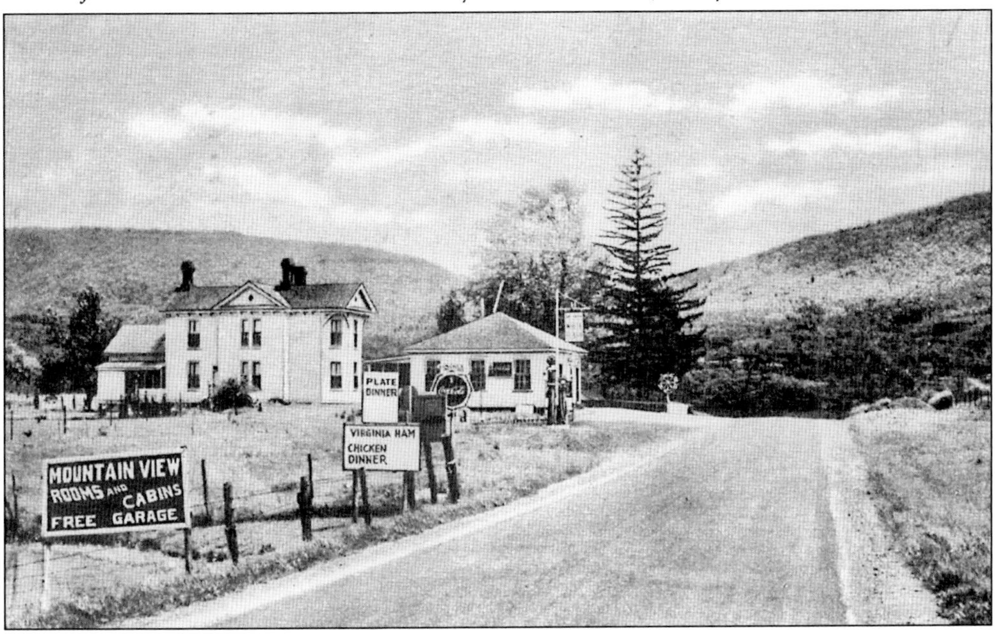

The Mountain View Tourist Home and Tea Room, one mile east of town on Route 211, provided travelers with home-cooked meals and also sold gas and oil as needed in the 1930s. During the 1940s, the Mountain View was owned and operated by Ralph and Helen (Rice) Bingham, and the home survives today on Lee Highway. (Dan Vaughn.)

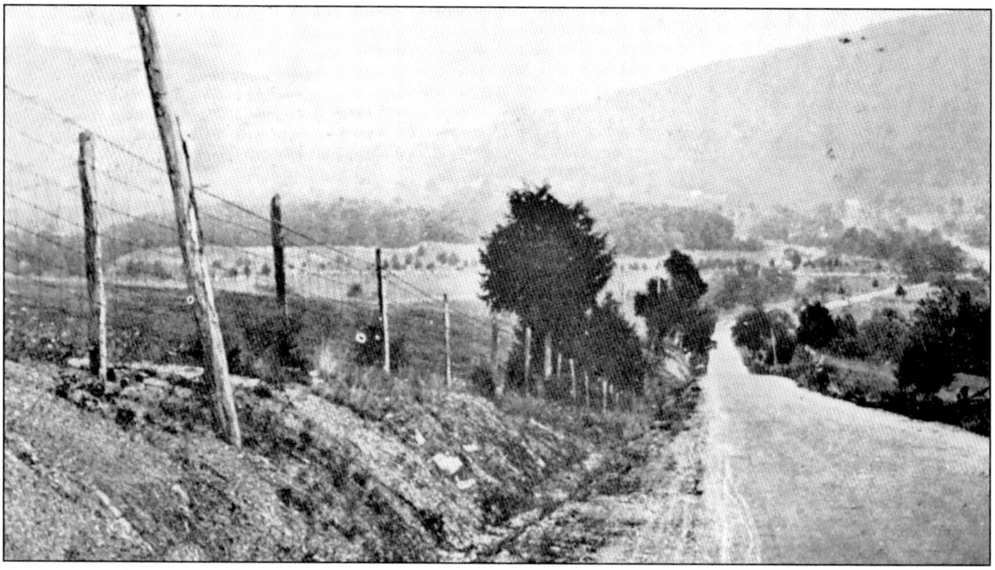

Cedars mark an easterly view to the New Market Gap along the old trail of Stonewall Jackson. His famed Valley Campaign of 1862 passed down this road. His army camped right above Smith Creek during the campaign. During the course of the Civil War, troop camps and cavalry clashes took place along these foothills. Today the road, now called Route 211, is fully paved but still follows most of the same path as this early-20th-century view of the Massanutten Range. (Nancy Branner Stewart.)

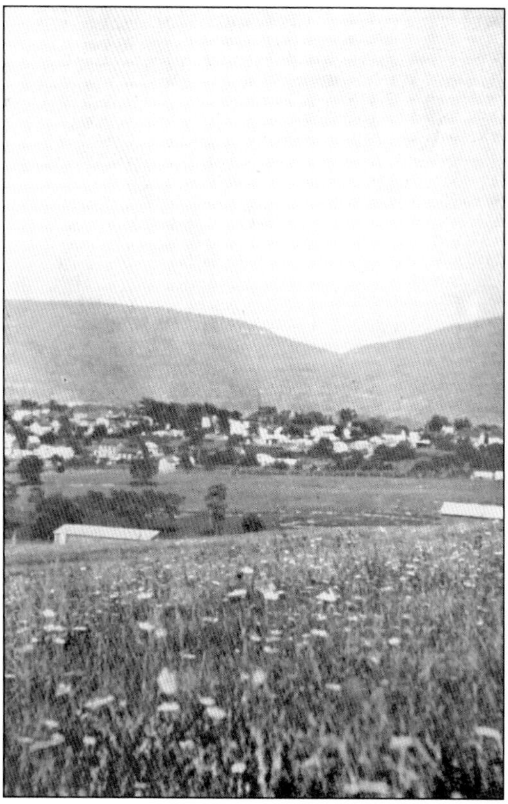

Looking on the quiet vistas around New Market, the fertile hay fields still remain as they have for generations. The moody and dramatic beauty of the valley endures, but for how long? It is springtime in this photograph on Shirley's Hill adorned with flowers, where so many men perished during the climactic battle that raged there for two days in 1864. During the years, many farmers would plow the fields, finding constant reminders of the past, whether it be shards of Schweinfurt pottery, a Native American axe, or a button dropped from a Civil War soldier, all reminders of peace and a time of conflict. (Nancy Branner Stewart.)

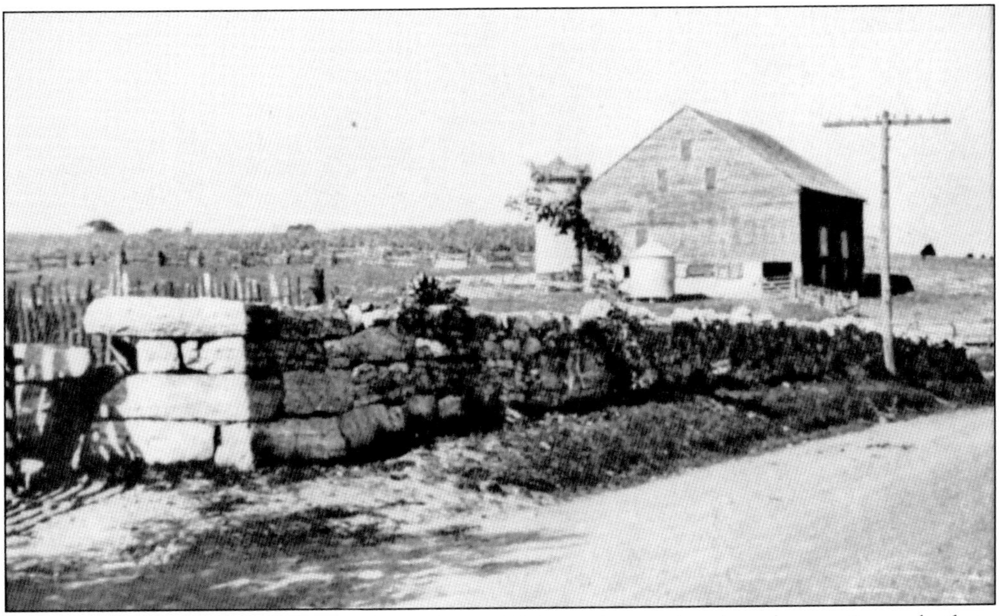

The John W. Rice bank barn stands solidly in 1900 on the north edge of town. It was built in 1854 and survived Union general Phillip Sheridan's 1864 burning of the valley. The structure was razed in April 1926, making way for construction of the Pythian Sisters' Orphan's Home. The local paper laments its passing, noting, "Thus another old landmark . . . has been removed to give room for the march of improvement in our Val'ey." (Private Collection.)

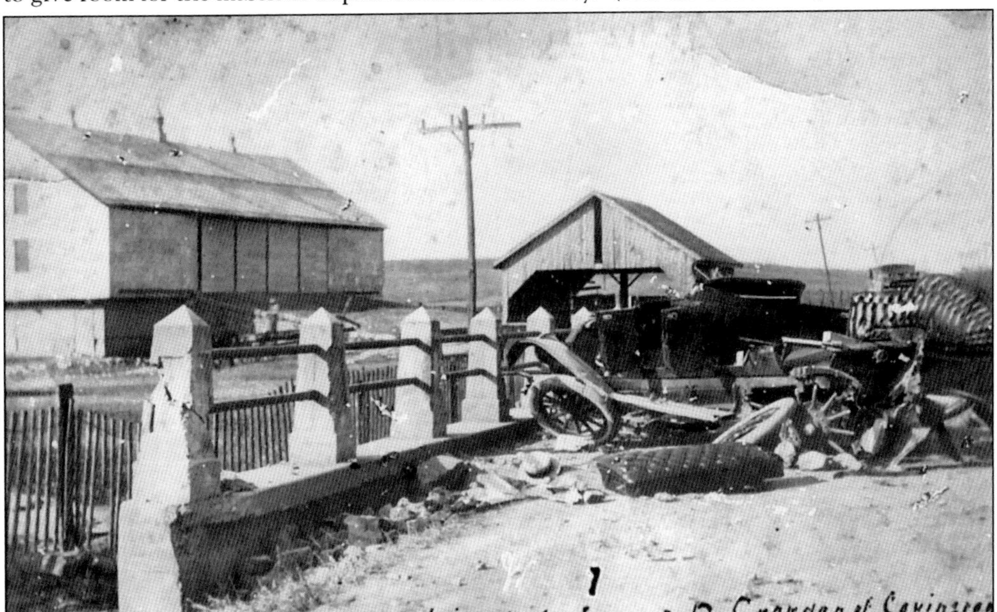

This terrible wreck c. 1912–1914 on the Valley Pike was just four miles south of town by an old barn (no longer standing). The wreck was reviewed by a local sheriff's deputy because it was a fatal accident that killed James D. Crowder of Covington, Virginia. Note the gruesome image includes a man's straw hat that may have been a macabre prop by the photographer. (Edward "Casey" Billhimer, Dan Vaughn.)

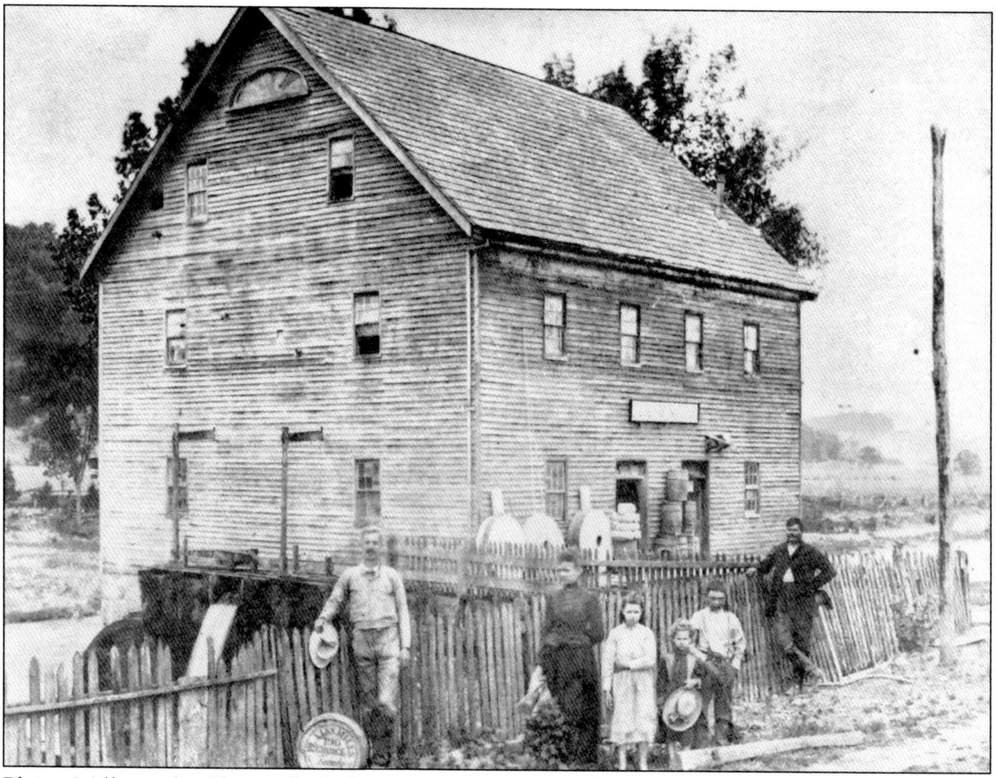

Plains Mill, on the Shenandoah River near town, served the community for many years. This early, 1890s view shows the family that operated the mill as well as some of the different wheels that could be changed out to provide the consistency of product needed by the customer. (Nancy Branner Stewart.)

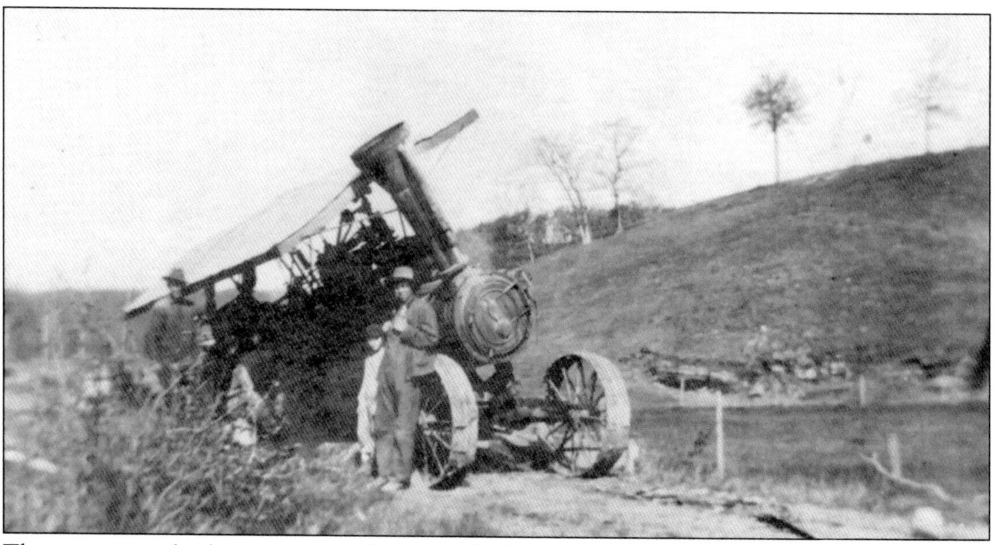

The camera caught this accident in 1918 at the bridge at Smith Creek. This steam engine belonged to a J. L. Golladay, and it appears that the axle has broken in a rut on the rugged road to Luray (now Highway 211 East). Judging from the eagle standing on the globe on the front end of the boiler, the steam tractor is a Case brand. (John H. H. Graves.)

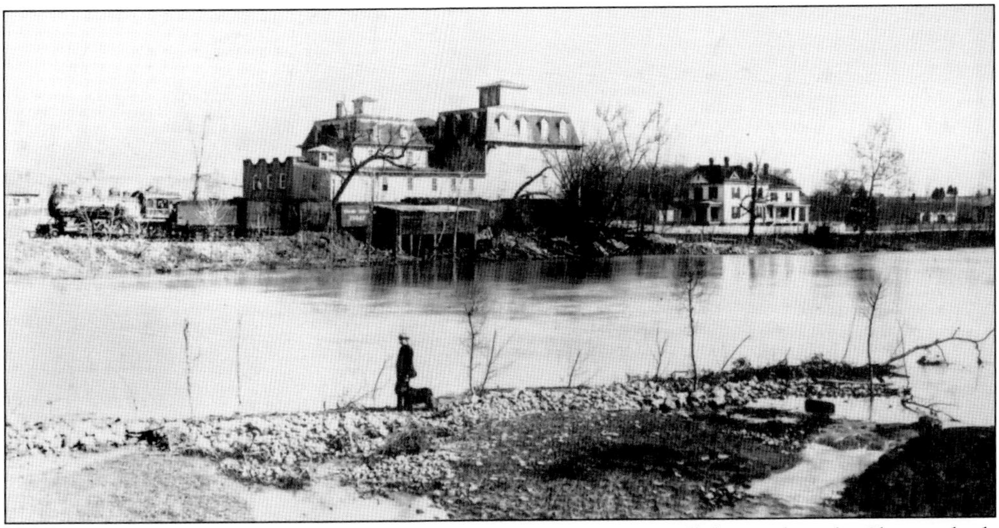

Here is an early-1900s view of the large and prosperous Manor's Mill, located on the Shenandoah River's west bank. Built in the 1870s, the mill processed grain and lumber for the area. A railroad spur connects the mill with the nearby B&O main line, and a train appears ready to leave for market. Dave Tuck of Strasburg is the train's engineer about the time of the photograph. In the foreground, Ott Emswiler walks his dog, Shep, along the east bank. Unfortunately the mill burned on March 26, 1926, leaving only the concrete foundations still visible today along the river. (James A. Litten.)

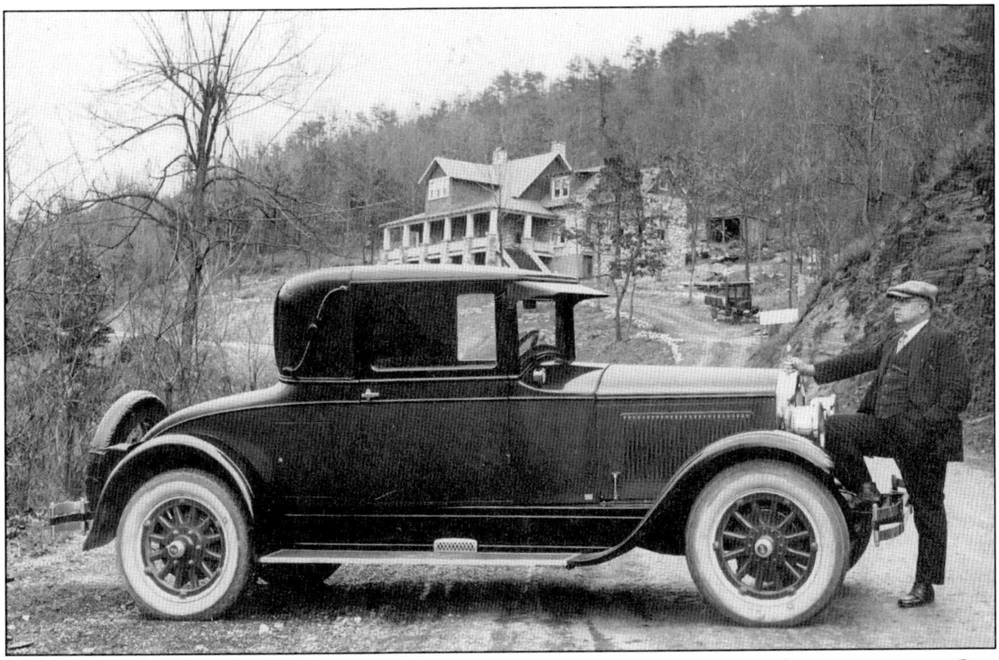

Dr. W. C. Shirley poses with his new car, thought to be a Buick, just below the Massanutten Gap east of town. The house may have been owned by H. B. Long Sr. Better known as a musician than as a dentist, Dr. Shirley was fond of having such pictures taken every time he obtained a new means of transportation. (Nancy R. Long.)

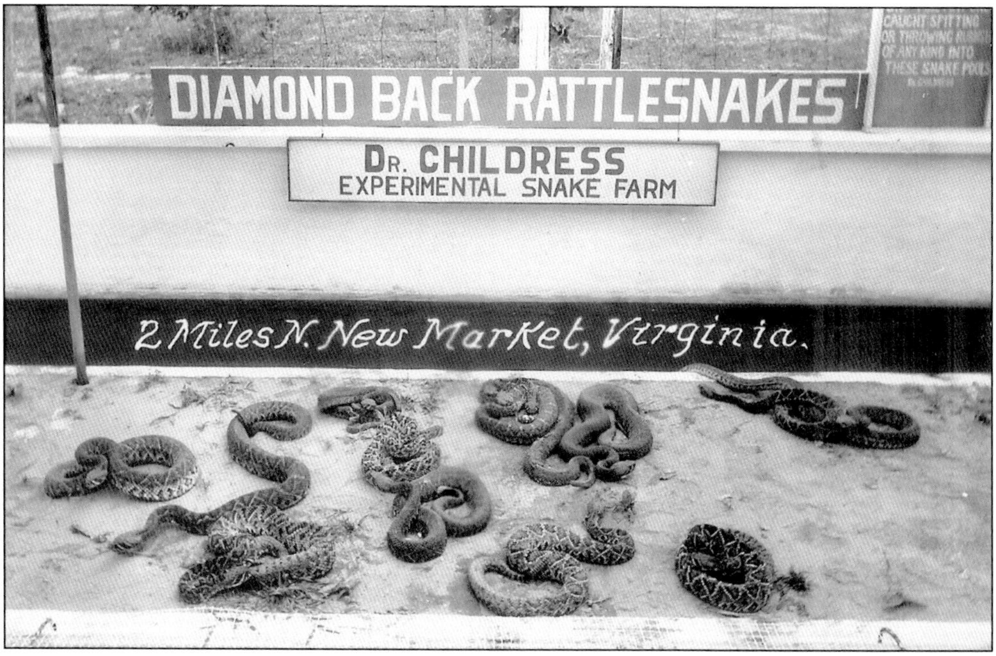

Diamondback rattlesnakes gather around for a slithery pose at Dr. Childress Snake and Monkey Farm. The farm, located on Rude's Hill north of town, was in operation from the 1940s to the late 1960s as a small tourist attraction. He had exotic forms of both monkeys and snakes. Locally the Eastern timber rattlesnake is generally not as long as the diamondback, but it is much more venomous and aggressive than its wiggly, western cousin. (Edward "Casey" Billhimer, Dan Vaughn.)

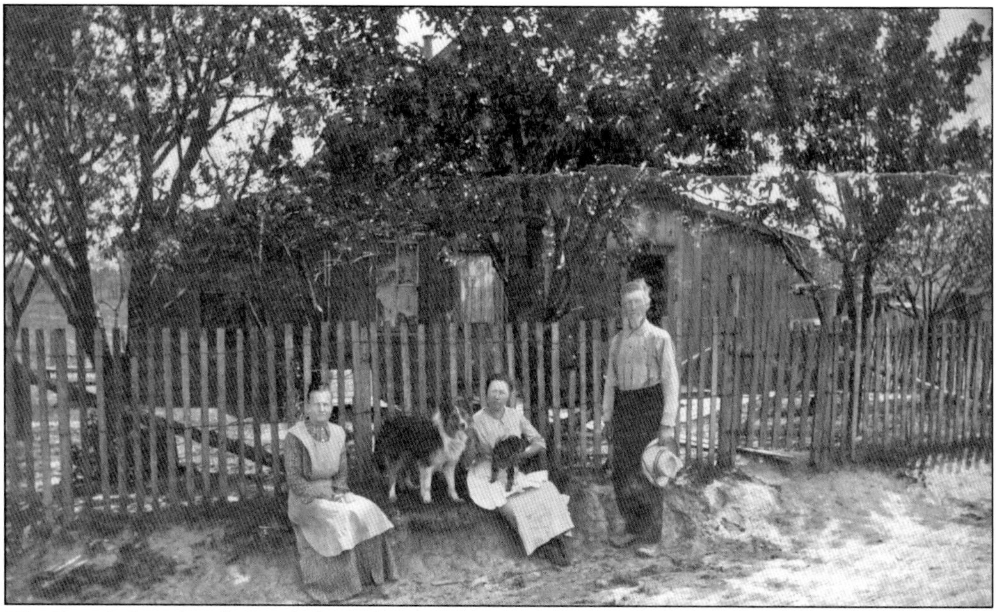

The Dingledine family lived along the road on this simple, small farm just west of New Market. Mr. Dingledine died young, leaving his wife and three little girls behind to carry on. The Dingledines were not wealthy folks, and the children nobly helped their mother out by being farmed out for work in other homes to survive. (Nancy Branner Stewart.)

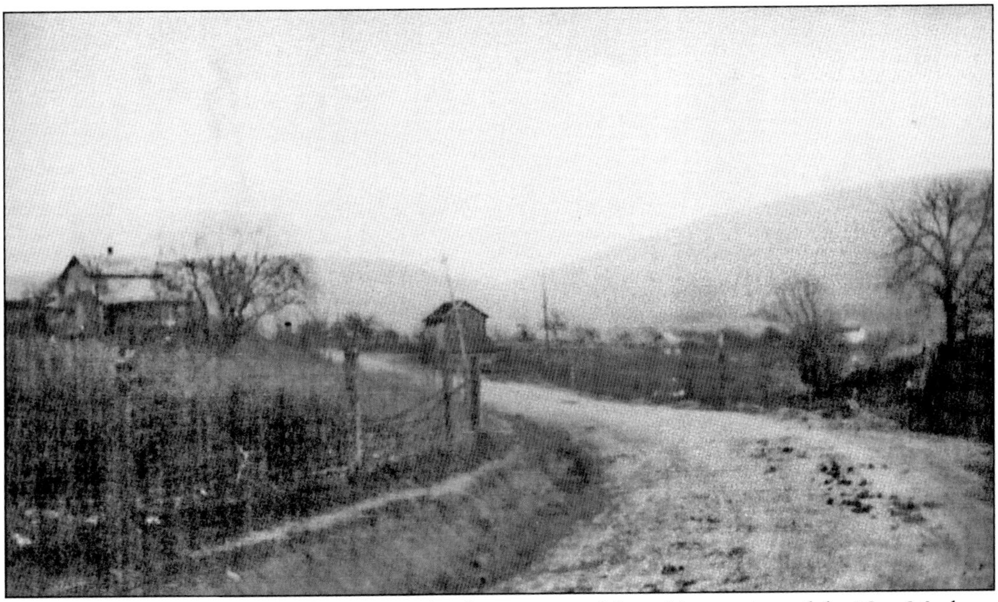

The New Market Gap in the distance is the destination of this older section of the New Market–Sperryville Turnpike just outside of town in the 1920s. In the mid-1950s, the old turnpike's connection to the Valley Pike was relocated several blocks north. That relocation forever changed the economy, character, and flow of traffic through town. The Gap lines up with Brock's Gap to the west and Thornton Gap to the east and is the only crossing readily available in the 50-mile length of the Massanutten Mountain. (John D. Crim.)

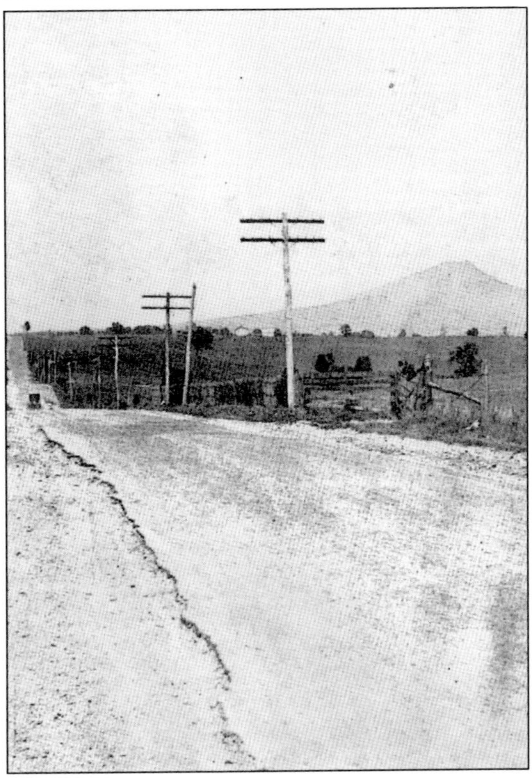

The old Valley Pike appears as it looked facing north about 1925. In the background, the old Massanutten Peak looms over the Shenandoah Valley in all her splendor. This mountain view is still a familiar site today, unchanging when entering and departing the area around New Market. (Nancy Branner Stewart.)

Consistent with our mission to preserve history on a local level, this book was printed in South Carolina on American-made paper and manufactured entirely in the United States. Products carrying the accredited Forest Stewardship Council (FSC) label are printed on 100 percent FSC-certified paper.

MADE IN THE USA